Melodramatic Landscapes

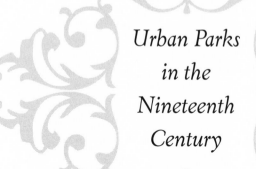

Urban Parks
in the
Nineteenth
Century

HEATH MASSEY SCHENKER

Melodramatic Landscapes

UNIVERSITY OF VIRGINIA PRESS
CHARLOTTESVILLE & LONDON

University of Virginia Press

© 2009 by the Rector and Visitors of the University of Virginia

All rights reserved

Printed in the United States of America on acid-free paper

First published 2009

9 8 7 6 5 4 3 2 1

LIBRARY OF CONGRESS CATALOGING-IN-PUBLICATION DATA

Schenker, Heath.

Melodramatic landscapes : urban parks in the nineteenth century / Heath Massey Schenker.

p.   cm.

Includes bibliographical references and index.

ISBN 978-0-8139-2842-5 (cloth : alk. paper)

1. Urban parks—History—19th century. 2. Urban parks—France—Paris—History—19th century. 3. Chapultepec (Mexico City, Mexico—History—19th century. 4. Central Park (New York, N.Y.)—History—19th century. I. Title.

SB481.S34 2009

712'.509034—dc22

2009009425

Contents

Acknowledgments

THE RESEARCH FOR THIS BOOK BEGAN IN the magnificent parks themselves and turned into a treasure hunt through musty archives and splendid historic reading rooms, from the Bibliothèque Historique de la Ville de Paris to the New York Public Library to the Archivo Histórico de la Ciudad de México. I am extremely grateful for the assistance I received along the way from both institutions and individuals. I wish to acknowledge, first and foremost, the support of the University of California, Davis, where I am a member of the faculty. In addition to the research funding I received through the Agricultural Experiment Station of the College of Agricultural and Environmental Sciences, I was very fortunate to be awarded two sabbaticals, one in Paris and one in Mexico City, and a fellowship at the UC Davis Humanities Center, during which I conducted major research for this book. An additional subsidy from the university, awarded while I was department chair, enabled me to continue research on the book while fulfilling my administrative duties. Finally, UC Davis provided a subvention for the publication of this book, without which the generous number of illustrations would not have been possible.

I also want to acknowledge the many librarians and archivists who helped me locate historic resources in Paris, Mexico, and New York, and the efficient staff of the Interlibrary Loan Department at Shields Library, UC Davis, who made it possible to consult many important resources at home. María-Teresa Zaldívar, of the Smurfit Company, provided a much-appreciated complimentary copy of the limited-edition book, *Chapultepec: Historia y Presencia*, edited by Mario de la Torre, when my tattered photocopies of relevant chapters disintegrated beyond legibility. I am particularly indebted to Diane Cary, my research assistant during the final stage of this project, for her efficient online searches and capable management of the reproductions and permissions process. Without her support at that crucial point, I seriously doubt the manuscript would have made it to press! I also want to thank Karen Olson for her careful attention to detail in readying the manuscript for submission to the publisher, and Jung-yen Chang and Gerrie Robinson, graduate students at UC Davis, for their help during early phases of the research.

It has been a pleasure working with the editorial staff at the University of Virginia Press. Boyd Zenner's immediate and unflagging interest in this book sustained it, and me, through the long process of getting to print. I am delighted that this book will be a part of the list she has been developing at the press focusing on the sociocultural history of the built environment. Susan Murray provided meticulous copy editing. Mark Mones and Angie Hogan capably shepherded the book and the illustrations into print.

Finally, I thank my husband, Dr. Marc B. Schenker, who enthusiastically shared those sabbaticals in Paris and Mexico City, and my wonderful daughters Yael, Phoebe, and Hilary, who remind me that the landscape is always changing.

Chapter 1 originally appeared as "Parks and Politics During the Second Empire in Paris" in *Landscape Journal* 14(2):201–19, Fall 1995. Portions of chapter 3 were previously published in "Pleasure Gardens, Theme Parks, and the Picturesque" in *The Landscapes of Theme Parks: Antecedents and Variations*, Dumbarton Oaks Colloquium on the History of Landscape Architecture 20, edited by Terrance Young and Robert Riley (Dumbarton Oaks, Washington, D.C., 2002, 69–89), and in "Central Park and the Melodramatic Imagination" in the

Journal of Urban History 29(4):375–93, May 2003, while portions of chapter 4 originally appeared as "Why Urban Parks: A Matter of Equity" in *The George Wright Forum,* the journal of the George Wright Society, 19(2):39–45, 2002 (and are republished here by permission). I wish to thank the editors and publishers of these books and journals for permission to incorporate this material into the present book.

Melodramatic Landscapes

Introduction

OFFICER MEANEY YESTERDAY, WHILE ON
duty in the upper portion of Central Park, espied a large bonfire blaz-
ing brightly in the woods. He approached the burning pile, and was
astonished to discover a middle-aged man, apparently immersed in
deep thought, standing with his back to the burning brushwood,
warming his coat-tails, and seemingly unconscious of his surroundings and position. In close proximity to the bonfire was a curiously-
constructed hut, built without any regard for architectural design, and
composed merely of several rough-hewn logs of wood, mingled with
freshly-cut branches of trees, which, being entwined around the logs,
helped to support and brace them. In this romantic residence, the
interior of which contained neither furniture nor bedding, the stranger
had determined to reside, at least temporarily, away from the strife and
busy turmoil of the great Metropolis.

—*New York Times*, 28 December 1877

The foregoing incident occurred not long after Central Park opened
to the public in New York. Episodes like this, reported in the popular

Footprint of Central Park, New York, in its urban context. (USGS aerial photographs compiled by Erik Schorr, 2003)

press, reveal that in the nineteenth century, large urban parks such as Central Park were something of an enigma to their intended audience. With their pastoral landscape scenery incongruously situated in urban areas, parks were a new cultural phenomenon and required some interpretation for a public unschooled in the finer distinctions of the romantic sensibility. Park designers anticipated certain reactions from the public and tried to orchestrate certain types of behavior in parks; however, not everyone responded as expected. The man with the bonfire, encountered by Officer Meaney, either missed the cues devised by park designers or willfully ignored them. Wandering onto a stage set depicting rural scenery, perhaps he mistook it for the real thing. In any case, his romantic residence did not correspond to the particular vision expressed in Central Park. No doubt Officer Meaney escorted the man from the scene and removed all traces of the bonfire. Yet incidents like this attest to the cultural ambiguity that attended urban parks at their inception in the nineteenth century.

Today a powerful cultural mythology surrounds urban parks such as Central Park, so that it seems almost unremarkable that meadows and forests should exist in the midst of dense urban surroundings. Yet one has only to consider how much profit has been forfeited, or try to imagine circumstances that would permit Central Park to be replaced by high-rise condominiums and fashionable shopping and dining districts, to realize that this park embodies durable cultural values. It is truly astonishing that such a large tract of rural landscape has been retained in the midst of the modern urban matrix of New York City, occupying some of the most valuable real estate in the world, defying strong social and economic pressures to envelop and develop it over the past 150 years. Even more remarkable is the fact that comparable parks can be found in cities around the world, most dating to the same time period, all similar in design and equally sacrosanct. The popularity of these parks transcended national, cultural, and political boundaries in the nineteenth century. Parks from this period have survived radical changes of government and ideology and become national treasures around the world. In more prosperous cities, these parks have been well maintained over the years. In cities with fewer resources, they are slowly decaying, relics of more prosperous times. But regardless of their current condition, these parks are still widely regarded as marks of civic distinction. They are a lasting

A rustic path in Central Park, New York.
(Photograph by the author, 2004)

footprint from the nineteenth century, and collectively they represent
a cultural institution that continues to enjoy extraordinary, international allegiance.

Urban parks were elaborate productions in the nineteenth century, among the most visible and most lauded of the new public institutions that transformed urban landscapes on an international scale,
from European capitals to far-flung colonial outposts. As cities grew
exponentially over the course of the century, reflecting a global shift
from agricultural to industrial economies, civic leaders conceived new
civic institutions and instituted urban renewal projects on an unprecedented scale.[1] Like other urban amenities dating to the same
period, such as new sewers and sanitary-water delivery systems, new
civic buildings, tree-lined boulevards, and shopping arcades, public
parks signified modernity and bourgeois prosperity. Both a sign and

a source of civic pride, they were bright green jewels in the new urban fabric of the nineteenth-century industrial city.[2]

Some of the larger parks included museums, outdoor theaters, bandstands, botanical gardens, zoological gardens, and other cultural institutions, but, above all, parks were stylized representations of rural countryside inserted into the heart of the city. The landscape of these parks was quite formulaic, employing a naturalistic landscape style that had become popular among the propertied classes throughout Europe. The formula included groves of trees, large areas of open lawn or meadow, artificial lakes, streams and waterfalls, meandering paths, and frequent benches affording pleasing vistas. This basic blueprint was adaptable to widely disparate locations, and could be adjusted to local culture and regional environmental conditions. Layers of imported topsoil converted sand dunes into lawns. Steps carved into rocky terrains enabled rustic rambles. Marshes were drained and scoured to become naturalistic lakes. Thousands of imported trees and shrubs replaced indigenous species to complete the desired landscape effect.

Walking along a tree-shaded path beside an artful artificial lake in the Bois de Boulogne in Paris or Central Park in New York—or in a great number of other parks dating to this era around the world—one experiences a similar reverie. The city vanishes from view, both literally and figuratively. The pace slows. The air seems fresher. The sky seems bluer. Patterns of leaves reflect in the water. Very often, being in such a park induces a change of mood. These landscapes were designed to be restful and relaxing, and they are remarkably effective in producing this effect. If we allow ourselves to surrender to their magic, we are transported out of the grit and bustle of the modern city into an artfully staged countryside where everyone is at leisure. Like the man with the bonfire in Central Park, we imagine ourselves in nature, even though we may know better.

This book is a cultural study of these nineteenth-century parks, viewed as an international phenomenon. My goals for this work are to explain why these parks were so widespread and so similar around the world; to explore the cultural meanings embodied in the generic park landscape, as well as some of the differences that distinguished one park from another; to analyze the goals and ambitions of park designers; and, particularly, to describe how audiences received these parks in different locations. As a landscape architect, I am well aware that nineteenth-century urban parks represent a period of extraordinary largesse in the provision of public open space. These parks have set a high standard for subsequent practices in my profession.[3] Yet, in subsequent years, urban parks of this type have come to be viewed as somehow natural, rather than as extremely clever and manipulative fabrications. And they are too often assumed to represent timeless values rather than values forged and anchored in a particular period in the past. For this reason, because these parks have attained such mythological status, I believe they need to be examined more critically. The cultural critic Roland Barthes, who extensively studied the structures and mechanisms of bourgeois mythology, confessed to a "feeling of impatience at the sight of the 'naturalness' with which newspapers, art and common sense constantly dress up a reality which, even though it is the one we live in, is undoubtedly determined by history."[4] I share this impatience when I read much of the historical literature on urban parks, a literature that often discusses parks uncritically, as if referring to some sort of natural phenomenon.

There are many ways to explore the history of nineteenth-century parks, ranging from the aesthetic to the political, social, and economic. It would be impossible in one volume to cover so large a subject and address the many different points of view and many individual parks that should be considered in such a history. Therefore, this book cannot claim to be a comprehensive history of urban parks in the nineteenth century. Rather, it is a collection of essays, each focusing on a specific park, or series of parks, in a particular city and exploring how and why this cultural phenomenon took hold in such very different locales. My hope is that these essays will contribute to a better understanding of nineteenth-century parks as an international cultural phenomenon, and perhaps serve as a catalyst for subsequent studies of parks by others working in different settings and bringing various interpretations to bear on the subject. An important aim of the book is to focus attention on the urban park as a historical cultural phenomenon that deserves much more serious attention from scholars of cultural and social history, as well as historians of urban design. Recognizing that the writing of history is always an interpretive process, I begin by discussing some of the theoretical frameworks that have shaped this study.

Bourgeois Landscapes

The contrast between the rustic landscape of nineteenth-century urban parks and their hard-edged urban surroundings has become more pronounced with time. Cities have become denser and more vertical, enclosing these parks in glass, steel, and masonry walls that are a formidable backdrop to the park landscape. Conspicuously contrasting the country and the city, and epitomizing *rus in urb*, nineteenth-century urban parks continued a venerable tradition in Western culture. Raymond Williams, in an extensive study of this tradition of opposing the country and the city in English literature, pointed out that the tendency to represent these two ideas in "what are loosely called symbols or archetypes" has historically been more marked in times of rapid and momentous change. Particularly in periods when the countryside has changed quickly, archetypes representing a rural ideal have proven appealing, perhaps addressing a deep-seated societal desire for stability. But Williams argued that such archetypes should be resisted and recognized as historically specific, pointing out that "the country and the city are changing historical realities, both in themselves and in their interrelations."[5] In the nineteenth century, industrial capitalism was rapidly transforming both the urban and the rural landscape at an extraordinary rate, and the phenomenon of the urban park should be understood in the historical context of this transformation, particularly in relation to the social and cultural changes that industrial capitalism produced in cities. The urban park is rooted in nineteenth-century bourgeois culture and is a product of industrial capitalism.

Roland Barthes' theories of bourgeois myth are particularly helpful as a framework for understanding how large areas of simulated rural countryside came to seem so natural in the midst of dense urban areas in various corners of the world. A basic premise of this study is that, like many of the phenomena that Barthes analyzed, nineteenth-century parks are cloaked in bourgeois mythology. Barthes' analysis of the process of "naturalization," by which bourgeois culture per-

The formal garden at Vaux le Vicomte, an example of
French landscape design in the seventeenth century.
Garden designed by Andre le Notre. (Photograph by
the author, 1993)

petuates itself, is particularly apropos to these parks.[6] From their
inception, parks have represented and promoted certain bourgeois
norms and values as though they were universal, including the value
of having a large patch of simulated nature in the city, the particular
aesthetic framework for appreciating that patch of nature, and the
set of behaviors and social interactions deemed appropriate in that
setting.

Although in the nineteenth century parks were intended to represent the so-called natural landscape in contrast to the cultural landscape of the modern city, they were not at all natural. They were clever
stage sets representing certain ideas about nature, the country, and the
city. Creating and maintaining the illusions in these parks always

MELODRAMATIC LANDSCAPES

required considerable ingenuity, great expense, and a certain willingness to suspend disbelief on the part of the public. The standard park blueprint, applied around the world in this period, evolved out of a discourse on landscape aesthetics that flourished among the landed aristocracy in England during in the eighteenth century. It is important to understand something of this discourse as a background to the story of public parks in the nineteenth century.

Since the Renaissance, an international exchange of ideas, plant materials, and technologies had enriched both thinking about gardens and garden-making among members of the propertied classes in Europe. The lavish gardens of royal palaces and aristocratic estates, from the fifteenth to the nineteenth centuries, reflected many influences, from the rediscovery and reinterpretation of classical ideas about nature and gardens in the Renaissance, to new currents that filtered in from the European colonies and Asia. As thinking about gardens evolved and new ideas circulated throughout Europe, the locus of innovation shifted, from Italy to France to England.[7] This complex

View of La Crescenza, Claude Lorrain, 1648–50. In the eighteenth century, English gardens were designed to evoke scenes like this. (© Metropolitan Museum of Art, Purchase, The Annenberg Fund Inc. Gift, 1978.205)

A seamless vista from Stowe to the pastoral landscape beyond the garden's boundaries. (Photograph by the author, 1998)

history of European gardens is the foundation on which the familiar landscape of public parks rests.

To understand the aesthetic of nineteenth-century public parks, it is most relevant to focus on the innovations in landscape design that occurred in England in the eighteenth century. A new naturalism in landscape design developed in the eighteenth century in England. This new style evolved in contrast to the elaborate design of French baroque gardens, a fashion that had reached an apogee under Louis XIV. At the end of the seventeenth century, the French baroque garden style was considered the height of sophistication among the European aristocracy, including the English. Gardens designed in this style were geometric in plan, with perfectly straight, tree-lined avenues (*allées*) and intricately patterned planting beds (*parterres*). In the early eighteenth century, rejecting the French style as too artificial and contrived, the English upper classes began to transform their extensive private estates into naturalistic representations of pastoral landscape. They created garden scenery inspired by classical poetry and by paintings of the Italian countryside by popular landscape painters such as Claude Lorrain and Salvator Rosa.

By the end of that century, this pastoral style of landscaping was increasingly identified as the "English" style. Most of the French-

The garden at Stowe, a classic example of eighteenth-century English land-scape design. (Photograph by the author, 1998)

style *parterres* and *allées* on English estates had been removed and replaced by expanses of grass, framed by dense copses of trees. Vistas from the great houses no longer followed an arrow-straight trajectory to the horizon, mimicking Versailles; instead they encompassed great sweeps of pasture dotted with grazing livestock and punctuated by natural-looking lakes. The grazing animals were kept in check by an ingeniously disguised ditch, called a *ha-ha*, bringing the pastoral landscape right up to the edge of the terrace in close proximity to the drawing rooms of great country manor houses.

Landscape aesthetics became a subject of intense interest among the English upper classes in this period, and the new, English-style garden was linked to philosophy, poetry, and the visual arts in a rich intellectual discourse. Through this discourse, English gardens be-came inextricably bound up with politics. Great gardens have always had political meanings embedded in them. Most obviously they rep-resent the social status and political power of their owners. The extraordinary garden built by Louis XIV at Versailles is a case in point. But a somewhat different and more subtle association arose between landscape design and politics in England in the eighteenth century. This is well illustrated by the great park at Stowe, the country estate of the Viscount Cobham. Cobham began to envision a new landscape at Stowe in 1713, after returning from the War of Spanish Succession, the final war stemming from the imperialist ambitions of Louis XIV of France. Cobham and his cohort were Whigs, political and ideological descendants of the leaders of the Glorious Revolution of 1688, who proudly claimed credit for establishing a constitutional monarchy and fostering political freedoms in England. Over the course of its development, the landscape at Stowe became a tribute to the Whig political agenda, as interpreted by Cobham and his circle.

Rejecting the French style of landscape design, which came to be associated not only with the French monarchy but with monarchist ambitions in general, prominent English landowners such as Cobham sought to establish a unique English-style landscape more responsive to, and reflective of, nature. This landscape style signified, for Cobham and others in his circle, the more "natural" evolution of political reform accomplished in England without recourse to violent political revolution, such as the one that occurred across the channel in France, the specter of which haunted English politics throughout the century. In marked contrast to the formal and obviously artificial French garden, with its rigid geometries, the garden ultimately realized at Stowe was "a picture of idealized nature, whose elements [were] grass and trees and water, with buildings carefully sited to give accents to the view and allow the wandering eye a resting place."[8]

The iconography at Stowe linked the Whig political agenda to ancient Greece as the classic model of participatory democracy. Stowe's bucolic scenery paid homage to a long line of pastoral poets, from Theocritus to Milton. Its Temple of Ancient Virtue, housing statues of Homer, Socrates, and Epaminondas, faced a Temple of British Worthies, filled with busts of the heroes of the struggle against the Stuart monarchists as well as the artists, scientists, and philosophers whose ideas provided the philosophic foundations for the Glorious Revolution. Thus, the garden at Stowe, with its more "natural" style of landscape design, came to signify not just the consolidated political power of its owner, but a new kind of politics, more broadly participatory and inclusive. Gardens like this set the stage for the "natural" style of landscape design to link up with the idea of "natural" rights.

The naturalistic, English style of landscape design started as a rarefied experiment on a few great English estates such as Stowe, but became increasingly popular among the propertied classes in England

Mr. & Mrs. Robert Andrews, Thomas Gainsborough, ca. 1748–49. (The National Gallery, London; Bought with contributions from the Pilgrim Trust, the National Art Collections Fund, Associated Television Ltd., and Mr. and Mrs. W. W. Spooner, 1960)

over the course of the eighteenth century. New wealth, produced by manufacturing and trade, enabled more and more people to purchase country property and a series of enclosure acts permitted landowners to claim and enclose the former commons of the traditional English countryside and remove the land from agricultural production. By the end of the century, much of the old, working, rural landscape in England had been replaced by new estates laid out in the newly fashionable style to look like pastures and woodland. An estate designed in this popular fashion became a mark of distinction, and many bourgeois land owners had their portraits painted with their newly landscaped country properties in the background.[9]

The irony of this transformation has been widely noted by historians. As Susan Lasdun has succinctly put it, "paradoxically the 'natural' style that finally resulted in landscaped parks which scarcely differed from the 'common fields,' altered nature more than the tastes of any previous age. Besides the razing of villages and the re-routing of roads, great tracts of earth were contoured, acres flooded, woods uprooted, and rivers dammed. The creation of ever greater heights of

Edenic sublimity was an aristocratic pastime prevalent enough by the early nineteenth century to have produced a welter of literature both praising and satirizing it."[10]

As the old, agrarian English landscape, with its rustic commons, unmanaged woodlands, and meandering country lanes, dwindled over the course of the eighteenth century, nostalgia for it grew. The English upper classes discovered a new affection for wildness and rusticity, as opposed to the gently pastoral landscaping that had been so popular on large estates earlier in the century. This nostalgia consolidated into a new aesthetic, the so-called Picturesque, which gained popularity toward the end of the century. "Picturesque" broadly meant suitable for a picture, but there were many nuances and fine distinctions to be made among various picturesque effects. The Reverend William Gilpin, a major proponent of the Picturesque, published a series of popular guidebooks to picturesque sites throughout Great Britain, and middle-class tourists began to follow his tours on their holidays. The tours included natural sites, such as rocky ravines and waterfalls, as

Gothic House Landscaped in a Picturesque Manner, Thomas Hearne. Engraving, plate 1 from Richard Payne Knight, *The Landscape* (London: P. W. Bulmer & Co. and sold by G. Nicol, 1794). (Courtesy of Cambridge University Library)

South View of the Coronation Fair in Hyde Park, June 28, 1838, on the occasion of the opening of this royal park to the public. (Guildhall Library, City of London)

well as particularly fine examples of naturalistic landscaping on the larger estates. Other proponents of the Picturesque, such as Uvedale Price and Humphry Repton, advocated for wilder, more rustic effects in estate landscaping, and such effects became fashionable and began to appear on landscaped country properties.

The discourse on landscape aesthetics in England in the eighteenth century is important background to nineteenth-century public parks because England, as the most advanced industrial nation in the world, set the tone and served as the model for bourgeois taste and fashion around the world in the nineteenth century. The first public parks were actually former private estates, located in or near growing cities, that gradually opened to the public. London led the way in this, with a string of Crown properties in the West End opening to the public on a fairly regular basis for special days as early as the seventeenth century.[11] It is not merely coincidental that this process mirrored the gradual reduction in the power of the monarchy in England and the introduction of parliamentary reforms; that is, as government

Public Gardens of Melbourne

These [Melbourne] gardens are not in themselves well kept. They are not lovely, as are those of Sydney in a super-excellent degree. Some of them are profusely ornamented with bad statues. None of them, whatever may be their botanical value, are good gardens. But they are large and numerous, and give an air of wholesomeness and space to the whole city. They afford green walks to the citizens, and bring much of the health and some of the pleasures of the country home to them all. One cannot walk about Melbourne without being struck by all that has been done for the welfare of the people generally.

(From Anthony Trollope, *Australia and New Zealand*)

Illumination of Fitzroy Gardens in Honor of the Arrival of the Prince, Nicolas Chevalier. *Illustrated Australian News,* 20 December 1867. (Latrobe Picture Collection, State Library of Victoria, Australia)

opened up to the people in England, the formerly exclusive estates of the ruling class also were made accessible to the public. At first Crown properties were opened only to the aristocracy for special events, such as coronations, but gradually, both conceptions of "the public" and the number of public occasions expanded, until by the nineteenth century many former Crown and aristocratic properties were permanently converted to public ownership, officially proclaimed public parks, and opened to a public that gradually grew to span the social spectrum by the end of the nineteenth century. The naturalistic landscaping on the former Crown properties in London served as model for new parks created on the Continent and in colonial cities around the world.

During the second half of the century, large-scale migrations from countryside to city and increasing movement of populations across national boundaries created exponential population growth in cities around the world. International proliferation of finance and trade capitalism produced a powerful, new international bourgeoisie, and as new democratic institutions succeeded older, hereditary forms of government worldwide, civic leadership consolidated into the hands of this elite business class, joined by members of the newly formalized professions. The new civic leadership assumed control of civic affairs as self-appointed guardians of the public interest, as well as arbiters of public taste, manners, and mores. This book views urban parks as a product of the international bourgeois culture that flourished in cities in the nineteenth century.

Urban parks were one means by which the new bourgeois social order asserted itself in cities. In the capitals of new nations emerging from colonial rule in the nineteenth century, entirely new parks were created and modeled after older, formerly aristocratic parks in European capitals, signifying and solidifying lingering cultural ties to Europe.[12] Lacking former estates to convert, new civic governments created the large new parks by appropriating various properties from multiple owners, in a process involving eminent domain and real-estate speculation. A large urban park became not only a mark of civic distinction, but also an important factor in national and international competition among cities for business investment. By the end of the century, nearly every modernizing city had added a large, naturalistic park, both to signify modernity and to attract members of the growing business and professional class. As community leaders in San Francisco put it, in a petition calling for such a park in that city in 1865: "the great cities of our own country, as well as of Europe, have found it necessary at some period of their growth, to provide large parks, or pleasure grounds for the amusement and entertainment of the people. . . . Until some provision is made to meet this need, however successful and impressive the business growth of San Francisco may be, it will not be an attractive and impressive place for families and homes."[13]

In many ways, the public park, as a nineteenth-century public institution, illustrates the theory of the liberal, bourgeois public sphere outlined by Jürgen Habermas in *The Structural Transformation of the Public Sphere*. Habermas postulated a liberal, bourgeois, public sphere composed of private citizens coming together by means of various new institutions, ranging from cafés to a free press, to shape civil society in the public interest; that is, in the interests of finance and commercial capitalism in the aftermath of the Industrial Revolution. According to Habermas, however, the liberal, bourgeois public sphere attained its fullest realization in the eighteenth century, and then disintegrated in the nineteenth century in the face of competing special interests, monopolistic capitalism, and social regulation. Habermas's critics have offered differing interpretations of the public sphere, particularly in the nineteenth century, arguing that the transformation of the public sphere in this period is better described as multiple publics competing in a process of class formation and social differentiation, and that much of the groundwork for the public sphere, as it operates today, was laid in the nineteenth century.[14] The public park, as a nineteenth-century civic institution, straddles this debate. Invented by powerful private citizens and public officials, and intended as public spaces in which citizens representing a cross-section of society could associate voluntarily, their interactions governed by public opinion and decorum, public parks were conceived to help shape civil society in the public interest. Thus, in many ways, the public park can be viewed as a model institution of the liberal, bourgeois public sphere. Yet, from their inception, public parks served as staging grounds for various competing publics and were shaped by competing special interests.

This book conceptualizes the urban park as a public stage on which complex processes of social differentiation played out in the nineteenth century, both figuratively and literally. These processes can be understood at both the global and the local scale. On the one hand, at the global scale, each park was part of an international phenomenon, an example of a prototype that proliferated widely in this period as a product of bourgeois culture, shaped by the big ideas, large cultural narratives, and social movements of the nineteenth century. On the other hand, at the local scale, each park was also a unique cultural production, with a particular set of managers and directors and a distinctive cast of characters drawn from the local pool.

Melodramatic Landscapes

Melodrama, or what cultural historians of the nineteenth century have termed the "melodramatic imagination," offers an illuminating framework for understanding and explaining various aspects and institutions of nineteenth-century culture, including the urban park. The literary critic Peter Brooks coined the term "melodramatic imagination" in a seminal study of the melodramatic form in literature. He argued that in the nineteenth century melodrama was much more than a popular genre of literature or a form of theater; it was "a mode of conception and expression, a certain fictional system for making sense of experience, a semantic field of force" that affected nineteenth-century culture in innumerable ways.[15] In other words, Brooks argued that melodrama was a pervasive cultural discourse in the nineteenth century, a set of narratives and themes that helped the nineteenth century understand itself. As such, the melodramatic imagination is a helpful framework for explicating a cultural institution such as the urban park in the nineteenth century, particularly in the United States, where parks were conceived as instruments of moral reform by a civic-minded elite whose goal was to shape and refine American society in a period of rapid social change.[16] The melodramatic imagination offers a framework for understanding not only how urban parks were conceived, but the way they actually worked as instruments of reform in the democratic United States, that is, how they embodied and transmitted certain moral messages and how the public received and responded to those messages.

In this book, I use the melodramatic imagination as a framework for explicating Central Park in New York, which was developed and took root in the decades surrounding the American Civil War. Political and social structures were fraying as the war approached, and were in disarray after the war ended. It was a time of high political and social tension in the United States, and it was obvious to nearly everyone that American culture was in a period of transition. Other historians have characterized this period in American culture as theatrical and have attributed this theatricality to a generalized state of social and cultural upheaval. Karen Halttunen, for example, has determined that in the nineteenth century there was "a growing acceptance by the American middle classes of the underlying theatricality of all their claims to genteel social status."[17] In her study *Theatre Culture in America*, Rosemarie Bank observed that melodrama offered Americans in the nineteenth century "a way of acting and a legitimization of performing outside as well as inside playhouses." In that connection, Bank writes of the need to scrutinize "not only the performances scripted by the author(itie)s, but those valorized by the actors themselves."[18] Applying this to public parks, the users of parks can be considered as both actors and audience in a public performance. Certainly, the way people acted in the parks and reacted to them is an important part of the historical record. The daily performances that occur in parks may be scripted by the authorities, but the actors have considerable influence over how these performances play out.

Designers and promoters of public parks in the nineteenth century were well aware of this dynamic and expressed some anxiety about the unpredictable nature of public behavior in the parks. A history of these parks that leaves out public reception of them and ignores how people actually used them would be incomplete, equivalent to reviewing a play without witnessing the staging of it. The audiences for these parks were large and diverse and left far fewer traces than those who mounted the productions. Yet in the press, in drawings and photographs, in private correspondence, journals, and even contemporary fiction, a sense of the public reception for the parks emerges. My goal is to examine the parks in this book from various points of view, to get a sense not only of the goals of the parks' designers, but also a sense of the special interests and agendas that shaped these parks, the range of people involved, and the public reception of each park in as much complexity as possible.

Most histories of nineteenth-century parks have tended to venerate a particular park and/or park designer, downplaying the complex tangle of social and political processes that have actually produced these public landscapes. A notable exception is *The Park and the People*, by Roy Rosenzweig and Elizabeth Blackmar, which explores the multifaceted social history of Central Park in New York, from its inception in the middle of the nineteenth century, to the end of the twentieth century. This work, while respectful of Central Park and the individuals who made it happen, also reveals the many competing ideologies and special interests that have shaped this park from its inception to the present day. Rosenzweig and Blackmar aim to explain Central Park from various points of view, including that of the park's designers, real-estate developers, financiers, politicians, laborers who built and maintained the park, the park police, and many different people who have used it. I have aimed for this broader kind of perspective in exploring the nineteenth-century history of the parks discussed in this book.

Structure of the Book

The three major chapters in this book focus on Paris, Mexico City, and New York. I have selected these particular cities because they all have large and significant parks dating to the nineteenth century, parks that were internationally recognized at the time and are well preserved today. These three cities represent three very different cultural, political, and geographical contexts for parks in this period, yet they are all connected historically. While each park's story is unique, these narratives also represent major episodes in the larger history of the public park as a nineteenth-century cultural institution, illustrating how the urban park began, evolved, and became what it is today.

The first chapter is about the parks created in Paris during the Second Empire. This chapter explores the motivations for building these parks, how they were developed, and the public's reception of them. The argument advanced in this chapter is that the parks created during the Second Empire in Paris were caught up in and reflected the sometimes contradictory and ideologically inconsistent politics of Napoleon III. Public parks played an important role in maintaining a precarious balance among various competing political interests and competing social classes in the aftermath of the revolution of 1848. Spaced over the increasingly delineated social map of Paris, the parks anchored certain strategic neighborhoods, forged new identities for *quartiers* in the newly annexed area surrounding the old city, which nearly doubled its size, and brought those areas into a net of social and political influence cast over the city by Baron Haussmann, prefect of the Seine. Haussmann was appointed by Napoleon III early in his tenure and charged with the enormous project of renovating Paris to make it into a modern, industrial city. The parks were an effective symbol of modernity, as well as a clever political tool, and they are one of the most remarkable legacies of the Second Empire in Paris.

Chapter 2 focuses on Chapultepec Park, in Mexico City. Even more than the Paris parks of the Second Empire in France, Chapultepec Park occupies a site sanctified by momentous historical events prior to its conversion into a public park. While this chapter focuses primarily on the transformation of Chapultepec into a bourgeois park in the late nineteenth century, as background to this transformation it addresses the previous history of the site, from the arrival of the Mexicas (precursors of the Aztecs) at Chapultepec around 1270; through the golden age of the Aztec city of Tenochtitlán, when Chapultepec was a retreat for the Aztec rulers and a site of religious ritual, including human sacrifice; through the Spanish conquest, the colonial period, and the struggle for national identity that followed. The transformation of this site into a European-style park began with the brief French intervention (1864–67), but occurred mainly during the Porfiriato (1876–1911), when the development of the park became the special province of José Limantour, minister of finance under the dictator Porfirio Díaz. This chapter explores the influence of both indigenous Mexican and European cultures on Chapultepec and shows how the park served as an emblem of the Porfiriato, reflecting its ambitious economic and nationalist agenda and its overt social controls.

Central Park, in New York, is the third park examined in depth. Much has been written about this venerable park, which was the first of its kind in the United States, and which spawned scores of similar parks in other North American cities during the second half of the nineteenth century. This chapter takes a new look at this well-studied park, exploring precedents set by commercial pleasure gardens and the influence of the "melodramatic imagination" on its design, its de-

Central Park, New York. (Photograph by
Marc B. Schenker, 2004)

velopment, and its reception by the public. Commercial pleasure gardens preceded public parks in New York as popular settings for outdoor leisure. Privately owned, these establishments vied for clientele by offering increasingly elaborate landscape effects, events, and performances. At the beginning, commercial pleasure gardens appealed to a range of visitors, but by the mid-nineteenth century, they were attracting a mostly working-class audience. Eventually they evolved into actual theaters, their history preserved in names such as Madison Square Garden and Niblos Garden. In contrast to these commercial gardens, Central Park was conceived and designed as a more natural, more bourgeois, and less theatrical setting for outdoor leisure. But in this chapter I argue that Central Park was also, in its own way, a theatrical production. A comparison of the park to popular moral reform melodramas playing in New York theaters at the time finds many parallels and evidence of the melodramatic imagination at work in both the theater and the new park. This analysis of Central Park, framed by the melodramatic imagination, reveals how the park navigated cultural, political, and social tensions in a social and political context quite different from that of France and Mexico in this period.

Throughout this book, as a counterpoint to the three main stories focusing on Paris, Mexico City, and New York, sidebars offer nineteenth-century accounts of parks in various cities around the world. Some of these sidebars offer additional insights about the parks in Paris, Mexico City, and New York. Others refer to parks in other locations. I have selected these vignettes—all drawn from primary sources—to represent diverse points of view on these parks in the nineteenth century, from the perceptions of the designers and civic leaders who promoted the parks, to those of journalists and critics. Included are accounts of park users, artists, photographers, and others who chronicled their experiences and impressions of the parks in the nineteenth century. These sidebars are intended to make the parks come alive in their nineteenth-century context and to offer a running counterpoint to the larger themes running through the text of this book. The sidebars are like subplots, expanding on the main narratives, adding drama, or providing comic relief. While it may be futile to try to avoid the mythologizing tendency inherent in a study of this sort, the sidebars are meant to serve as a check on the propensity to explain these parks only in terms of powerful social agendas or theatrical metaphors. The idiosyncratic and personal accounts included in the sidebars illustrate how, even as they were under construction physically, these parks were under construction culturally. This is still true of parks today. This book is part of that process.

Parks in Paris
during the
Second Empire

ÉMILE ZOLA'S NOVEL *LA CURÉE*, SET IN
Paris at the height of the Second Empire, opens with a traffic jam in
the Bois de Boulogne.[1] As an interminable parade of elegant carriages
makes its way slowly around the lower lake of the park, the landscape
serves as a charming background for the fashionable bourgeoisie who
are the subject of Zola's novel. The scenery unfolds, revealing the two
islands in the lower lake with their "pleasing" cliffs, joined by a bridge.
Foliage drapes from the grand old trees like "curtains," framing views.
Great lawns sweep down to the water's edge like "immense grass car-
pets." Zola's language portrays the park as an artful backdrop to the
social drama in the foreground: "This corner of nature, this decor that
seemed freshly painted, was bathed in a light shadow, in a bluish
vapor that gave to the distance an exquisite charm, an air of adorable
falsity."[2]

Émile Zola wrote twenty novels in the series *Les Rougon-
Macquart: Histoire naturelle et social d'une famille sous le Second
Empire.* His intention was to create a complete chronicle of life during
France's Second Empire, under the regime of Napoleon III. Each

The Champs-Élysées. Engraving from Adolphe Joanne, *Paris-Diamant* (Paris: Hachette, 1872).

novel in the Rougon-Macquart series focuses on a different segment of French society. In *La curée*, the second novel of the series, the main events take place in the 1860s, at the height of the rebuilding of Paris under Napoleon III, and the main characters are the bourgeoisie who made fortunes on real-estate speculation in this period of unprecedented urban development. It is a tale of glittering, conspicuous consumption, decadent lifestyles, and dubious morals. The bottleneck of vehicles described by Zola was, in fact, a daily occurrence in the Bois de Boulogne at the height of the Second Empire. Paris guidebooks recommended that tourists go to the park in the late afternoon to see the daily spectacle of high fashion and stylish carriages for which Paris was famous during that period.[3]

Completely refurbished, the Bois de Boulogne was a showpiece of the new Paris created by Napoleon III during the Second Empire. It was one of the first design projects completed under Louis Napoleon's reign, and the emperor took a personal interest in the transformation of the former royal woods into a public park. The success of the new park gave impetus to the transformation of other former royal gardens into public parks: the Bois de Vincennes, Parc Monceau, and the Jardin du Luxembourg were similarly remodeled and opened to the public in the 1860s. Toward the end of the Empire, Parc des Buttes Chaumont and Parc Montsouris were designed in a similar style. Each had sinuous avenues, serpentine lakes, waterfalls, grottoes, and other picturesque effects in the so-called English style. The parks were jewels in the precious fabric of the new Paris. They were part of the city's new face, along with architectural monuments and new boulevards, all woven into the grand project of rebuilding Paris as a modern city, "capital of the world." Yet, not everyone welcomed the face-lift. The preface to Edmond Texier's 1867 novel, *Paris, capitale du monde*, opens with a lament for the old Paris, before Haussmann's renovations: "When, towards 1852 or 1853, the material transformation of Paris began on a vast scale; when small, timid punctures were succeeded by immense, gaping holes, demolished houses by demolished *quartiers*, we didn't understand at first that as the old city tumbled down it was taking with it the ancient mores, old habits, ancient traditions."[4]

Baron Haussmann, prefect of the Seine, bore the administrative responsibility for the rebuilding of Paris under Napoleon III, including the new parks. The baron's *Mémoires* are an important primary source from the period, especially valuable to historians since most of the official records of the period were destroyed in a fire in the Hotel de Ville in 1871. In the *Mémoires*, Haussmann emphasized the importance of the new public parks, identifying them as a particularly innovative aspect of the modernized city: "The creation of promenades, parks, gardens, squares especially for public use is nearly without example before the second half of this century. Constantly preoccupied with improving life for the classes the least favored by fortune, particularly concerned with conditions of health and the well-being of the urban population, the emperor Napoleon III gave the impetus, as all the world knows, to this beneficial undertaking of which the results are visible and admired by other nations."[5]

The baron's reference to those "least favored by fortune" contrasts with the image of the Bois de Boulogne sketched by contemporary guidebooks and painted so vividly by Zola, raising the question, For whom *were* the parks actually intended?

Certainly the story of these parks is more multifaceted than that told in the baron's *Mémoires*. This work, written from an ignominious retirement after the fall of the Empire, must be read as a useful but

A Socialist View of the Thiergarten

You may stand in the Thiergarten in Berlin, and here roll by the handsome carriages with jingling harness and liveried footmen. Very comfortable people lounge on the cushions. The women have diamonds and costly dresses; the men have white soft hands. At one side of the park is a long line of costly palaces. . . . And on the river there is a barge going slowly by. A man takes a long pole to the bow and drives it down to the bottom of the river, and sets his shoulder to the end. Then he struggles slowly toward the stern, pushing with all his strength upon the pole. On the deck of the barge, inside the gunwale, are crosswise cleats upon which he clings with his feet as he pushes. He crawls slowly along, bent far over, his head below his knees. . . . So, inch by inch, he fights his way to the stern. There he takes his pole from the river and moves forward to the bow again. And you see how his toil has distorted his face and twisted his body, and you look at him and wince. And he takes his pole and limps back to the bow. The birds are singing in the garden, the trees are handsome in the sun, there are vistas down the avenues, somewhere a band is playing. Evidently he sees none of these things and hears none. Birds and green grass and the blessed sun mean nothing to him. Brutal toil has obliterated the sense of them. The handsome carriages go by, full of laughing people; a Prussian officer, brilliantly dressed, rides down the bridle path.

Dozing in the Shade, in the Thiergarten, Berlin. Engraving from Henry Vizetelly, *Berlin under the New Empire: Its Institutions,* vol. 1 (London, Tinsley Brothers, 1879).

(From Charles Edward Russell, *Why I Am a Socialist*)

biased account of the renovation of Paris under the Second Empire.[6] The politics of the Second Empire involved a delicate balancing of class and political interests, maintaining a tenuous peace for twenty years between the Revolution of 1848 and the bloody suppression of the Paris Commune in 1871. Haussmann resigned in 1870, when the chorus of criticism of his methods for financing public projects reached such a pitch that he became too much of a political liability to the emperor. The defeat of the Franco-Prussian War brought about the end of the Second Empire shortly thereafter. But how did the parks fit into the changing social configuration of Paris as it was reshaped under Haussmann's direction? What did the English style of the parks signify in this context? Whose political interests did the parks serve? How did "the public" view the parks? How were they used and by whom? These parks were indeed "admired by other nations," but they cannot really be understood without understanding the particular political and social context that produced them in Paris at this time. They are bound up in, and reflective of, the political conflicts and internal inconsistencies that characterized Napoleon III's administration.[7] In this context, the symbolism of those remarkable stage sets described by Zola is more complex than has generally been recognized by the parks' many admirers and imitators.

The Rebuilding of Paris

Haussmann's tenure spanned the years from 1853 to 1870, and the legacy of those years includes an extensive network of new roads, new parks and squares, new public buildings, new sewers, and a new water-delivery system. The process of rebuilding the city during the Second Empire has sometimes been called the "Haussmannization" of Paris. The prefect of the Seine was a skilled administrator whose task was to realize the emperor's vision. He worked directly from an original plan for new boulevards and monuments sketched by the emperor himself, who "fancied himself something of an architect."[8] As a career bureaucrat, Haussmann held a series of posts in the provinces before being appointed prefect of the Seine by the emperor. As prefect he directed a large bureaucracy. The individual contributions of those who worked on the rebuilding project in various capacities within this bureaucracy cannot always be determined from historical records.[9]

However, Adolphe Alphand was in charge of the design and construction of parks, squares, and boulevards under Haussmann, and his later account, *Les promenades de Paris*, is the primary reference on the parks. Jean-Pierre Barillet-Deschamps, as chief gardener for the city, provided plants and played a large role in the design of the parks. As prefect, Haussmann bore not only the major responsibility for the rebuilding project, but also the brunt of public criticism, since he was the figure constantly in the public eye.

In 1852, Paris was still largely a medieval city, a haphazard warren of narrow, crowded streets with open sewers and very little open space. Encircled by the eighteenth-century "wall of the *fermiers généraux*" (tax collectors), which controlled tax collection on goods entering the city, Paris had grown by filling in available space, becoming more and more densely populated.[10] Most working-class quarters of the city were still tight-knit communities, providing necessary services to inhabitants, who rarely ventured beyond the familiar territory these quarters afforded.[11] As the population of Paris grew during the eighteenth century, increasing social-class stratification occurred, initially within buildings rather than by district. Ground floors were occupied by businesses and commercial establishments; bourgeois living quarters occupied the lower floors, while poorer, working-class tenants were installed in the garrets.[12]

During the early nineteenth century, increasing class separation occurred by district. Newer fashionable housing began to appear in the western half of the city. These wealthier quarters were adjoined by some of the worst slums, however. A particularly impoverished and unsightly area occupied the space between the Louvre and the Tuileries Palace, and the center of the Île de la Cité, between the Palais de Justice and Notre Dame, was another dark hole of poverty. Stretching eastward from the Rue Montmartre was the working-class district that is the setting of Zola's novel *L'Assommoir*, the most well-known and widely translated novel of the Rougon-Macquart series, which tells the story of the gradual descent into abject poverty of a working-class family in eastern Paris, roughly between 1850 and 1870. The heroine, Gervaise Macquart, is a laundress. Her husband is a roofer who, in his younger days, profits from the construction boom in Paris, but after an accident suffered while working, takes to drink and gradually sinks into destitution.[13] Like Gervaise in the novel, residents of this

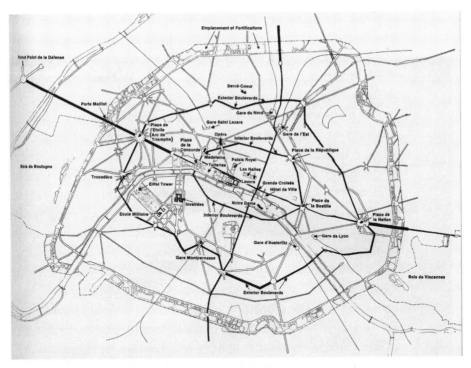

Map showing the extension of the limits of Paris to the outer ring of fortifications in 1859. Line drawing from Norma Evenson, *Paris: A Century of Change* (New Haven: Yale University Press, 1979). (Courtesy of Yale University Press)

area lived in decrepit tenements above tiny shops and workshops. Artisans and pieceworkers produced the fashionable clothing, jewelry, and metalwork for which Paris was world-famous. Such densely populated, poor districts were not only a breeding ground for disease (Paris experienced a devastating cholera epidemic in 1848 that killed nineteen thousand people) but also the source of successive popular uprisings during the first half of the nineteenth century.

In 1859–60, the size of Paris was nearly doubled with the annexation of the surrounding area that lay between the toll boundary of the *fermiers généraux*, at the line of the present second ring of boulevards, and an outer ring of fortifications that had been erected in the 1840s about a mile beyond. In contrast to the densely populated central districts, the newly annexed zone was more sparsely populated. This area figured prominently in plans for rebuilding the city during the Second Empire. During the 1850s and 1860s, the population of Paris nearly doubled, fed by a large influx of workers from the provinces lured in part by the prospect of jobs created by the rebuilding projects. Most of the growth occurred in the newly annexed areas. At the same time, the central districts decreased in population, as slums were razed to make way for civic improvements.[14]

At first, new boulevards and squares overlaid a facade of modernity on a city that remained largely poor and disheveled behind the modern facade. Regulations that accompanied the new building program sometimes emphasized appearance over substance. For example, a decree of 1852 required cleaning or repainting of buildings at least every ten years, but no regulations controlled living conditions in new buildings, so many builders erected crowded, poorly ventilated apartments, creating tenements behind new facades.[15] In the beginning, many Parisians welcomed the improvements. The new circulation system promised to alleviate traffic congestion, facilitate crosstown communication, and open up neighborhoods to light and air. New boulevards were enlivened by the spectacle of Parisians from all walks of life. Condemnation of buildings to make way for the new boulevards provided an official excuse for removal of some of the worst slums. Many workers benefited from jobs provided by the new building projects. Approximately 20 percent of the Parisian labor force was employed in the building trades in the mid-1860s, during the height of the rebuilding projects. New sewers and a new water-delivery system accomplished perhaps the most important transformation, not only enhancing the appearance of the city streets but improving public health and sanitation.

The condemnation of buildings to put through the new wide boulevards displaced poor tenants, crowding them into nearby areas of substandard housing, or pushing them out of the city center to the plains of La Villette or the hill of Belleville in the newly annexed zone to the east. The new plan favored development of bourgeois districts in the center and to the west.[16] Industry consolidated in areas to the northeast and the south in the annexed zone and beyond the city limits. The effect of the rebuilding project was to push the working classes and industry out of the city center, ultimately creating a bourgeois core.[17] Shifts in the social configuration of the city began in the early part of the century; many of the trends blamed on

Construction in Paris during the Second Empire. *Élargissement de la rue
Soufflot,* Stablo. Engraving after a drawing by Ch. Chegaray, 1876. (Courtesy
of Agence Roger-Viollet)

Haussmannization—such as the shift of the city to the west and displacement of the poor from central districts—were, in fact, already
well under way before the coup d'état. But the policies of the Second
Empire reinforced these trends.[18]

It is unlikely that a rebuilding project of such grand scale could
have been accomplished under a less authoritarian regime.[19] Yet dis-
sonant voices were heard, increasing in volume as the relentless evic-
tions and demolitions, the din of construction, the dust, and the disruption took their toll on Parisians. Again Zola captures the mood, in
L'Assommoir, when Gervaise, the working-class heroine, expresses
annoyance in reaction to the emperor's "improvements," which create
gaping holes in the old district where she has lived and worked all her
life. She is sometimes "furious at having to step over building materials, paddle about where pavements [are] not finished." Her husband
engages in daily arguments with their friend, a policeman, about the
rebuilding of the city: "The former went on and on about the Paris

demolitions, accusing the emperor of building palaces everywhere so as to pack the workers off into the provinces, and the policeman, white with suppressed anger, riposted that, on the contrary, the emperor's first thoughts were for the workers, and that he would demolish the whole of Paris if necessary, simply to make work for them."[20]

Nineteenth-century criticism of the rebuilding of Paris has been thoroughly documented by historians.[21] I summarize some of the general arguments here. Critics charged that the emperor was rebuilding Paris as a bourgeois city, filling the money coffers of bourgeois speculators, evicting the working classes from the center of the city. They charged that the new, wide boulevards were really intended to improve national security, making barricades more difficult to erect and facilitating access by government troops to *quartiers* where disturbances might arise.[22] Some mourned the colorful, tight-knit old neighborhoods. They noted that the rebuilding process inevitably changed the social structure of the city. *Quartiers* that had existed for centuries were torn down or broken up by new streets, and the result was increasing segregation by social class. Political opponents of the Empire pointed out conflicts between official explanations for the transformation of Paris and the actual results, charging corruption and favoritism and ascribing political motives.

Artists and intellectuals charged that the new boulevards and uniform facades created a monotonous and alienating effect. Haussmann was accused of "puerile taste."[23] Those who lived through the process of reconstruction were often nostalgic for the twists and turns of the old city. They joked about Haussmann's penchant for straight lines. Edmond de Goncourt wrote in his journal: "I am a stranger to what is coming, to what is, as I am to these new boulevards without turnings, without chance perspectives, implacable in their straight lines, which no longer smack of the world of Balzac, which make one think of some American Babylon of the future."[24] Parisians found relief in satirical humor. There was no escaping the fact that Paris was experiencing a great face-lift, but some weren't sure whether the end result would be worth the discomfort and disruption.

Théophile Gautier described the scenery of the new Paris, with its ghostly skeletons of half-demolished buildings, as a "mosaic of ruins," and observed: "Paris is getting dressed and wishes to show herself to the world in her best finery," while Baudelaire wrote:

Old Paris is no more (the form of a city changes
faster, alas, than a mortal heart); . . .

Paris changes! But nothing of my melancholy
has lifted! New palaces, scaffoldings, blocks,
old outer districts: for me everything becomes allegory
and my cherished memories weigh like rocks.[25]

Throughout much of the contemporary commentary about the rebuilding of Paris ran a strong vein of cynicism about the motives behind the rebuilding project. The regime of Napoleon III, with its glamorous Imperial court and its satellite society of *nouveaux riches,* was broadly characterized as frivolous and corrupt. Zola evoked this atmosphere in *La curée:* "The grand preoccupation of the society was to know with which amusements to kill time. . . . Paris sat down at the table and dreamed dirty jokes for dessert. Politics was appalling, like a dangerous drug. Weary spirits turned toward scandal and pleasure. . . . There was, at the depth of the crush, a muffled sighing, the nascent noise of hundred-sou pieces, bright laughter of women, the faint tinkling of china and kisses."[26] Bourgeois speculators made fortunes in real estate by buying and selling properties in the path of new boulevards and new parks. In such an atmosphere of heady speculation some Parisians, especially intellectuals, voiced cynicism about the ulterior motives of those in charge of the rebuilding process. Haussmann's unorthodox methods for financing public improvements came under increasing scrutiny, and eventually charges of fiscal irresponsibility forced his resignation.[27]

The political ideology of the Second Empire was inconsistent and contradictory, reflecting Napoleon III's efforts to maintain a tenuous balance between various competing political interests. Eventually he alienated everyone. Writing in 1852, Karl Marx noted that Louis Napoleon's mission was to maintain "bourgeois order." The emperor saw himself as the standard-bearer of the middle class, yet he also had to keep the peasants and the lower classes happy and, to this end, characterized himself and his regime as representing the *lumpenproletariat,* to which he largely owed his election. According to Marx, "this contradictory task of the man explains the contradictions of his government, the confused groping about which seeks now to win, now to humiliate first one class and then another and arrays all of them uniformly against him, whose practical uncertainty forms a highly comical contrast to the imperious, categorical style of the government decrees, a style which is faithfully copied from the uncle."[28]

The strategy of contradiction and conciliation that Marx described worked for twenty years, but ultimately could not sustain the Second Empire. Napoleon III had been brought to power by a coalition of provincial peasants and industrial capitalists united against aristocrats, monarchists, landowners, and clergy in their desire to expand industry, transport, and trade and to free up credit and land.[29] As emperor, he tried to maintain the support of this mercurial coalition, but during the life span of the Empire political opposition shifted and regrouped. The original political support that had brought Napoleon III to power eroded during the course of the Empire. In a period of rapid industrialization, class definitions and political allegiances were in a state of flux. A strictly economic determinist definition of class is not adequate to explain the shifts and turns of political allegiance and the emergence of the Republican opposition that eventually brought down the Second Empire. The rapidly expanding industrial bourgeoisie exerted increasing social influence, as well as political and economic power. The established political opposition—the old financial bourgeoisie and remnants of the aristocracy—found opportunities to profit from collaboration with the Bonapartist regime. Peasant support was alienated by Napoleon's promotion of capitalist industry.[30] Throughout these shifts in political opposition, the rebuilding project in Paris provided a visible focus for a relentless current of criticism, as Louis Girard notes, "almost always inspired by political passion."[31]

Parks and the Social Reconfiguration of Paris

The Paris parks played a key role in the social reconfiguration of the city during the Second Empire, helping to reshape both a new physical reality and new public perceptions of the social map of the city. Introducing green spaces into the fabric of urban life, parks played a role in improving public health, or at least the perception of public health, in the city. Anchoring key districts, the parks served as focal points for emerging social identities attached to various districts, showcasing new social distinctions, but also blurring social boundaries by affording new opportunities for social classes to mingle. Perhaps most importantly, parks were intricately bound up with real-estate develop-ment, offering lucrative opportunities for speculation and profiteering, as well as fashionable new addresses for the upwardly mobile.

In *Les promenades de Paris*, Alphand proclaimed parks and park-ways essential to public health in the modern city: "Public gardens [and] wide, planted streets where air can circulate freely are absolutely necessary in the interior of large cities in respect to health. The prog-ress of science and of man requires the most hygienic conditions inside and near dwellings. This is, above all, important for the populations of cities."[32] Public health benefits were cited by both Alphand and Haussmann as general justification for public expenditures on parks, tree-lined streets, and squares.

Scientists in England, France, and Germany had made connec-tions between poverty and disease in the years leading up to 1848. France led the world in developing public health survey methods in the early nineteenth century. Louis René Villermé, a French physi-cian, published a study in 1828 correlating poverty and mortality in Paris by district, and relating public health to the different living conditions of the different social classes. Villermé's work was used by Edwin Chadwick to focus attention on the need for a systematic study of public health in England, which led to the extensive surveys con-ducted by the Poor Law Commission in the 1830s and 1840s and the publication of an extensive report, in 1842, on the sanitary conditions of the working class in Great Britain.[33] These studies led to increasing acceptance of an association between the conditions of poverty— crowded, unsanitary living conditions, stagnant air, foul water, etc.— and disease. Yet, the mechanisms by which diseases were transmitted remained poorly understood and in dispute for most of the nineteenth century. There were two competing theories. The miasmatic theory held that epidemics of infectious disease were caused by the state of the atmosphere (miasma). An unhealthy atmosphere was thought to be a function of poor sanitary conditions. Many nineteenth-century public health advocates, such as Edwin Chadwick in England, held this view, hence their focus on sanitary improvements. The other theory attributed disease to specific contagia; this was the strict con-tagionist position and led to the bacteriological discoveries at the end of the century. The contagionists called for the use of quarantines and isolation to control disease outbreaks. Anticontagionists opposed such

The Pont des Îles in the Bois de Boulogne. Lithograph from Adolphe Alphand, *Les promenades de Paris* (Paris: J. Rothschild, 1867–73). (Courtesy of Special Collections, University of Virginia Library)

methods, for various reasons, including the hardship they imposed on the poor. Scientifically, neither theory had a strong enough body of evidence to be conclusively proved until the end of the century. Certain important pieces of information supporting the contagionist theory had not yet been discovered, such as the role of human carriers and insect hosts.[34] Sutcliffe notes that contemporary theories of public health favored the "anti-contagionist hypothesis," which attributed the spread of disease to environmental causes such as dirt, poverty, overcrowding, and poor sewers, as well as foul air. The fresh air and sunlight afforded by the new, wider street corridors and parks were therefore assumed to contribute to public health.[35]

Nicholas Green's analysis of environmental thinking in the early part of the nineteenth century offers additional insight. Green noted that "Paris was seen as a map where moral and social meanings were read into the contrasting quarters of the capital. Yet, despite the efforts of hygienists and planners, these spaces were never kept wholly apart. In the minds of metropolitans, diseased and dangerous Paris was always threatening to invade *their* habitat, to infiltrate *their* field of vision."[36] Green's study of environmentalism in the first half of the century sets the stage for understanding the official thinking about parks during the Second Empire. In the 1840s, "environmentalist discourse projected urban space as a topography whose potentially healthy features, like air, light and running water, were to be maximized against incursions of disease and decay. . . . imagining gardens as concentrated enclosures of wholesomeness, moral as well as physical, as breathing holes . . . where all classes and ages of the population could enjoy themselves *appropriately;* where, *secure,* they could immerse themselves in the goodness of air and light and restorative exercise."[37] The network of parks and boulevards laid over the city in the ensuing decades helped keep diseased, dangerous, and unhealthy Paris under control. Inserted strategically around the city, parks did provide fresh air and pockets of greenery, but they also had a more symbolic significance, which becomes apparent in the context of the changing social configuration of the city.

On the plan of Paris as reconstructed during the Second Empire, the parks occurred in a balanced spatial configuration. This spatial arrangement was not only related to the social map of the city, but also had political connotations. The Bois de Boulogne to the west, just beyond the fortifications, found its counterpoint to the east in the Bois de Vincennes, also just beyond the fortifications. Parks Monceau, Buttes Chaumont, and Montsouris formed a triangulation that not only held the city center in check, but asserted a new focus on the annexed zone after 1860. Each of the parks corresponded not only to a specific area of the city, but to an emerging map of social and political identities. The Bois de Boulogne on the western edge of the city related to the shift to the west of the centers of finance and commerce, a shift already under way by the time Napoleon III came to power. The Champs Élysées, extended via the Avenue de l'Imperatrice to the Bois, followed a momentum set in motion by Haussmann's predecessors. Parc Monceau, at the inside edge of the annexed zone, also on the western side, formed the focus of a newly fashionable bourgeois neighborhood and was soon surrounded by new residences. As the western bourgeois districts prospered, the eastern districts became increasingly identified as working-class. The renovation of the Bois de Vincennes became necessary to reestablish political equilibrium; as Haussmann noted in his *Mémoires,* it "became necessary to create

Plan of Paris at the end of the Second Empire, showing the Bois de Boulogne on the west and the Bois de Vincennes on the east. Lithograph from Adolphe Alphand, *Les promenades de Paris* (Paris: J. Rothschild, 1867–73). (Courtesy of Special Collections, University of Virginia Library)

in the east of Paris, conforming to the generous designs of the emperor for the working-class population of the new eleventh and twelfth arrondissements, and for the workers of the Faubourg Saint-Antoine in particular, a promenade equivalent to that which had been given to the west, to the rich and elegant districts of [the] capital."[38] On the political map of Paris, the Faubourg Saint-Antoine was one of those zones of uncertainty that persisted as a nagging political worry for the government. It had been a particularly important scene of riots and barricades during the suppression of the national workshops in June 1848.[39] Providing an equivalent pleasure ground for the working-class districts to the east balanced the political map. Buttes Chaumont to the northeast balanced Parc Monceau, and Parc Montsouris brought in the south.

Just as the parks were balanced spatially on the plan of Paris, so they were balanced throughout the life span of the Second Empire. The Bois de Boulogne was the first to be transformed, with major renovations occurring between 1852 and 1856. The Bois de Vincennes and Parc Monceau were both acquired by the city in 1860, after the city's expansion. Renovation of Parc Monceau was finished in August 1861, followed by renovation of the Bois de Vincennes from 1860 to 1863. Buttes Chaumont was acquired and constructed between 1864 and 1867. Although the property for Parc Montsouris was acquired in 1867, the park was not completed until 1878, after the end of the Empire. The chronology of the parks suggests shifting political necessities. In the 1850s, Napoleon III invested heavily in western Paris. This investment, perceived as support of financial privilege, alienated both the working class and the newly emerging industrial bourgeoisie. The later parks, created in the 1860s in working-class strongholds, courted the workers but contributed to increasing alienation of both the old financial bourgeoisie and the newly emerging industrial bourgeoisie, who feared a working-class threat to established social order.[40]

The political necessity of equitable distribution of parks over the map of the city had been demonstrated to Louis Napoleon in London, where he had been impressed by the royal parks of London's West End, particularly Hyde Park. He had these in mind as a model when he ordered the precedent-setting transformation of the Bois de Boulogne from a royal woods traversed by straight avenues to a public park with sinuous promenades and serpentine lakes.[41] He may also

A place of refreshment in the Bois de Vincennes. Lithograph from Adolphe Alphand, *Les promenades de Paris* (Paris: J. Rothschild, 1867–73). (Courtesy of Special Collections, University of Virginia Library)

have been aware of English agitation in the 1830s over the issue of creating a park for London's East End equivalent to the royal parks serving the affluent West End. The efforts of social reformers, fueled by declining land values in the East End, finally produced Victoria Park, which opened in 1846.[42] A similar disparity in social conditions as well as land values existed between the east and the west of Paris. The daily spectacle of high fashion in the Bois de Boulogne after its renovation heightened the contrast between the eastern and the western districts in Paris.

In contrast to the glamorous new Bois de Boulogne, the renovation of the Bois de Vincennes, which came later, was a rather pale imitation by most accounts, receiving less detailed descriptions in contemporary guidebooks, often relegated to an appendix. Haussmann confessed to embarrassment about the lesser quality of the Bois de Vincennes, especially given the fact that its renovation cost five times as much as the Bois de Boulogne.[43] Alphand, although he emphasized the comparability of the two parks, devoted 148 pages and 29 plates in *Les promenades de Paris* to the Bois de Boulogne, while

Rotten Row, London

The "Nilometer" of the season is the Park, and by the state of the Park an experienced person would at once know the period of the year. "The Park" is a piece of ground about three hundred yards long and fifty wide, between Hyde Park Corner and Albert Gate. This space contains part of a carriage drive, part of the celebrated riding path called Rotten Row, three walking paths, and some flower beds. The uses to which it is put during the season are various, viz., riding, driving, walking, and sitting.

And first of riding. As we have only to do with the season, we will say nothing of the riding before twelve o'clock, which goes on all the year round in fine weather. But in "the season" between that hour and two o'clock a class of riders appear who do not show in any number except during that period, viz., members of Parliament, "leisured" fathers with their daughters, and a sprinkling of "young men."

The horses of this epoch are very superior to those of the preceding. Papa may be there seen riding his hunter, which he does not summer in the country. But the great time for the Park is in the evening, when every one rides who can scrape together four legs and a saddle. People then wear their smartest clothes and ride their smartest hacks—bits of horse-flesh for which £500 or £600 may have been given. Young ladies, who

---

38 pages and 17 plates sufficed to cover the Bois de Vincennes. Guide-books sometimes echoed the government's explanation that the Bois de Vincennes was created as a "valuable place of resort and recreation [for] the inhabitants of the eastern quarters of Paris."[44] Engravings of the park in *Les promenades de Paris* depicted well-dressed people strolling, but Vincennes never rivaled the Bois de Boulogne as a fashionable rendezvous. As one guidebook noted, although Vincennes had been "thoroughly transformed" into "an English park with bowling greens, lakes, streams, waterfalls, etc. . . . between the two there is a notable difference, even to the most unobservant—the difference

The English Take Their Pleasures Sadly. Harper's New Monthly Magazine,
May 1886.

have been resting during the day, appear, and are joined, if the
authorities permit, by their cavaliers. The throng is so large that
most of the riders walk—a process that is also more convenient for
saluting and general conversation.

(From "The London Season," Harper's New Monthly
Magazine, May 1886)

that there is between Hyde Park and Woerlitz Garten. One is animated, noisy, glittering during the seven days of the week, while the
other is silent and deserted except Sundays when the bourgeois and
the workers of Faubourg Saint-Antoine go there for entertainment and
amusement."[45]

Class distinctions were a subject of endless speculation during the
Second Empire, and the flow of people of different classes, mixing and
mingling in public spaces, offered a mesmerizing spectacle of modernity. The Bois de Vincennes, like the Bois de Boulogne, became a
stage on which a parade of Parisians provided a fascinating show,

especially on days when the racetrack drew large crowds. At the races in Vincennes, "the spectacle becomes curious, because it is double: inside the racetrack, in numerous carriages, installed as at a restaurant, dandies and their lady-friends sip champagne with an excessive familiarity . . . lacking taste and sophistication; outside the racetrack, a malevolent crowd, alien to the extravagant luxury of these hussies and the outrageous impertinence of their companions. And the return, through the Faubourg Saint-Antoine! This merits viewing by the *flaneur* who wants to get to hate a part of humanity, and [hold] in contempt, the other half."[46]

Parks and Real Estate

Real-estate speculation flourished during the Second Empire. The older, established bourgeoisie played their traditional role, as bankers and financiers, while new fortunes were invested in the newly annexed zones by real-estate speculators and industrial entrepreneurs.[47] The relationship between the parks and real-estate speculation deserves closer scrutiny. New parks signaled expectation of residential real-estate development, and in terms of financial rewards, the parks benefited bourgeois real-estate investors. In *Les promenades*, Alphand listed costs for each of the parks, and in each case those costs were offset by resale of properties to private investors.[48] Although Alphand's figures may not have been completely accurate, they indicate that the financing of the parks was based on estimates of increasing property values and the expectation of lucrative returns for the state, both in sales of adjacent property and increased tax revenues.

The expectation that parks would increase adjacent property values was based on the early success of the Bois de Boulogne. Alphand noted that not only was the Bois de Boulogne project economically advantageous to the city and the state because increased property values around the park yielded higher revenues, but it also greatly benefited private investors in the vicinity of the park. The value of adjacent properties, according to Alphand's estimate, increased from between 1.5 and 6 francs per meter to between 20 and 100 francs per meter. He pointed out 487 expensive new villas constructed in the environs of the park. In the case of the Bois de Vincennes, however, Alphand estimated the value of property for resale at only 8 francs per

Entrance to Parc Monceau, flanked by elegant new residences. Lithograph from Adolphe Alphand, *Les promenades de Paris* (Paris: J. Rothschild, 1867–73). (Courtesy of Special Collections, University of Virginia Library)

meter.[49] Real-estate values around the park at Vincennes fell victim to economic and social disparities that were becoming more firmly outlined on the Paris map. As Haussmann noted, returns on real estate on the east side of Paris could not be expected to match those on the west.[50]

Real-estate transactions surrounding Parc Monceau worked to the advantage of both bourgeois speculators and the city, but the story, when it became publicly known, caused a smear on the prefect's reputation. Formerly the estate of the Duc d'Orléans, the property was in a state of neglect in 1861, when work commenced to turn it into a public park. Napoleon III had declared the park public property in 1852. According to Alphand's explanation in *Les promenades*, Parc Monceau offered an opportunity to conserve for the public a ready-made park in the center of a quarter that was being transformed.[51] He was no doubt referring to the fact that the Boulevard Malesherbes was already under construction and would be a major connector between the center of Paris and the new bourgeois district that was developing around Parc Monceau. At the time the park was transferred to public ownership, a large parcel of the property was sold as lots, and this transaction was surrounded by rumors. According to Haussmann's account, the city sold a large parcel of the park to businessman Émile Péreire, who served as intermediary between the descendants of the Duc d'Orléans and the state when the property was acquired in 1852.[52] When Napoleon took the park from the descendants of Louis-Philippe, the Duc d'Orléans, this assertion of eminent domain proved an embarrassment to the baron, who had been a classmate of Louis-Philippe's oldest son at the prestigious Collège Henri IV, and felt an obligation to look after the family's interests. Haussmann arranged, through Péreire, to pay a large indemnity to the family (more than 9 million francs). In return for his services as intermediary, Péreire was allowed to buy the "extra" land from the city—land not included in the corridor for the new boulevards or the area for the public park—for 8.1 million francs, which paid back the city for most of the indemnity.[53] Elegant and expensive hotels were subsequently built on these lots, and Péreire realized a large profit.[54] This kind of arrangement gave the office of the prefect of the Seine a bad name.

The new residences surrounding Parc Monceau replaced open fields and farmland. A bird's-eye view of the park included in *Les promenades de Paris* showed large areas around the park still undeveloped. The district was still quite remote from the crowded, central neighborhoods of Paris, and many of the new mansions built nearby had private gardens of their own. The park offered another setting for promenading in the afternoons, another place to watch a parade of "elegant feminine silhouettes promenading with their parasols and their dreams in a universe of bowling-greens."[55] According to one guide, Parc Monceau had its own special public, composed of families of independent means living in the area, servants of nearby households, local housewives with their children, and young men "in riding boots who hide behind the willows in order to be better observed by the ladies for whom they hold a special interest."[56]

In *La curée*, Zola showed the protagonist, Aristide Saccard, becoming rich by buying and selling properties around Parc Monceau and along the corridor slated for Boulevard Malesherbes. In the novel, Saccard picked up inside information about upcoming public projects by keeping his ears open around the Office of the Prefect of the Seine. It was not coincidental that Zola placed Saccard and his wife, Renée, in an ostentatious new villa on a lot abutting Parc Monceau.[57] A fashionable address near the park signaled success for the *nouveaux riches* who prospered during the Second Empire. Haussmann himself noted that the renovation of Parc Monceau "made this promenade the most luxurious and . . . the most elegant of Paris."[58]

In contrast to Parc Monceau, Buttes Chaumont was located in a working-class district, part of the newly annexed zone on the northeast side of Paris. The site between La Villette and Belleville was acquired by the city in 1863. Both Haussmann and Alphand considered it to be an intolerable blemish within the new boundaries of the city.[59] Formerly a quarry, and later used for the deposit of nightsoil, it emanated foul odors that were carried great distances by prevailing winds. Buttes Chaumont presented a challenge to Alphand's skill as an engineer and designer. The precipitous chalk cliffs offered dramatic possibilities, but required complete regrading and reconstruction to create an artificial lake, terraces for planting trees, lawns, and promenades. The final park, with its great butte rising out of the lake and crowned by a rotunda, its cavernous grotto, and its plunging waterfalls, remains one of the most remarkable monuments of the Second Empire.

As previously noted, politically motivated critics charged that Haussmann's improvements forced the working classes to evacuate the city center. Many of those evicted moved to areas such as the plains of La Villette or to Belleville, in the eastern part of the *petite banlieue*—that is, the annexed zone recently incorporated into the expanded city.[60] Buttes Chaumont was located in this area, between Belleville and La Villette. One of Haussmann's most persistent critics, Louis Lazare, pointed out that the areas on the outskirts of Paris did not enjoy the level of services that were provided to the renovated central districts and the new districts to the west. Lazare described conditions in these areas as follows: "Artisans and workers are shut up in veritable Siberias, crisscrossed with winding, unpaved paths, without lights, without shops, with no water laid on, where everything is lacking. . . . We have sewn rags onto the purple robe of a queen; we have built within Paris two cities, quite different and hostile: the city of luxury, surrounded, besieged by the city of misery."[61] In engravings of the park published in *Les promenades de Paris*, one sees the contrast between elegant ladies and gentlemen promenading at leisure along the shores of the lake, and in the background, large areas of open countryside and industrial chimneys giving off lazy plumes of smoke, reminding one that this is La Villette and Belleville, not the fashionable west side of Paris. William Robinson noted: "From this park, the surroundings of which are by no means attractive, you can look over nearly all Paris. The approach to it from the central parts is shabby for Paris, and on the way some idea of what the city was before the splendid improvements of the past ten years."[62] The area described by Robinson was in a state of flux. Industries in the area had previously been outside the boundaries of the city and had enjoyed exemption from city taxes. Now they were within the new urban limits and subject to city taxes. As the city began developing the annexed zone, industry relocated further out, to areas such as the Plaine Saint-Denis, a process encouraged by Haussmann.[63]

In his *Mémoires,* Haussmann implied that the proposal for Parc Montsouris, the last park of the series, was related to expenses incurred in constructing Buttes Chaumont: "The relative enormity of the figures [from Buttes Chaumont], which no important resale of land came to relieve, put my administration in pressing need to create, as planned, in the south of Paris, another park, in order to procure in the extreme quarters of the thirteenth and fourteenth arrondissements some of the equivalent advantages to those that Parc des Buttes-Chaumont had given to the new districts of the north city."[64] Both financial and political motivations supported the decision to produce this final park. By the time he proposed Parc Montsouris, Haussmann faced mounting criticism of his handling of public funds. The park represents both a last effort to offset some of the costs incurred by the other parks and an attempt to court political support in the southern districts. Parc Montsouris, with its curving walks and a lake, fit the formula; it was an appropriate counterpart to Parc Monceau although not as dramatic as Buttes Chaumont.

In only one instance was public resistance audibly voiced and organized against proposed park improvements. A controversy erupted over plans to renovate the Jardin du Luxembourg in 1865. The emperor authorized cutting off a portion of the park along the western and southern edges to make way for new boulevards. Loud public protests ensued. One night at the Odeon Theater, the emperor and empress faced a hostile crowd of protestors. Afterward, the emperor decided to preserve the western side of the garden, but proceeded with plans to

MELODRAMATIC LANDSCAPES

A view of the rotunda at Parc des Buttes Chaumont, with factories in the background. Lithograph from Adolphe Alphand, *Les promenades de Paris* (Paris: J. Rothschild, 1867–73). (Courtesy of Special Collections, University of Virginia Library)

cut off the nursery on the south. Several petitions, one with more than ten thousand signatures, were presented to the Senate in 1866. Protestors charged that the government planned to sell land cut off from the park to balance the budget; next they would be selling off lots in the Tuileries! The Senate listened, but plans proceeded for the new boulevards on the west and south sides of the park. Protests about the Luxembourg garden "improvements" continued to be raised in the Legislative Body in 1868 and 1869.[65]

It is difficult to know what difference the parks made to the lives of the working classes. Opposition to the renovation of the Luxembourg garden came mostly from professors and students who frequented the gardens. Criticisms of the parks were written by intellectuals, artists, writers, and authors of guidebooks. The design of roadways in the parks indicates that many of the users were expected to come by carriage or on horseback. Parks also included extensive networks of walking paths, and promenading was not an exclusively

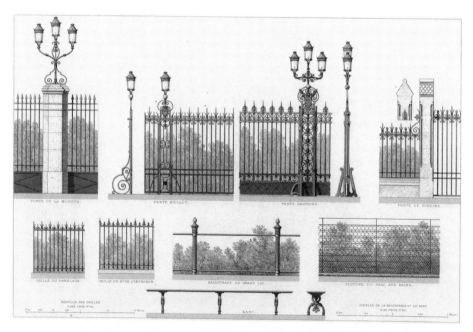

Designs for perimeter fencing, gates, and benches in the Bois de Boulogne. Lithograph from Adolphe Alphand, *Les promenades de Paris* (Paris: J. Rothschild, 1867–73). (Courtesy of Special Collections, University of Virginia Library)

upper-class pastime, but just as different areas of the city were associated with different social classes, different areas were frequented by different classes of promenaders.[66] Public transportation to the Bois de Boulogne and the Bois de Vincennes, mentioned in many guidebooks, would have been beyond the means of many working-class Parisians. Engravings included in Alphand's treatise depicted well-dressed middle- and upper-class visitors in all of the parks, including Buttes Chaumont. Social mores and class distinctions no doubt influenced patterns of use in the parks, and different kinds of events staged in the parks would have attracted different audiences. However, complete girding of the parks with grills, locked gates, and extensive *sauts de loup* (ha-has) indicates a high level of control over who used the parks and how they could be used. There were also pavilions designed to house park guards and live-in superintendants.[67] Herbert notes that in the Bois de Boulogne, "the working class was kept out of sight, quite literally unrepresented in imperial nature."[68]

MELODRAMATIC LANDSCAPES

The English Style and the Question of Taste

Questions of style and good taste preoccupied both designers and critics of the Paris parks. In the introduction to *Les promenades de Paris*, Alphand undertook a sweeping overview of garden design history. The purpose of this introduction was to demonstrate that landscape gardening could boast a venerable history as an art form, and to place the new parks of Paris in historical perspective. In undertaking this historic overview, Alphand stressed that history should be viewed as offering opportunities rather than constraints. He warned that "servile imitation of antiquity leads most often to reproductions that no longer suit our needs." Rather than copying historic styles, he urged his contemporaries to "analyze the creations of the past, separate the outmoded, and recognize the elements that are appropriate to the modern art [of landscape gardening]." After summarizing garden styles in ancient Asia, Egypt, Greece, Rome, and during the Middle Ages, the Italian Renaissance and the French Renaissance, Alphand arrived at the style he called "irregular or wild, said to be English." This style, he said, was inspired by the unique qualities of light and natural effects of nature found in northern parts of Europe, particularly England—inspired by "the genius of the place." It required "a negation of all that had preceded it," a complete abandonment of tradition. Looking at eighteenth-century attempts to adopt this style in France, Alphand found examples that he deemed "mediocre and very incomplete," mainly because he felt they were fussy and contrived in layout, crowded with ornaments, faux temples and antiquities, and generally lacking in sensitivity to the simple effects of nature. These early attempts at creating irregular or English-style gardens were guided, according to Alphand, "by ostentation more than by taste."[69]

Alphand argued that a garden, or *parc*, was ultimately a work of art. He believed that "natural accidents of the terrain" and effects found in nature should guide the landscape designer in creating, ultimately, a picture or series of visual images. While "nature furnished the grand lines," the task of the landscape gardener was to create "a melody of forms and colors" intended to please the eyes as, similarly, a work of music was created to please the ears.[70] Alphand's analogy to a work of art—a painting or a work of music—suggests that he saw himself creating in the Paris parks a visual spectacle, an experience

BIRKENHEAD PARK, ENGLAND

Opening of Birkenhead Park, in Liverpool, England. *Illustrated London News,* 10 April 1849. (Illustrated London News Picture Library, London)

The great charm of Birkenhead Park is its intricacy and quasi snugness; this latter quality Englishmen prize highly. I cannot, however, dismiss the Birkenhead Park without remarking the very great beauty of the sheets of water. From no point are the limits discernible; all is easy, graceful, and natural. . . . The walks by turns approach and leave the

similar to a performance or an exhibit of paintings. For Alphand, "picturesque" meant "like a picture," and the parks were designed accordingly, as a series of views unfolding before the spectator.[71]

Nicholas Green explored "the picturesque as an idea or style . . . in terms of its circulation as a set of commodities—produced, marketed, consumed" in nineteenth-century Paris.[72] From the dioramas that drew admiring crowds, to sales of landscape pictures and travel prints, to guidebooks designed to aid appreciation of picturesque effects, Green argues, the visual experience of "nature" was commodified and

margin of the lakes; at every ten yards a new vista presents itself; the intricacy produced by an apparently simple plan is marvelous! I made nearly a complete circuit of the first lake without knowing that I had done so; it was only by recognizing one of the bridges that I found out where I was. The entirely different aspect which the banks of the lake continually present is completely illusive. This work, in short, is in the highest style of art, and presents a marked contrast to the celebrated Bois de Boulogne at Paris, where the water is very much like an irregular canal; every part can be seen from one end, and the drives follow the margin with scrupulous and hideous exactness. The Bois de Boulogne shows the hand of the military engineer, not the fancy of the landscape gardener. Strange as it may appear, the French, with all their elegance of character and subtlety of *esprit*, are entirely without correct notions of landscape gardening. Since the time of Le Nôtre in the days of geometry, long straight avenues and square clipped gardens, they appear to have made no approach to better style. The reason, I believe, to be this: No Frenchman cares a straw for nature; no Frenchman ever leaves Paris from choice, or is ever without light-colored kid gloves, a Palais Royal cane, and varnished boots. Besides, they care too much for what they eat.

(FROM HOWARD DANIELS, "EUROPEAN PARKS")

became increasingly popular among the French bourgeoisie. Green notes that "from the beginning of the century, if not before, writers had exploited the image of nature as a privileged site for personal and poetic reflection. What was quite new to the 1830s was an analysis that situated the experience as romantic, modern and decisively urban." Illustrated travel books, *voyages pittoresques*, which were popular in this period, recounted excursions to various scenic parts of France, with emphasis on French history, overtones of nationalism, and a focus on topographic information. Consumption of the picturesque

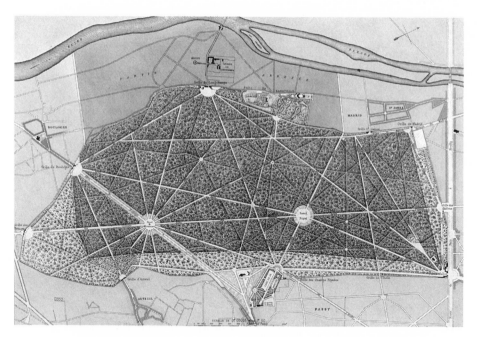

The plan of the Bois de Boulogne showing its formal design, before renovation during the Second Empire. Lithograph from Adolphe Alphand, *Les promenades de Paris* (Paris: J. Rothschild, 1867–73). (Courtesy of Special Collections, University of Virginia Library)

was governed by expertise of various kinds, and "struggles around a professionalizing landscape art laid down ground-rules for the relation between perception and representation which were registered across the spectrum of nature image-making from the 1820s to the 1850s."[73] In the process, the question of "taste" became important as a means for discrimination among various landscape effects. Alphand's argument, in *Les promenades*, in favor of the irregular, or English, style is largely a defense of good taste: informed and expert discrimination among various landscape effects.

Alphand's treatise on the parks was illustrated by engravings of English precedents in public park design, including Regent's Park, Victoria Park, and Battersea Park in London; the Crystal Palace Park at Sydenham; and Birkenhead Park near Liverpool. Louis Napoleon's admiration for the London parks has been cited by historians to explain the choice of the English style for the Bois de Boulogne and subsequent parks.[74] But the relationship to English precedents is complex, "linked with the onset of the industrial revolution and the rapid expansion of Paris, and linked also with the dominant men of Paris, their clubs, their investments, and their dependence upon British precedent."[75] The English style of landscape gardening, increasingly associated with the conspicuous consumption of English *nouveaux riches* by the beginning of the nineteenth century, was satirized by arbiters of refined taste in England.[76] But a taste for British style, including gardens, flourished among the fashionable set of Parisian society at midcentury.

In terms of industrial development, France lagged behind England in the nineteenth century. During the Second Empire, however, industrialization occurred in France at a rapid rate, spurred on by the trade treaty signed between France and England in 1860, by the economic crisis of the American Civil War, during which no cotton was shipped to France from the United States, and by the rapid construction of a French rail network.[77] Over the time span of the Second Empire, industrial production doubled and the number of establishments using steam engines quadrupled. Industrial capital expanded rapidly. The English style of the new parks, incorporating racecourses and promenades, catered to the English tastes of the *nouveaux riches*, who prospered as a result of industrial expansion. The British were the chief investors in the expanding French economy, and British styles, manners, and taste became extremely fashionable among the newly wealthy Parisian industrialists. Horses, horse breeding, and horse racing were a major preoccupation of the dandies who set the tone for Parisian society during the Second Empire. The Jockey Club, which "set the fashions for Parisian males for two generations and was one of the principal conduits for the penetration of British manners," built the Longchamps racetrack in the Bois de Boulogne, negotiating a fifty-year lease with the city for a modest annual rent.[78] It was likely Napoleon III had in mind the riding paths in Hyde Park, such as the famous Rotten Row, when he transformed the Bois de Boulogne into an English-style park. All of the parks featured both pedestrian and equestrian paths, offering ample opportunities for fashionable display.

In spite of rapid expansion of industrial capital throughout France, Paris remained largely a city of artisans. The districts of Paris where artisans lived and worked, such as the Faubourg Saint-Antoine, were important sources of Napoleon III's political support. Yet one of

The plan of the Bois de Boulogne after its renovation into the more naturalistic English style. Lithograph from William Robinson, *The Parks, Promenades and Gardens of Paris* (London: John Murray, 1869). (Courtesy of Fiske Kimball Fine Arts Library, University of Virginia)

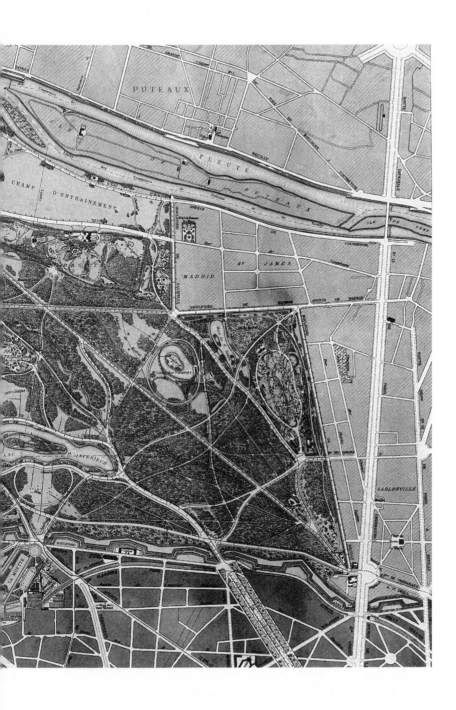

Haussmann's tasks was to give Paris a new image suited to a capital of an industrialized nation. The odd juxtaposition of Parc des Buttes Chaumont with its surrounding working-class district symbolizes these conflicting political necessities. Following the precedent of the Great Exhibition of 1851, which had established Great Britain's leadership of the industrial world, Napoleon III and Haussmann planned the Exposition of 1867 in Paris to establish France's presence as an industrialized power. Parc des Buttes Chaumont was timed to coincide with the opening of the Exposition and to impress visitors who would flood Paris in conjunction with the Exposition.[79] Marceca has argued that in Buttes Chaumont, nature had "a clearly subordinate relationship to the machine." But Grumbach notes that "the lesson of the Buttes-Chaumont is that the only true nature is the false one," and this seems a more appropriate reading.[80] Technology played an important role in the conception and construction of the park, but it was supposed to be a behind-the-scenes presence, like the mechanism that raises and lowers the scenery in a theater. "Nature" was intended to set a certain tone and to serve as a stage set. The parks, with their highly stylized renditions of nature, were an important element in the staging of modernity. Some visitors were dismayed by the too obvious technological effects at first, probably reacting, in part, to the newness of the parks. For example, there is William Robinson's description of Buttes Chaumont, published in 1869, merely two years after it opened to the public: "The entrance is not promising—a hard-looking porter's lodge, and a mass of badly-made rockwork face a mound, and from the rockwork springs an apparently quite unnecessary bridge. The rockwork is bad because, although superior in general design to the masses of burnt bricks that sometimes pass for it with us, it shows radical faults—presumption and unnaturalness. Instead of a true rockwork, something like a very puny attempt at reproducing the more insignificant ribs of Monte Campione is the result of plastering over a heap of stones. A hole is left here and there in this mass from which may spring a small pine or an ivy, but the whole thing is incapable of being divested of its bald artificial character."[81]

Robinson, although he admired some aspects of French gardening, was quite critical of the Paris parks, not only their construction and planting, but also their stylized picturesque effects. His disparaging tone is not surprising since English critics had been critical of

French interpretations of the English style since the late eighteenth century, when French estate gardens first began to show English influence. But Robinson's motivations are not as important here as his insight about the parks' contrived artificiality and relation to surrounding neighborhoods. To him, the parks looked too staged, too contrived, too hastily constructed. Perhaps even more revealing of public perception, Haussmann himself, in his description of Parc des Buttes Chaumont, referred to "the inevitable grotto," suggesting a kind of formula, or at least repetition of certain elements, in the design of the parks.[82]

The new parks were clearly perceived in some quarters as examples of bourgeois taste. Parc Monceau, for example, had originally been designed in the 1770s by the artist Carmontelle, a design criticized by Alphand in *Les promenades* for its fussiness.[83] Carmontelle's original conception exhibited a penchant for embellishment, including windmills, grottos, a rustic farm, ruined bits of classical architecture, lakes with islands, geometric flower beds laid out in different color schemes, fountains, statuary of all descriptions, greenhouses, a Turkish minaret and tents, to name only a few of its follies.[84] Alphand's design for Parc Monceau greatly simplified Carmontelle's layout and

The Grand Avenue of the Parc Monceau. Lithograph from Adolphe Alphand, *Les promenades de Paris* (Paris: J. Rothschild, 1867–73). (Courtesy of Special Collections, University of Virginia Library)

conserved only a few of the ancient architectural remnants, such as the Naumachia. Alphand also constructed a cascade, rockery, and grotto. The original ornate gates were restored and the rotunda, which originally marked one of the gates of the old wall of the *fermiers généraux*, was repaired and retained as an entrance to the park. The rest of the park, which encompassed only about 8.5 hectares, less than half of its original size, was laid out with curving promenades, undulating lawns, and plantations of trees—similar, although smaller in scale, to the Bois de Boulogne. A broad boulevard for carriages and horses traversed the length of the park.

Victor Fournel, another of Haussmann's persistent critics, derided Alphand's improvements both in the Bois de Boulogne and at Parc Monceau. He regretted the replacement of the old forest of the Bois de Boulogne with an "artificial paradise."[85] As for Parc Monceau, he charged that the engineer took every opportunity to reduce and diminish the old park, chipping away at it to create new boulevards and new house lots. The original private park was three times the size of the portion ultimately reserved for a public park.[86] He also ridiculed Alphand's so-called improvements:

> The new Parc Monceau is the most disastrous, the most distressing example of the system followed in the "restoration" of public gardens. It is once again M. Alphand who was here the executor of the great work of the city of Paris. The balance sheet of his improvements is easy to draw up: a boulevard that cuts [the park] in two, motor routes—why not a railroad?—to traverse it from part to part; a ridiculous cave with stalactites and stalagmites that resemble terra-cotta claws, and which are guarded by a live-in superintendent and by written signs, for fear that they might be broken; rivulets restored, cascades made new, a bleached white bridge, the great shady places destroyed, the silence and the mystery that one breathed there in older times, chased away for always; a banal, patched-up varnish and paint thrown on the ruins of the old park, and then, finally, a grille— there it is, this masterpiece summarized.[87]

Fournel's sarcastic description emphasized the banality of the renovation, as he saw it, compared to Carmontelle's original design. But Alphand defended his simplification of the original design in the name of good taste.

While guidebook authors were generally content to merely de-

A view of the lake and cliffs at the Parc des Buttes Chaumont. Lithograph
from Adolphe Alphand, *Les promenades de Paris* (Paris: J. Rothschild, 1867–
73). (Courtesy of Special Collections, University of Virginia Library)

scribe the recent "improvements" to the parks, at least one objected to
certain aspects of the of the Bois de Boulogne's renovation, on grounds
similar to Fournel's: "The Bois de Boulogne has ceased to be a wood;
they have felled without pity her most beautiful forests, and transformed them into logs to warm the boys of the offices of the ministries,
they have laid out with precision wide allées in place of small, sinuous
paths, shady and delicious, that were sought out with such eagerness
and for reasons so different by the loving and the melancholy."[88] Criticisms of the parks generally followed the same vein as criticisms of the
new boulevards and new architecture: their style was repetitive and
monotonous, reducing the individuality and charm of old landscapes
to a new formula, making it difficult to tell one park from another.

Conclusion

There can be no doubt that politics played an important role in
shaping the parks of the Second Empire in Paris. Spaced over the
increasingly delineated social map of Paris, the parks were critical to

The Route des Buttes in the Bois de Vincennes. Lithograph from Adolphe Alphand, *Les promenades de Paris* (Paris: J. Rothschild, 1867–73). (Courtesy of Special Collections, University of Virginia Library)

maintaining political balance, anchoring certain strategic neighborhoods, forging new identities for *quartiers* in the annexed zone, and bringing these areas into a net of social and political control cast over the city by Haussmann. Constructing and renovating parks, like the other public works projects during the Second Empire, allowed Napoleon III to mollify disparate political interests. The park projects provided jobs for the working class and a speculative real-estate market for bourgeois investors. But, in the end, the parks best served the interests of the bourgeoisie. The parks in the western districts (the Bois de Boulogne and Parc Monceau) were the most successful in terms of increasing real-estate values and providing public spaces that were well used and appreciated. The later parks reflect the mounting problems of Napoleon III's political regime: increasing debt and increasing political opposition.

Gaillard's general conclusion about the overall rebuilding project also applies to the parks specifically: "'Haussmannization' was less an exercise in urbanization than a research toward a point of equilibrium favorable towards the empire. This political strategy is revealed as

MELODRAMATIC LANDSCAPES

subtle, fragile . . . but it is impossible to say that . . . it didn't succeed."[89] Although the administration of the Second Empire did improve the lot of the working class in many ways, it most actively promoted the interests of the bourgeoisie. As Gaillard points out, ultimately the expansion of the middle class and the displacement of the city toward the west created a political counterpoint to the revolutionary tendency of the working classes in the eastern districts. This political balance, with the brief exception of the Commune, has been maintained in France ever since.

As for political meaning inscribed in the style of the parks, another nineteenth-century commentator provides insight. Henry Tuckerman, writing in the 1860s, analyzed French interpretations of Nature. His reading of those artificial effects helps clarify and explain political motivation behind nineteenth-century criticism of the parks. Tuckerman noted the French "ambition to pervert Nature and create artificial effects," remarking on "so many forms of the theatrical instinct and proofs of the ascendency of meretricious taste." Asserting that "this want of loyalty to Nature, and insensibility to her unadulterated charms . . . constitute[d] the real barrier between the Gallic mind and that of England," he concluded that "manufactured verse, vegetation, and complexions indicate[d] a faith in appearances and a divorce from reality, which, in political interests, tend[ed] to compromise, to theory, and to acquiescence in a military regime and an embellished absolutism."[90]

Tuckerman's analysis serves as a reminder that the ideological foundations of the Second Empire were never very secure; the notion of a people's empire had to be packaged in deception and false pretense. The parks, with their elaborately contrived effects, their artificial nature, their stylized, repetitive attractions, symbolized not only the English style in landscape gardening, but the political style of Napoleon III. As Herbert has noted, "the plan of the Bois [de Boulogne] is a perfect symbol of [Louis Napoleon's] reign: curving paths among specimen trees, ponds and lakes, inviting lawns, broad alleys for carriages, undulating terrain punctuated by slight eminences which provide views—all that would appear casual and carefree, remote from the impositions of authority. It was also a massive deception."[91] Finally, the double entendre of Zola's "air of adorable falsity" in the Bois de Boulogne is understandable.

Charges of bourgeois banality and images of adorable falsity apply to these parks in the unique political and social context of the Second Empire. The parks have become well-loved public spaces, often studied by landscape designers today, but to understand them historically it is necessary to return to Zola's Paris. His portrait of the Bois de Boulogne holds at least as much historical truth as Alphand's treatise or Haussmann's memoirs. Zola saw that the Bois de Boulogne offered Parisians a stage setting, a fantastic and unreal background for the drama of the Second Empire as it unfolded with all of its corruption, glamour, political maneuvering, and pretense. The rest of the parks were cast in the same mold, caught up in the scandals and political uncertainties of the Empire, shaped by political needs and social circumstances. The history of these parks is intricately bound up in "the effort at ideological unity involved in Haussmann's rebuilding, and . . . the degree to which that effort failed."[92] The parks received their share of criticism during the Second Empire because they were identified with an authoritarian political regime, reflective of bourgeois taste and mores, and surrounded by rumors of corruption and political favoritism. For contemporary critics of the political regime, such as Zola, the parks reiterated these meanings with monotonous regularity. Haussmann's and Alphand's versions of the public good and good design could not conceal from Parisians how much political expediency factored into the formula for public parks during the Second Empire.

Chapultepec Park & the Staging of Modern Mexico

¡Cuántos recuerdos despierta en la memoria el legendario bosque de Chapultepec!

¡Cuántos ensueños! . . . ¡cuántas ilusiones! . . . qué de encantos; de idilios y cuentos de amor! ¡Mas ¡ay¡ también evoca tristezas, también arranca lamentos, y lágrimas y sollozos y gritos de dolor!

[How many memories are aroused by the legendary forest of Chapultepec!

How many reveries! . . . how many dreams! . . . of enchantment, idylls and tales of love! Moreover . . . it evokes sadness and conjures up laments and tears and sobs and cries of sorrow!]

—Adolfo Prantl and José L. Groso, *La Ciudad de México*

Chapultepec Park in Mexico City is a prototypical nineteenth-century park, offering all of the amenities associated with parks of that period. A lush, green oasis in the city, it is laid out in the formulaic nineteenth-century style, with curving paths and drives, shade trees, serpentine lakes, and long, cool vistas offering respite from the gritty, hard-edged landscape of the modern metropolis. The modern park is primarily a legacy of the late nineteenth century, particularly the brief French-Austrian intervention (1864–67), when the puppet emperor Maximilian ruled Mexico, backed by Napoleon III of France; and the Porfiriato (1876–1911), when the dictator Porfirio Díaz presided over a prolonged period of political stability, backed by a progressive bourgeoisie with ties to Europe and the United States. Yet, to fully understand what this park represents in the continuum of Mexican history, and particularly the role it played in the construction of modern Mexican national identity in the nineteenth century, it is necessary to start further back in time. The site has been the locus of momentous events in Mexican history dating back to the Aztec period, and its ancient history figures importantly in the park's mythology.

Grasshopper Hill: Chapultepec in the Pre-Hispanic Landscape

The human history of the high valley that contains present-day Mexico City began about seven thousand years ago when humans settled down to an agricultural existence on the shores of the shrinking lake that had once filled the valley.[1] As the ancient lake receded, a rocky promontory surfaced on its southwest shore, with freshwater springs issuing from its base. This promontory was a landmark valued by early inhabitants of the valley, both for its strategic geography and for the clear, freshwater pools at its base. It afforded protection and a natural vantage point for surveillance of the surrounding countryside in a period when warring cultural groups were vying for supremacy in the area. The Aztecs (Mexicas) arrived at this promontory in the 1270s. Their arrival is recorded in several Aztec codices produced during the early Spanish colonial period by native artists in the pictorial pre-Hispanic style. At some point, the promontory was given the name Chapultepec, which, in Nahuatl, means "grasshopper hill" (*chapulin*, "grasshopper"; *tepetl*, "hill"). One explanation of the name is that grasshoppers were abundant there; another is that the hill has the shape of a grasshopper. A red carneolite grasshopper found in the large spring-fed pool at the base of the hill, and now residing in the National Museum of Anthropology, is said to represent "the god of the forest" of Chapultepec.[2]

The Aztecs began to build the fabled floating city of Tenochtitlán in Lake Texcoco, near Chapultepec, around 1325, constructing the city's foundations by anchoring floating islands of woven reeds, called *chinampas*, in the marshy shallows at the edge of the brackish lake. Tenochtitlán depended on the springs at Chapultepec for freshwater, which was conveyed by an aqueduct constructed around the middle of the fifteenth century.[3] Under a series of aggressive leaders, the Aztecs expanded and consolidated power, and by the mid-fifteenth century an alliance between Tenochtitlán and two other city-states in the region, Texcoco and Tlacopan, controlled most of central Mexico. During this period, the Aztecs built a temple and an observatory on the hill of Chapultepec and apparently used the site for sacred ceremonies, including ritual human sacrifice. The *Códice florentino*, or *Historia general de las cosas de Nueva España* (*General History of the Things of New Spain*), a sixteenth-century codex, refers to a large altar stone on the hilltop and asserts that the Aztecs sacrificed human victims there to appease water deities. Diego Durán's *Historia de las Indias de la Nueva España e islas de tierra firme* tells of a group of young men from Tenochtitlán sacrificing a group of slaves in the forest

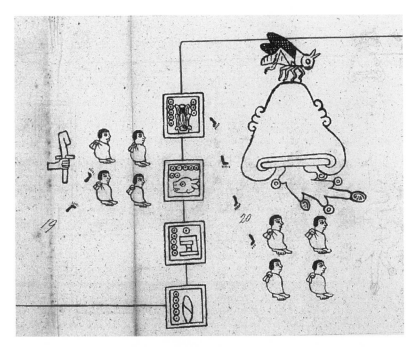

Detail of an Aztec codex showing the arrival of the Aztecs at Chapultepec. From the *Códice Boturini: Tira de la Peregrinación Azteca*, 1530–41. (Courtesy of Mapoteca Manuel Orozco y Berra, Mexico City)

of Chapultepec, and records that the Aztec ruler Moctezuma I, shortly before his death in 1469, asked his brother, Tlacaelel, to oversee the carving of their exploits into stone at Chapultepec. Excavations at the base of the hill in 1975 uncovered an ancient pool and water channels, gardens, sculptures, and carved reliefs indicating a villa and sanctuary devoted to the Aztec rain god. These excavations confirmed the use of Chapultepec by the Aztecs of nearby Tenochtitlán, not only as a source of freshwater, but also as a retreat for Aztec rulers.[4]

The city of Tenochtitlán was an impressive testament to Aztec culture. At the time of the Spanish conquest, Tenochtitlán had around 200,000 inhabitants. Only four other cities in the world had populations of 100,000 or more at that time: Paris, Venice, Milan, and Naples. Seville, the port city from which the Spanish conquistadors sailed for Mexico, had a population of around 40,000 in 1520. By 1580, when it had become Spain's largest city, Seville had a population of only a little more than 100,000. In fact, the Valley of Mexico had one of the largest concentrations of population in the world in the sixteenth century. The magnificent island city of Tenochtitlán was a wonder of its time. Encompassing about five square miles, it was laced with canals plied by canoes laden with cargo. Pedestrian streets and market squares teemed with activity. It was a city of imposing temples, impressive residences, and lovely gardens, including a royal botanical garden. A zoo with wild animals fascinated Hernán Cortés and his men. Three causeways connected the island city to the shore, including the causeway to Chapultepec, which also supported the freshwater aqueduct.[5]

Chapultepec under Colonial Rule

When the Spanish arrived in Mexico, they were appropriately amazed by sight of Tenochtitlán, noting "the magnificence, the strange and marvelous things of this great city . . . so remarkable as not to be believed."[6] The freshwater springs of Chapultepec played a decisive role in the Spanish conquest of Tenochtitlán in 1521; indeed, the aqueduct from Chapultepec proved to be the Aztec city's Achilles heel. Bernal Díaz del Castillo, lieutenant to Cortés, recounted how Cortés discovered that Tenochtitlán was supplied with water from Chapultepec and ordered his men to surround the island, destroy the aqueduct, and lay siege to the city. The famous Nuremberg map, attributed to

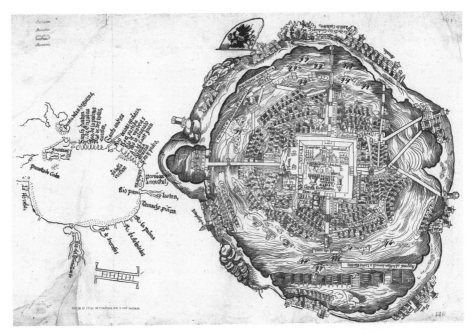

Map of the island city of Tenochtitlán, 1524, attributed to Hernán Cortés.
(Courtesy of Mapoteca Manuel Orozco y Berra, Mexico City)

Cortés, shows the hill of Chapultepec to the west of the island city, its springs and the aqueduct supplying freshwater. After the conquest, the Spanish built the new colonial Mexico City directly on the ruins of the old Aztec capital. They also rebuilt the aqueduct from Chapultepec and continued to use it to supply water to the city for many years.[7]

Following the conquest, several among the conquistadors coveted Chapultepec, which was an attractive site for a villa with its panoramic hilltop vistas, fabled crystal springs, and the venerable forest of Moctezuma cypresses that grew around the springs at the base of the hill. Apparently in response to various land claims and disputes, in 1530 the Spanish Crown decreed the site to be public property of Mexico City and the city's official water source in perpetuity. Prior to this decree, due to concern about contamination of the water supply, a town council meeting on 18 February 1527 had approved cutting down part of the ancient grove of cypresses around the springs, to prevent contamination of the pools from leaves and roots. When the springs began to dry up and the supply of freshwater dwindled, this removal

The cascading fountain in Mexico City, supplied by aqueduct from Chapultepec. Lithograph from C. Castro et al., *México y sus alrededores: Colección de monumentos, trajes y paisajes* (Mexico City: Establecimiento Litográfico de Decaen, 1855–56). (Courtesy of Bancroft Library, University of California, Berkeley)

of trees was blamed, in retrospect, for damaging the water supply rather than protecting it.

The water of Chapultepec did not remain pure for very long after the Spanish conquest. Two aqueducts originated in Chapultepec and supplied Mexico City during the colonial period. One, known as Tlaxpana, originated in the Santa Fe springs northwest of Chapultepec. Its construction began under Viceroy Juan de Mendoza y Luna, Marquis of Montesclaros, who governed from 1603 to 1607, and was finished under Diego Fernández de Córdoba, Marquis of Guadalcazar, in 1620. The Tlaxpana aqueduct had two brick conduits: the upper conduit carried potable water from Santa Fe, and the lower one carried water from Chapultepec. The water from the lower conduit was not used for drinking unless filtered first. The other aqueduct from Chapultepec, known as the Belén aqueduct, originated in the forest pools in Chapultepec and ended at a baroque fountain in Mexico City, the Fuente del Salto del Agua (Waterfall Fountain). The Belén aqueduct was finished under Viceroy Antonio María Bucareli y Ursúa in 1779. It carried only water from Chapultepec, and many historical documents refer to its water as unhealthy. Water from both aqueducts was sometimes diverted during the colonial period for the use of private estates along the way, causing shortages in the rest of the city.[8]

As colonial Mexico City grew, obliterating the remains of the vanquished Aztec capital, the Spanish viceroys used Chapultepec for recreation and retreat from the city. They fenced in a sizable area to protect the city's water source and keep poachers out of the forest. Don Luis de Velasco, the second Spanish viceroy, built a pleasant villa at the foot of the hill, where the old Aztec structures had fallen into ruin. He used it for his own leisure and invited prominent citizens to ride, watch bullfights, and partake of sumptuous banquets. In 1624, Viceroy Rodrigo Pacheco y Osorio began to use the villa at Chapultepec to receive and entertain new viceroys arriving to take up posts in the city. Over the ensuing years, these ceremonies became so extravagant that the Crown suspended them in 1739. Following this decree, the viceroys' villa at Chapultepec slowly fell into disrepair. In 1784, an explosion at a nearby gunpowder factory reduced it to a ruin.

In 1785, work commenced on a new structure to replace the viceroys' ruined villa. The project was authorized by the Crown and supervised by Viceroy Bernardo de Gálvez. Because the old location near the pools had been damp and plagued by mosquitoes, the new structure was situated on top of the hill. Crenellated parapets and towers contributed to the new structure's image as a castle: El Castillo de Chapultepec. The year 1785 is sometimes remembered as the "hunger year" because a national agricultural crisis caused widespread famine in the countryside. Many farmers migrated to Mexico City that year, unable to subsist in the parched farmland. Some were put to work on the new castle at Chapultepec. When Viceroy Bernardo de Gálvez died in 1786, the construction of the castle continued for a while under the succeeding viceroy, but halted in the fall of 1787. Gálvez's plans for the shrubbery in the castle garden had included a topiary rendition of his personal motto: "Yo solo, Don Bernardo de Gálvez" (I alone, Don Bernardo de Gálvez), casting some doubts on his intentions and lending credence to suspicions that he may have been harboring thoughts of revolution.

The property was put up for auction by the Crown in 1788, but there were no takers. A judge at city hall, overseeing water issues, objected to the sale and pointed out that the property had belonged to the city since 1530 and was the source of the municipal water supply. He suggested that the building be adapted for use as a hospital for smallpox epidemics; however, this suggestion was never implemented. In subsequent years, city ministers dismantled the building for their personal profit. The unfinished structure languished for the rest of the century and throughout Mexico's prolonged war for independence (1810–21) and was damaged further by an earthquake in 1819. When the War of Independence ended in 1821, Augustín de Iturbide, the first leader of independent Mexico, contemplated using Chapultepec as a residence, but he never got beyond ordering some Bohemian crystal with the inscription "Palace of Chapultepec."[9]

The War with the United States and Los Niños Héroes

Following Iturbide's brief interest, the castle languished until 1841, when Joaquín Velázquez was commissioned to renovate the structure for use as a military academy, setting the stage for the subsequent events that took place there during the final U.S. offensive of the Mexican-American War, on 12 and 13 September 1847. For many Mexicans, these are the most momentous events associated with Chapultepec. The U.S. army had defeated the Mexicans at Veracruz and then won intense battles at Contreras and Churubusco, on the outskirts of Mexico City. After U.S. forces breached Mexican defenses

Attack on the Castle of Chapultepec, N. Currier, 1848. Engraving. (Courtesy of Library of Congress)

at the Molino del Rey, just west of Chapultepec, the castle remained the last Mexican stronghold; it was defended by about one thousand troops and the young cadets of the military academy. This small band of loyal defenders confronted some eight thousand attacking troops. Final resistance in the fierce battle came from the cadets of the military academy, most of whom died in the fighting. After mounting a fierce defense, Gen. Nicolás Bravo surrendered to Gen. Winfield Scott on 12 September 1847.[10]

Historians of Mexico recognize the 1847 battle of Chapultepec as representing both the humiliation of defeat for Mexico and the birth of modern Mexican nationalism. The young cadets who gave their lives in that battle against impossible odds were immortalized as *Los Niños Héroes,* and became a national symbol of bravery and loyalty, especially one young man, Juan Escutia, who reportedly wrapped himself in a Mexican flag and threw himself over the parapets of the castle rather than surrender to the U.S. troops.[11] A monument to these young fighters was erected at the base of the hill and ever since has been the locus of nationalistic celebrations and pilgrimages on 13 Sep-

The Valley of Mexico viewed from the heights of Chapultepec, with the castle in the foreground. Lithograph from C. Castro et al., *México y sus alredededores: Colección de monumentos, trajes y paisajes* (Mexico City: Establecimiento Litográfico de Decaen, 1855–56). (Courtesy of Bancroft Library, University of California, Berkeley)

tember each year. Chapultepec Castle, which suffered severe damage during the battle in 1847, was quickly repaired and continued to be used as a military academy.

The French-Austrian Intervention: Maximilian and Carlota

In the years following Mexican Independence, Mexican politics was characterized by bitter and prolonged conflict between conservatives and liberals. Conservatives, who were generally large landowners, members of the clergy, and remnants of the colonial elite, favored autocratic and centralized government and tended to support home markets and a controlled economy. Liberals, who were generally smaller landowners, professionals, and bureaucrats, were more populist, advocated land reforms, and were more interested in developing Mexico's links to a growing international capitalist market. The conflict between conservatives and liberals produced more than thirty-five changes of government between 1821 and 1864. When Benito Juárez won the presidential elections in March 1861, following the War of Reform, it was a liberal victory following on the heels of forty-two years of political instability, and the country was in financial crisis, with a bankrupt treasury. European creditors began demanding payments, and Juárez declared a two-year moratorium on foreign debts. Great Britain (under Queen Victoria), Spain (under Queen Isabella II), and France (under Napoleon III) signed a pact, the Convention of London, agreeing to occupy the Mexican coast and try to collect on the debts. Spain and England apparently intended only to protect their existing claims, but Napoleon III of France saw in Mexico an opportunity to advance his imperialist ambitions. He wanted to establish a monarchy in Mexico to counterbalance the power and influence of U.S. republicanism in the Americas. When the Spanish and the English realized that the French agenda went beyond collecting debt, they ordered their troops home and effectively withdrew from the pact. A month later, the French army invaded Mexico. This was in blatant defiance of the Monroe Doctrine, which had declared, in 1823, that future attempts to colonize the American continent by European powers would be treated as acts of hostility. However, as Napoleon III had calculated, the United States was too preoccupied by its own Civil War to do anything about events in Mexico. In a battle that would reverberate through Mexican history, the Mexican army defeated the French at Puebla on 5 May (Cinco de Mayo), with General Porfirio Díaz in charge of the Mexicans' Second Brigade. However, the French army regrouped and gathered reinforcements and a year later attacked again, laying siege to Puebla for two months until, finally, the city surrendered. President Juárez realized that the Mexican army would not be able to defend the capital, so he ordered the troops to withdraw to San Luis Potosí. The French took Mexico City without opposition and set up a provisional government.

Following this victory, Napoleon III persuaded the Archduke Maximilian, brother of the ruling Hapsburg emperor of Austria, to serve as emperor of Mexico, backed by France. Maximilian agreed, on condition that his appointment be approved by Mexican vote. Mexican conservatives, who had continued their opposition to Juárez's liberal government, rigged an election and informed Maximilian that he had been overwhelmingly approved by popular vote. Maximilian gave up his right of succession to the Austrian crown, and, in a pact with Napoleon III, agreed to pay all back expenses incurred by the French troops during the invasion, as well as future salaries of the French troops that would remain in Mexico until 1867, under his command, to support his new regime. This agreement tripled Mexico's foreign debt. It also illustrates the mixture of ambition and political naiveté that Maximilian brought to his new post. Maximilian sailed for Mexico with his young wife, Carlota (Charlotte), daughter of King Leopold of Belgium. As the Mexican historian Justo Sierra memorably described the situation, Maximilian "was about to become the protagonist of a drama, but a drama ending in tragedy, for he was neither a politician nor an administrator nor a soldier: he was a dreamer, a poet. Charlotte had all the common sense in the family; he [Maximilian] saw everything in a theatrical light, as a stage effect."[12]

The drama of the short-lived empire played out quickly. When they assumed the reins of government in Mexico, Maximilian was thirty-two years old and Carlota was twenty-four. They were idealistic as well as ambitious. Although Maximilian was descended from a venerable line of kings in Europe, he had a reputation for liberal thinking. Along with many of his supporters, he talked of establishing a "democratic monarchy" in Mexico, as a provisional government on the way to a "democratic republic." His liberal ideas soon put him in conflict with many of his conservative supporters in Mexico, those who had actually brought him to power. He advocated a free press and religious tolerance. To learn more about the country, he took several long tours of the provinces, appearing in regional dress and eating regional food. However, Mexican liberals were not sympathetic to him, as they opposed a foreign-imposed monarchy for obvious reasons. Maximilian made more enemies than friends, alienating his conservative political base with his liberal views and failing to gain support among the liberals who were skeptical of his talk of a liberal monarchy. He was, by nature and by lack of experience, hopelessly ill-prepared to govern in the unstable political climate of midcentury Mexico, and soon became fatally embroiled in Mexican politics, unable to please either the liberals or the conservatives.[13]

The puppet empire lasted only three years. As the North began winning the Civil War in the United States, Benito Juárez appealed

(Left) The Late Maximilian, "Emperor of Mexico." Harper's Weekly, 20 June 1867. (Right) Execution of the Emperor Maximilian, Meija, and Miramon, at Querétaro, Mexico, 19 June 1867. Harper's Weekly, 10 August 1867.

for and received support from the U.S. Congress and began to muster an opposition army. After Lincoln was assassinated, Andrew Johnson's secretary of state, William Seward, began to pressure Napoleon III to pull out of Mexico, and Juárez was allowed to buy arms in California. The French, also under pressure in Europe, began to withdraw troops in late 1866, leaving Maximilian in an untenable position. Appeals to Napoleon III by a series of envoys from Mexico, including Carlota herself, were turned down. Maximilian passed up several opportunities to abdicate, and his dwindling army ultimately suffered defeat by Juárez, who denied all appeals for leniency and put Maximilian and two of his officers to death by firing squad, on 19 June 1867. Carlota, still in Europe trying to muster support for their failing Mexican enterprise, descended into madness and spent the rest of her life in confinement, claiming to be the empress of Mexico.[14]

Maximilian's execution was intended by Juárez as a definitive blow to imperialist ambitions in Mexico, and it successfully put an end to outside political and military intervention in Mexican affairs once and for all, but Maximilian's death by firing squad haunted Mexico, particularly Mexico's progressive elite, for the rest of the century. Juárez resumed power as head of a short-lived liberal democratic republic. As the country tried to pull itself together, outraged Europeans labeled Maximilian's execution an act of barbarism and painted

A sketch for a proposed architectural improvement to the baths in Chapultepec Park, ca. 1865–66. (Courtesy of Mapoteca Manuel Orozco y Berra, Mexico City)

Mexico as an uncivilized wilderness. Maximilian's death, and the subsequent international reaction to it, became important factors in shaping Mexican national identity, as Mexican politicians and intellectuals struggled to redraw a national image shadowed by lingering memory of the violent ending to the French intervention and the European reaction that followed.[15]

The arrival of Maximilian and Carlota, in May 1864, had opened a new chapter for Chapultepec. The secluded hilltop castle appealed greatly to their romantic sensibilities, reminding them potently of Miramar, their beloved castle in Trieste. They immediately preferred Chapultepec to the more ponderous National Palace in the center of Mexico City. Maximilian wrote to his brother a month after his arrival in Mexico: "We live by turns in the vast *palais nacional* [*sic*] in the city, an old and venerable building with eleven hundred windows, and at Chapultepec, the Schönbrunn of Mexico, a fascinating country residence on a basalt crag, surrounded by Montezuma's famous giant trees, and offering a prospect the like of which for beauty I have seen perhaps only at Sorrento."[16] Within eight days of their arrival in Mexico City, Maximilian and Carlota took up residence at the hilltop castle, although the building was remote and barely habitable. The first night Maximilian reportedly slept on a billiard table, and Carlota and her ladies-in-waiting had their beds made up on the terrace to escape the dust and vermin inside.[17] However, the superb views the terrace commanded over the valley of Mexico apparently outweighed the discomforts. It was, by all accounts, a spectacular panorama, including the sparkling waters of Lake Texcoco backed by the magnificent volcanoes, Popocatepetl and Ixtaccihuatl; the capital city in the near distance; and above all, "that boundless, infinite, over-arching sky."[18] Maximilian began to refer to the castle at Chapultepec as Miravalle and to remodel it into a Mexican counterpart to Miramar. He added a wide, covered corridor commanding the view, replanted the castle gardens, and embellished them with statuary, fountains, and urns, among other improvements. Repairs and renovations to the castle and grounds commenced under the direction of the Mexican architect Ramón Rodríguez Arrangoiti, but European architects were also engaged, including Carl Gangolf Kayser and Julius Hofmann, from Vienna. Furniture and art objects from Europe graced the interior. The castle had three levels, with kitchens, servants, and storage on the lower levels, and the emperor, empress, and their entourage on the upper levels. Maximilian also constructed the spiral drive, paved with stones, that still serves as the approach to the castle, with thirty gas lamps on iron columns lighting the way.[19]

According to one view of Maximilian's tenure on the hill, an "imperial farce took place in Chapultepec; in its most amiable aspects it had a touch of spectacle and operetta. The Emperor could feel almost as if he were in Europe, he could impose European etiquette and sleep in peace. The Chapultepec Hill was an oasis, decorated for the Archdukes."[20] However, by the standards of many of Maximilian's European contemporaries, the architecture and furnishings of the castle were rather austere. One visitor noted that, although "this castle on the rock will always have an imposing effect at first sight; yet, as a piece of architecture, little can be said in its favor. It is a long, rambling, two-storied building, terminated towards the city side by two badly-proportioned towers, unequal in size, and quite destroying the *ensemble;* and besides has, to my thinking, been more than ever disfigured by the glaring colours with which its walls have been painted."[21]

The Countess Paula Kollonitz, lady-in-waiting to the Empress Carlota, described the "Burgher-like simplicity and great discomfort of the Imperial residence." According to her, although the views were indeed spectacular, the residence itself was "unpleasing, and its arrangement uncomfortable," and the rooms were drafty and prone to flooding from the poorly situated garden terrace. Nevertheless, she reported the emperor telling his entourage that, "in the moments of difficulty . . . nothing had so much power to cheer and strengthen him as the wonderful harmony of [that] view."[22] Maximilian wrote to his brother the Archduke Karl Ludwig in a letter dated 26 July 1864: "At Chapultepec we are quite alone and very retired, and live even more quietly and simply than at Miramar. In town, moreover, we very seldom give dinners; we almost always have our meals alone and see nobody in the evenings. . . . The so-called entertainments of Europe, such as evening receptions, the gossip of tea-parties, etc., etc., of hideous memory, are quite unknown here, and we shall take good care not to introduce them."[23]

Maximilian enjoyed the simple pleasures afforded by the beautiful forest at Chapultepec, riding most mornings in the park and bathing regularly in the ancient pools. According to the memoir of his personal secretary, Maximilian would pay the customary five pesos to use the baths and swim for fifteen or twenty minutes at midday, while four guards kept the public away.[24] A zoo and an aviary were added during Maximilian and Carlota's tenure. Perhaps bowing to political necessity, Carlota adopted the French empress Eugenie's habit of hosting a reception each Monday evening at Chapultepec, with music and dancing. Invitations to these evenings were coveted by members of Mexican high society; however, Maximilian did not attend regularly, often leaving Carlota to play the role of hostess on her own.[25]

Work on the park during Maximilian and Carlota's residency included removal of undergrowth in the forest and new plantings of cedars and pines to add variety to the ancient forest. The great grove of Montezuma cypresses (*Taxodium mucronatum*) that grew at the base of the hill around the pools of Chapultepec had entered a prolonged period of decline following the Spanish conquest, due to the gradual drying up of the springs and marshes that were their natural habitat. Yet, by all accounts, these trees remained a remarkable sight. According to the *Galván Almanac*, in 1838 there were about three hun-

The Chapultepec Cypresses. Engraving from Elisée Reclus, *North America*, vol. 2 of *Mexico, Central America, West Indies* (New York: D. Appleton and Co., 1891).

dred great cypresses standing like sentinels at the entrance to the park, the largest with a circumference exceeding 15 *varas* (about 41 feet), another measuring 14 *varas* (about 38 feet) and many others over 12 *varas*. The Nahuatl name for this tree is *ahuehuete*, which translates roughly as "old tree of the water," reflecting its water-loving nature and the venerable age the species commonly attains. This species dates to the Mesozoic era, between 100 and 200 million years ago, and once dominated the area. It is one of the longest-living trees in the world, with a normal life span of five hundred years; a specimen in Oaxaca (the famous Tule tree) is estimated to be over two thousand years old. It is very difficult to artificially reproduce this species, a difficulty that was known in the nineteenth century. The *Galván Almanac* noted that in the previous century, only eight had been successfully reproduced from seed.[26] Yet, some of the Chapultepec cypresses were removed in the nineteenth century, and at least one great specimen met its demise during Maximilian's tenure.[27] Nineteenth-century travelers, poets, and painters much appreciated the magnifi-

The Bucareli Promenade in Mexico City, with the Chapultepec aqueduct in the distance. Lithograph from C. Castro et al., *México y sus alrededores: Colección de monumentos, trajes y paisajes* (Mexico City: Establecimiento Litográfico de Decaen, 1855–56). (Courtesy of Bancroft Library, University of California, Berkeley)

cent cypresses at Chapultepec. Paul Duplessis, the French writer of popular westerns, in his romanticized account of Mexico, *Aventuras Mejicanas* (1862), wrote about the magnificent cypresses: "they were of such proportions, that they came close to the grandeur of fantasy's creations: when these old trees contemplate their leaves, green as tears, in the murky reflection of the swamps, they become even more melancholic."[28]

Maximilian and Carlota began the transformation of Chapultepec into a modern park, not only by means of the physical changes they made to the castle and forest, but by enveloping the site in a veil of European romanticism that selectively blocked out some of its ancient history, while enhancing other aspects that were more in keeping with European cultural ideals. Maximilian's tenure in Mexico coincided exactly with the transformation of Paris that was occurring under Napoleon III, and the changes he made to both Chapultepec

The town of Tacubaya. Lithograph from C. Castro et al., *México y sus alrede-dores: Colección de monumentos, trajes y paisajes* (Mexico City: Estable-cimiento Litográfico de Decaen, 1855–56). (Courtesy of Bancroft Library, University of California, Berkeley)

and Mexico City mirrored the renovations in Paris in many respects. Perhaps most importantly, Maximilian laid out a broad, straight, eucalyptus-lined avenue that was often compared to the Champs Ély-sées, linking Chapultepec to the city and providing a suitably grand arrival experience for visitors to the imperial residence. Maximilian called the new boulevard Emperor Drive; later the name was changed to Paseo de la Reforma. The new avenue created a major new axis on the western side of the city, through terrain that was still largely un-developed. Along this four-lane avenue, a series of circles marking major intersections afforded opportunities for nationalistic monu-ments and fountains. With the great park at its western terminus, Paseo de la Reforma became the spine of modern Mexico City, giving momentum to a shift of the wealthy toward the west side of the city, a movement that would gain force subsequently, under the Porfiriato.

Just south of Chapultepec was the leafy village of Tacubaya. Important visitors during the French intervention would often combine a visit to Chapultepec with a stop in Tacubaya, where "men with heavy purses" had built villas and country houses. Residents of this wealthy enclave included a number of foreigners involved with various enterprises in Mexico, such as "Mr. Barron, an Englishman . . . the Rothschild of these parts," whose country house was reputed to be "in perfect taste," and Antonio Escandón, founder of the Mexican Railroad.[29] The proximity of Chapultepec to Tacubaya, a fashionable residential area on the west side of Mexico City, mirrors the location of the Bois de Boulogne on the west side of Paris and the location of the London parks in the wealthy West End. Later in the nineteenth century, under the Porfiriato, the relationship between Chapultepec and high-end real-estate development would be fully exploited.

It is said that Juárez spent only one night in the Castle at Chapultepec, in July 1867, after taking over the government following Maximilian's downfall.[30] Perhaps Chapultepec was too associated with Maximilian for the Juárez government to be comfortable there. In fact, the park became somewhat of a political issue in the notoriously partisan Mexican press during the brief Juárez administration. Because of Maximilian and Carlota's love of Chapultepec, it had become a symbol of the French intervention in Mexico, not just politically but also culturally. With the new boulevard linking it to the city, patterned on the Champs Élysées, Chapultepec represented the introduction of French urban design to the Mexican capital. Some members of the Mexican elite, ardent capitalists who saw progress in terms of material development, had welcomed French influences in Mexico. They sought to make Mexico more modern by introducing trends and fashions from Europe and the United States. These so-called progressives rejected many Mexican traditions as backward or primitive. They felt that these traditions held Mexico back, slowing what they saw as inevitable progress.[31] A debate about Chapultepec in the press, following the end of the French intervention, reflects the beginnings of the culture wars between traditionalists and progressives that would engage Mexican society for the rest of the nineteenth century and into the twentieth.

Less than six months after Maximilian's death, on 12 November 1867, *El Constitucional* reported on the destruction of trees in the park at Chapultepec and blamed this on forest guards. Apparently some measures were taken to protect the park, because the following summer an article in *La Revista Universal* protested a special permit required for access to the forest: "This magnificent property, which Maximilian so beautified, and which could be considered on a par with the most famous European royal sites, belongs to the Nation. However, as it is now being cared for by an inflexible guard who prohibits both Mexicans and foreigners to enter, it has simply been reduced to the President's weekend resort. . . . At the time of the last empire, a numerous crowd spent moments of genuine recreation in Chapultepec; today, democracy does not allow these innocent amusements, and by tomorrow, according to their own rights, they will prohibit people from entering the Alameda park or the garden at Mexico's main square."[32] Two days later another article, in *El Diario Oficial*, asserted that there was really no prohibition on use of Chapultepec Park; it was just a matter of requesting a permit, which was available to anyone who asked. Another periodical, *La Opinión Nacional*, weighed in on 19 August in favor of the permit process because, "with the excuse of visiting the castle or spending a day in the forest, many people came in and destroyed the flowers, took away the plants, and even got to the point of stealing the locks on the doors and the curtains from the windows."[33]

The claim that, during the short-lived empire, large crowds had been able to recreate in the park, whereas "today, democracy does not allow these innocent amusements," seems politically motivated, as does the response. In fact, although Chapultepec was used by a certain segment of the public during Maximilian and Carlota's tenure, its distance from the poorer parts of the city, and the presence of imperial guards, protected it from broad public use. Those who felt welcome because of their social standing, and who either lived in the vicinity or had the means to get to the park, used it to exercise their horses, picnic under the great trees, and, perhaps, bathe in the pools. Following the end of the Empire, they took a proprietary interest, not just in the park itself, but in what it represented. It stood for a particular type of landscape scenery, the appreciation of which was becoming a mark of distinction among the Mexican and foreign bourgeoisie who frequented it. It was becoming associated with certain leisure activities that were increasingly popular among the Mexican elite, such as horseback riding, picnicking, and later in the century, bicycling.[34] The articles in

The Road from Tacubaya to Chapultepec. Lithograph from C. Castro et al., *México y sus alrededores: Colección de monumentos, trajes y paisajes* (Mexico City: Establecimiento Litográfico de Decaen, 1855–56). (Courtesy of Bancroft Library, University of California, Berkeley)

the press debating how the park should be used and who should be allowed to use it reflect the beginnings of a new way of thinking about the park. It now represented modern urban design, like the parks in Paris, and would become increasingly important as a symbol of modernity under the Porfiriato. It is likely that the government instituted more control over access and use of the park at this time, because the castle was no longer regularly occupied and fewer castle guards were available to police it. It was still well beyond the city limits, and, with the exception of nearby Tacubaya, it was surrounded by haciendas and small, poor indigenous communities. Yet the politicizing of this issue in the press, as early as 1868, foreshadows the transformation of Chapultepec into a showplace for the progressive elite who would soon become powerful under the regime of Porfirio Díaz.

The Porfiriato

Porfirio Díaz won the presidential election in 1876 with solid liberal credentials. As the young general who led the Mexican army to victory over the French on 5 May 1862, Díaz was a national hero. During the French intervention, he had solidified his liberal image as a leader in guerrilla warfare against the French army that supported Maximilian's regime. In his first term as president (1876–80), Díaz brought Mexico back onto the international stage and set the country on the path to modernity. He reestablished diplomatic relations and trade with most of Western Europe and Latin America, as well as the United States. He began a process of putting the Mexican economy back together, streamlining the bureaucracy, attacking problems of smuggling and lawlessness along the U.S. border, and establishing regular payments on foreign debt. In 1880, at the end of his first term, he honored the term limits established in the liberal constitution of 1857, and stepped down. Four years later, in 1884, he was eligible to run again and was easily reelected. After that, he maintained a tight hold on the presidency, ignoring constitutional term limits, until 1911, when a popular uprising forced his resignation. Díaz is credited with boosting Mexico into the modern era during his thirty-five-year rule; the Porfiriato is the period when, by most accounts, Mexico became a modern state. However, this transformation came at considerable social cost, which has tainted Díaz's legacy.

When Díaz came to power in 1876, Mexico was a rural, undeveloped nation, its abundant natural resources largely untapped. The industrial and scientific revolutions that had transformed Europe and the United States had barely touched Mexico. The country had been mired in political strife and internal upheaval for years: the presidency had actually changed hands seventy-five times in the fifty-five years since Independence. One of Díaz's primary goals was to convince foreign investors, who had been scared off by the years of political instability, that Mexico was stable enough to warrant investment. His government enforced order and peace throughout the country, and Mexico entered a long period of economic growth. The regime developed the mining and petroleum industries; doubled manufacturing; built railroads throughout the country; replaced horses and mules with steam, water, and electric power; introduced the telephone and the automobile; and generally improved Mexico's image—and self-image—enormously.

The prolonged peace under the Porfiriato produced marked population growth in the country, from 8.7 million in 1874 to 15.2 million in 1910. Mexico City grew even more remarkably, doubling from 200,000 in 1874 to 471,066 in 1910.[35] During the Porfiriato, Mexico City experienced an extraordinary transformation, as the national government spent large quantities of money in the capital, constructing a modern tramway system and fixing the drainage problems that had plagued the capital since the Aztec era. Other urban improvements that contributed to quality of life included new potable water systems, sewage systems, hospitals, and schools. Older streets were paved, and many broad, new boulevards were built. Banks and foreign companies constructed new buildings, new department stores opened, and elegant shops appeared. The Alameda, a public square dating to the colonial period, was a rustic and sometimes dangerous place in the 1860s. By the 1880s, it had been expanded and outfitted with fountains, trees, and walkways. Electric lights were installed there in 1892, and it became a pleasant place for the middle and upper classes to stroll and listen to music. Three theaters—the Principal (built in 1753), the Arbeu (1875), and the Fine Arts Palace (early 1900s)—put on plays by Racine and Shakespeare and hosted European companies performing Puccini and Verdi operas.[36]

Although the country benefited in general from improvements instituted by Díaz, the economic prosperity enjoyed by hacienda owners, industrialists, developers, bankers, and others in the upper class during the Porfiriato did not trickle down to the lower classes. A very small, but conspicuously wealthy, upper class prospered enormously. Representatives of foreign companies from the United States and Europe who invested heavily in Mexico also profited handsomely. But social inequity increased greatly in both rural areas and in the cities, where populations swelled with rural migration. A land law of 1883, intended to encourage foreign colonization of rural Mexico, gave land companies the right to survey public lands for subdivision and rewarded them for doing so by giving them, free, up to one-third of the land surveyed along with the option to purchase the rest of the surveyed land at bargain prices. If landowners could not produce proof of ownership, their land was declared public. The indigenous population particularly suffered, as the *ejidos*—traditional public lands owned and administered by indigenous villages—were often undocumented. The practices enabled by the land law consolidated land into few hands, and a powerful elite class of *hacendados* emerged, con-

The Alameda in Mexico City in the 1850s. Lithograph from C. Castro et al., *México y sus alrededores: Colección de monumentos, trajes y paisajes* (Mexico City: Establecimiento Litográfico de Decaen, 1855–56). (Courtesy of Bancroft Library, University of California, Berkeley)

trolling vast resources. By the end of the Porfiriato, a few hundred fantastically wealthy families controlled most of Mexico's best land. Some of the larger landholders owned haciendas encompassing more than 1 million acres. Many peasants, forced off their own lands, either joined the work force that supported the enormous haciendas or moved to the city in search of work. The hacienda system employed over half of all rural Mexicans by 1910. Millions of rural Mexicans became much worse off under the often harsh conditions on the haciendas. Average daily wages remained the same during the nineteenth century, but the prices of staple foods increased. The cost of corn and chile more than doubled, and beans cost six times more in 1910 than in 1800. Conditions on the haciendas were often bleak for laborers, who were dependent on the hacienda management for everything as the government provided nothing in the way of social services. Education and health care were nonexistent in the countryside. The *hacendados* themselves spent little time on their haciendas. Profits from the countryside were largely spent in Mexico City during the Porfiriato.[37]

The mechanisms for maintaining order and enforcing peace under the Porfiriato included a strong military, trained at the reorganized

Military Academy in Chapultepec, by instructors who were sent to observe at West Point and at the French officers' school at St. Cyr. During the peaceful era of the Porfiriato, the military enforced the law of the land and helped administer the country. The *rurales*, a rural police force established by Juárez prior to the French intervention, became an effective, and feared, force in maintaining order in the countryside. As Díaz's loyal guardsmen, the *rurales* also served as a check on the military. The regime maintained an illusion of democracy while exerting tight control over political processes, including censoring the press, tampering with elections to favor the regime's supporters, and rewarding supporters with political favors and economic benefits. Díaz appointed political opponents to remote diplomatic posts to get them out of the way, and relocated ambitious generals frequently to keep them from developing strong political support in a particular location.

The intellectual foundations of the Porfiriato were articulated by the *científicos*, whose scientific positivism was based in the ideas of Auguste Comte and influenced by John Stuart Mill, but also by Herbert Spencer, whose ideas about social Darwinism underpinned some of the *científicos'* social attitudes. The *científicos* put their faith in scientific progress and technological innovation and advocated stronger ties to Europe and the Unites States as a means to modernize Mexico. They took a paternalistic view of the large indigenous population of Mexico, believing that the future of the country lay in the hands of the *criollo* class (Mexican-born people of Spanish descent). Justo Sierra, founder of the conservative newspaper *La Libertad*, secretary of education, and first rector of the national university, was one of the main articulators of the *científico* position. He defended the authoritarian Díaz regime on the grounds that it was necessary for Mexico to have a period of strong government to enforce structural reforms, both economic and social. Once those reforms were firmly in place, Sierra held, it would be possible to broaden democratic participation. As a liberal educator, he believed that social and cultural factors, more than biological determinism, held back the indigenous population, and argued that they could become productive citizens with the proper education. However, schools built during the Porfiriato were all in the cities and served mostly the *criollo* population, and two million indigenous people still were not speaking Spanish by the end of the

Porfiriato. The philosophy of the *científicos* translated into policies that marginalized the poor in general, but particularly the indigenous population.

Mexico City became much more socially stratified during the Porfiriato. As in Paris and New York, appearances were important to signify social status, particularly for the emerging middle class in Mexico City, composed of skilled artisans, government bureaucrats, clergymen, low-ranking army officers, professionals, small businessmen, and neighborhood merchants. Dress, neighborhood of residence, and attendance at certain social events helped differentiate the middle class from a lower class only recently left behind. While the upper classes enjoyed a lavish lifestyle and demonstrated their status in a daily parade along Paseo de la Reforma, displaying fine carriages, horses, and the latest European fashions, the middle class also developed a fine-tuned awareness of the markers of social distinction, such as dress and manners. All things French became fashionable among the upper class, from clothing, furniture, and cuisine, to French governesses. Everyone who was anyone wanted to be seen at French comic opera or at the French Polo Club. The most coveted symbol of social status among the elite was membership in the exclusive Jockey Club, founded in 1881 to bring together the wealthiest and most powerful men in the capital for the purpose of promoting and building a track for horse racing.[38]

Like Paris during the Second Empire, the Mexican capital had its famous *flaneur* during the Porfiriato. Manuel Gutiérrez Nájera, known as "El Duque Job," was to Mexico City as Baudelaire was to Paris. He wrote poetry and short stories heavy with French and English references, and turned a critical eye on the city. In one short story, "La novela del tranvía" (The Streetcar Novel), the protagonist sits in the back of a tram and observes the scene, speculating about the class, occupation, residences, and thoughts of various streetcar riders, gauging their station from their dress, speech, and manners. Besides dress and neighborhood, different forms of entertainment became associated with different social classes. For example, the *zarzuela*, a bawdy form of musical comedy, became popular, particularly among the middle class in the mid-1880s. Relying on vulgar dancers, risqué language, and satire, *zarzuela* entertainers portrayed different classes in stereotypical fashion: beggars, water carriers, dandies on horseback.

Disaster at Regent's Park, London

At the time of the disaster there were five hundred skaters, many of them ladies, on the ice, and at least three thousand spectators looking on from the shores; and the excitement and fun were at their highest. The entire expanse of ice, covering nearly an acre of water, gave way according to some, exploded according to others, and was agitated as if by an earthquake. The fatal cracks are described as shooting with sharp reports in every conceivable direction, and with such rapidity that it seemed as if

The Disaster at Regent's Park. Harper's Weekly, 2 March 1867.

The upper classes looked down on this type of theatrical entertainment as it became popular with shopkeepers and clerks.[39]

The physical geography of Mexico City represented the growing gap between the rich and the poor during the Porfiriato, as the wealthy moved gradually to the western districts of the capital. In the 1870s and 1880s, fashionable lodgings, shops, and businesses migrated from the older, established districts north and east of the great central plaza (el Zócalo) to the west side, along Plateros and around the spruced-up Alameda park. In the 1890s and 1900s, new suburbs developed along both sides of Paseo de la Reforma. That wide boulevard first laid out by Maximilian, from the Alameda to Chapultepec, became the spine of the new fashionable west side. In the new western districts along Paseo de la Reforma, European-style architecture and modern amenities afforded a sophisticated and urbane lifestyle for the upper classes.

MELODRAMATIC LANDSCAPES

the giving way was simultaneous in each direction. Within a minute the whole sheet of the ice over the full width of the lake gave way, and split up into fragments of a few yards square. A general rush was made for the banks. Unfortunately, this broke up the soft ice into still smaller pieces. About two hundred persons were struggling in the water, and screaming for help. A few, with great presence of mind, threw themselves flat upon the surface of the pieces of ice, and were thus instrumental in saving the lives of many of those in the water, as well as preserving their own until assistance came to them. The scene was most distressing for many minutes after the breaking of the ice: a multitude of people, among whom were several women and children, were struggling in the water, and trying to save themselves by holding the pieces of ice, and most of them screaming in despair. Of those on shore, a few were able to give prompt assistance to the nearest sufferers, and help them to scramble to land; but many were struck with horror and could do nothing but utter cries of lamentation.

(FROM *HARPER'S WEEKLY*, 2 MARCH 1867)

During the Porfiriato, American companies built the exclusive *colonias* of Cuauhtémoc, Juárez, and Roma, in partnership with local business and government officials. Real estate in Mexico City under Díaz's watch was a profitable investment, as "land prices along Reforma increased sixteenfold between 1880 and 1900."[40] Speculators and construction firms, such as the American-owned Mexico City Improvement Company, made large, quick profits. A very small, exclusive group of financiers and investors controlled most of the real estate and commerce in the capital and saw huge profits.

Meanwhile, artisans and laborers moved into the properties abandoned by the wealthy around the Zócalo, and these buildings were subdivided into tenements. The new suburbs of San Rafael and Santa María, built in the 1880s and 1890s, to the northwest of Paseo de la Reforma, provided housing for the emerging middle class. Peasants

The Viga Canal in Mexico City. Lithograph from C. Castro et al., *México y sus alrededores: Colección de monumentos, trajes y paisajes* (Mexico City: Establecimiento Litográfico de Decaen, 1855–56). (Courtesy of Bancroft Library, University of California, Berkeley)

immigrating from the countryside swelled large, sprawling, makeshift barrios to the east and south of the city center. These barrios were dense and without potable water, sewers, or paving. They were subject to flooding and typhus. The Viga Canal, which ran to the south between Xochimilco and the city, was a pleasure ground for eastside residents, with vendors selling food and flowers on the roadway bordering the canal and from boats laden with produce grown on the *chinampas* of Xochimilco. By the 1890s, the upper classes no longer visited the Viga Canal much, although the middle class continued to do so, especially on festival days.

Chapultepec became the showpiece pleasure ground of the wealthy, new western side of the city during the Porfiriato. Upon assuming office, Díaz reinstated the castle as a presidential residence, and the government commenced improvements to the building, redecorating the interior and making it suitable for the president's use. In 1877, a new entrance structure was built to the park, consisting of five ornamental iron arches with large gates that could be closed off. The Astronomical, Meteorological and Magnetic Observatory was inaugurated at the castle on top of the hill on 5 May 1878, and astronomers working there corresponded with colleagues at observatories in the United States (Harvard), Madrid, Paris, and other locations around the world. The instruments were relocated to Tacubaya in 1883, but the observatory structure remains to this day. In the pre-Hispanic era, some sort of observatory had existed on the hill; the first Spaniards described carved stones found on top, presumably linked to stars. Subsequently, during the colonial period, several proposals for reestablishing an observatory on the hill were never carried out. It seems appropriate that Díaz, with his *científico* ideology, would support the establishment of such a facility.[41]

When Díaz first became president, the park at Chapultepec was still rustic and undeveloped, located well beyond the borders of the city, underutilized by the public, its venerable trees uncared for and its springs drying up. An article in *El Siglo Diez y Nueve* in 1876, "Chapultepec, Impressions of a Traveler," criticized the neglect of the great forest by the authorities, noting hatchet marks and signs of fires in the trees.[42] Tomás Noriega, a Mexican naturalist, published a study of disease attacking the trees, in 1877, but apparently little was done to remedy the situation, and the ancient cypresses continued to decline. In 1881, "alarming clearings" were reported in the *ahuehuetes*, and the pools, no longer a sanctuary for swans and sea gulls, were reported to be green and stagnant, a hatchery for snakes and lizards, a detriment to the ancient forest, and a menace to public health.[43]

The baths at Chapultepec, so enjoyed by the emperor Maximilian, had long been one of its main attractions, particularly in the summer months. There was a large, deep pool and a number of smaller pools with "Pompeian-style" private rooms for those not wishing to bathe communally. The pools were filled with the clearest water from the springs, surrounded by gardens with sandy paths, and shaded by ash trees and weeping willows.[44] However, both the quality and the quantity of the water steadily declined over the years, and around 1880 the baths were closed. In 1887, they were leased by the city to a private party, Joaquín Romo, who proposed to reopen them in April of that year after making some improvements. This plan was well received by residents of the capital, particularly by those with nervous afflictions and anemia, as bathing at Chapultepec was thought to have medicinal benefits.[45] But the springs were drying up, and by 1892 only the large pool remained, opposite the streetcar depot for the Tacubaya line, on the edge of the park. New hydraulic works, used to pump water from the receding springs up to the aqueduct of Chapultepec, occupied the site of the smaller pools. These pumps were put into service on 29 December 1891.[46]

During the last decade of the nineteenth century, the Díaz regime accelerated improvements to the park. In 1889, the department of public works started a propagation garden near the old Molino del Rey (king's mill), west of the hill, to grow plants not only for Chapultepec, but for the whole city, and by 1894 the garden was reported to have 67,194 plants.[47] The zoo added animals, and additional facilities to house them, just south of the Reforma entrance to the park. There was a formal English-style garden immediately inside the entrance gates, with statuary, fountains, a duck pond, and a deer park, and the area around the foot of the hill, described by one guidebook as "a wild little park," still had "about 280 slender and gigantic cypresses, centuries old, picturesquely draped by nature with pendants of gray Spanish moss." The guidebook also mentioned a fragment of rock, the "Relief of Ahuitzol," at the base of the hill on the eastern side, a lingering remnant of the Aztec presence in the area.[48]

Around 1896, José Yves Limantour, finance minister under Díaz, began to assume an active role in management and development of the park. That year more than two hundred meters were added to the park and many new trees were planted. Limantour personally supervised the renovation of the old *cuerpo de guardia* (guardhouse), relocated to the foot of the ramp leading up to the castle, with the intention of maintaining more separation between the castle and the park.[49] The park was becoming a more popular destination for tourists and residents of the growing western districts of Mexico City. At twilight each day, a parade of fashionable carriages formed a festive *paseo*, starting at the Alameda and following Paseo de la Reforma into Chapultepec. In the park, the carriage route passed by the zoological gardens and, under the great *ahuehuetes*, circled the boating and duck ponds and followed the new avenues around the outer limits of the park.[50] In 1899, the press reported that the authorities were expecting a large

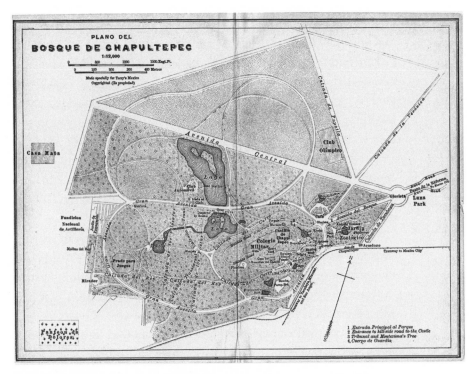

Plan of Chapultepec. From T. Phillip Terry, *Terry's Mexico: Handbook for Travelers* (Boston: Houghton Mifflin, 1909).

quantity of statues, marbles, and other artistic objects from Europe, to ornament the park.[51]

Limantour set up a formal commission, around 1900, to manage and improve the park, the Junta Superior del Bosque de Chapultepec. Frequently citing the Bois de Boulogne as inspiration, the commission completed the transformation of Chapultepec into a modern urban park. They pursued acquisition of land from private owners to increase the size of the park. An iron fence, with elegant grillwork, extended around the park, delineating its boundaries. Thousands of new trees were planted, mostly exotic species, along with acres of grass, enhancing the pastoral effect. New avenues included a carriage road circling the whole park and an extensive network of smaller roads and paths to accommodate pedestrians and equestrians. Small hills, grottoes, simulated ruins, and statuary from France, Belgium, and Switzerland provided interest and detail. The commission modernized the zoo, adding many animals and birds, kennels, and a deer enclosure made of whole tree trunks. The young architect Nicolás Mariscal, a protégé of Limantour, designed a handsome summerhouse with an elegant café-restaurant and classical grandstands for ceremonies. On 8 September 1900, *La Rotonda a los Niños Héroes* was inaugurated, a new monument to the young cadets of the Military Academy who gave their lives in defense of the country in 1847. Two new lakes were constructed and connected by a meandering canal deep enough to accommodate small boats. The lakes' design made use of a picturesque group of trees near the shore and included several islands and a rustic bridge.[52]

A blueprint plan of Chapultepec, dated 1906, a copy of which is currently housed in the Historical Archives of the City of Mexico, shows most of these improvements. In addition, the plan indicates a large polo field and automobile club to the west of the large, new lake. The automobile club, completed in 1908 at a cost of $35,000, purportedly included among its members some of the city's most aristocratic residents. The plan of 1906 also indicated an area designated for the future Club Olímpico at the eastern edge of the park, north of the Reforma entrance. A subsequent plan, dated 1913, shows the Olympic club fully developed, with ranks of tennis courts and a golf course north of Avenida Central. In the first decade of the twentieth century, as these plans show, the site was truly transformed into a typical nineteenth-century urban park. A naturalistic landscape, modeled on the Bois de Boulogne, had superseded the wild, ancient forest that had witnessed so many milestones on the way to modern Mexico. Similarities between Chapultepec and the well-known European parks were often pointed out in guidebooks for foreigners. For example, T. Phillip Terry, author of the popular English-language guidebook *Terry's Mexico*, noting "the steady stream of fine equipages and automobiles" starting at around 10 A.M., and the "many fine turn-outs and toilettes" that were "features of the afternoon (4–6) parade," added that, "in point of size and general attractiveness [Chapultepec] compares not unfavorably with the Bois de Boulogne, Hyde Park and similar European resorts."[53]

These improvements took time and travelers noted that the park was a work in progress during the decades flanking the turn of the twentieth century: "a beautiful, lake-dotted woodland intersected by

MELODRAMATIC LANDSCAPES

shaded walks, handsome and splendidly kept drives, running streams and parterres of perennially blooming flowers . . . being constantly enlarged." More than two hundred of the *ahuehuetes* still remained in the park in 1910, but the trailing Spanish moss (*Tillandsia asneoides*), which had formerly festooned the trees, giving the forest "a phantom-like appearance," had been removed because the moss was thought to sap the vitality of the older trees. The venerable trees were succumbing to the changes in their environment. Terry reported that, "decay has eaten into the heart of some of the patriarchs, and to preserve them clay has been inserted; to gain uniformity in appearance this clay has been adroitly tinted and ribbed and made to resemble the bark, so that near inspection is required to distinguish it."[54]

This description of the clay packed into the decaying cavities of the *ahuehuetes* could serve as a metaphor for urban planning in Mexico City under the Porfiriato. Many of the improvements to the city, including the transformation of Chapultepec into a modern public park, were carried out mainly with an eye for appearances, part of the government's strategy to create a modern national image that would help in attracting foreign investors. The massive social and economic reforms needed to truly convert Mexico into a prosperous, modern, industrial nation did not occur under Díaz, but the regime put on an impressive show of modernity. The capital, particularly the new west side, was the main stage for this show, and Chapultepec was a crucial player. Chapultepec already had the basic attributes on which to build a large, naturalistic park, and its location on the western edge of the city, at the end of Paseo de la Reforma, fit perfectly into the Porfiriato's grand scheme for the capital. The park became a showpiece in a new bourgeois city growing to the west of the old, problem-plagued city center. With Chapultepec as an anchor on the west, the elegant neighborhoods along Reforma filled in with handsome homes. As Terry noted, looking toward Mexico City from the slopes of Chapultepec, "the fine Paseo de la Reforma—the Empress Carlota's eucalyptus path—stretches like a plumb-line to the equestrian statue of Charles IV—whose predecessor's money built this glorious summer retreat. To the left and right of the paseo are the new homes of the capital's foreign residents."[55] Like the clay packed into the cracks in the ancient *ahuehuetes*, the new garden city on the west, with its impressive houses and its jewel of a park, hid the decay that was attacking the old city

La Glorieta en el Bosque

The families usually choose the picturesque forest [of Chapultepec] to rest on classical holidays, such as birthdays or any other reason for enjoyment. The group leaves by train, but up until fourteen years ago they used horse carriages and omnibuses. Young ladies enjoy themselves

A party in the forest of Chapultepec. Lithograph from C. Castro et al., *México y sus alrededores: Colección de monumentos, trajes y paisajes* (Mexico City: Establecimiento Litográfico de Decaen, 1855–56). (Courtesy of Bancroft Library, University of California, Berkeley)

and the cracks in the programs of the Porfiriato. In the comfortable western sections of Mexico City, it was easy to forget, or ignore, the growing social and economic problems of the rest of Mexico.

By 1892, Chapultepec was open to the public from 5:00 A.M. to 7:00 P.M. daily. In 1901, daily omnibus service to the park was inaugurated between 4:00 and 7:00 P.M., the first bus leaving from the statue of Carlos IV at the city-center end of Paseo de la Reforma at 4:00 P.M., and every twenty minutes thereafter until 6:20 P.M., the last omnibus departing from Chapultepec at 6:40 P.M.[56] This timing facili-

riding the horses which young lads, who do not like the railroad, have taken; lunch is eaten underneath the old cypresses, and later on the pools are visited; some dance, others talk about love, some admire the thickness of the trees, the pleasantness of the site and the beautiful perspective which the Valley offers from the various points of the hill; they comment about the towers and watchpoints which can be seen at a distance.

Dance! Dance! Is everyone's cry and unavoidable duty—Everybody must dance. And taking each other by the hand, the couples dance at the beat of the music, forming a cheerful scenery as the figures intertwine and separate. To rest from the fatigue, they wander about the paths of the forest and after a tiresome and happy day, almost at sunset, they return to the city, taking the public trains or carriages, while some ride their horses. During those picnics, musicians with their inseparable mandolins go their own way; nobody thinks of the rugs, the crystal chandeliers, nor of good table manners; there is no satin in the shoes, nor soft leather gloves to tightly wrap their hands; the servants are careful to see that the wine glasses are full and happiness quickly goes from their stomachs to their heads.

(FROM MANUEL RIVERA CAMBAS, *MÉXICO PINTORESCO, ARTÍSTICO Y MONUMENTAL*, TRANSLATED IN MARIO DE LA TORRE, *CHAPULTEPEC: HISTORIA Y PRESENCIA*)

tated public viewing of the parade of fashionable equipages that was a daily spectacle in the park. This daily display of wealth and fashion enhanced the national image that the Porfiriato cultivated. Guidebooks, presumably written more for tourists than for residents of the city, often mentioned this daily show.[57] One book described crowds of visitors arriving at the park in various conveyances: electric trams, ramshackle vehicles, elegant carriages with "fatuous lackies," on foot, horseback, or bicycle. This account appears to emphasize a mix of social classes, but the author devoted by far the most attention to the parade of fashionable, European-style carriages carrying beautifully dressed ladies on the roadways circumnavigating the park, representing "the richest and most luxurious of the capitalists," and included a society roster listing the most well-known individuals that park visitors might be lucky enough to spot in the parade.[58] It is doubtful that members of the working class used the park much for recreation. The increasing geographical segregation in the city kept them far away, and although tram service was available, the fare was prohibitive for most, ranging from five centavos within the city to thirty centavos to Tlalpan (outside the city). The average daily wage for unskilled labor in 1910 was around fifty centavos, and domestic servants made the equivalent of three to four U.S. dollars a month.[59]

Inside the park, strict surveillance controlled public use, as evinced by the following description:

> The early morning is the best time to visit the *parque;* then all is fresh and attractive, and a saunter through the almost deserted grounds is thoroughly delightful. Guide unnecessary. There is a lamentable dearth of free seats to be had; the spindle-legged chairs sitting in rows at various points (usually far from any beauty spot) are rented by the park custodians (who see to it that the visitor does not sit on the grass) at 5 c. the 1/2 hour. Mounted guards constantly patrol the avenues, and visitors are cautioned against any infraction of the rules relating to the picking of flowers, etc. In the early mornings of summer the President of the Republic and his wife may often be met strolling through the park. When the police-band plays (by the lakeside, usually at 10 A.M.) the music is well worth hearing.[60]

The obvious presence of guards throughout the park served as a deterrent to the lower classes; anyone deemed unsuitable would have been quickly removed from the premises. The modern Mexico City, of which Chapultepec was a showplace, was for the rich, and perhaps the middle classes, but not for the poor, who were viewed as a threat to both "health and morality."[61] The president and his wife would not have rubbed shoulders with the lower classes in the park. Just up the spiraling ramp, in the lavishly redecorated castle, General Díaz and Sra. Romero Rubio de Díaz, when in residence, entertained friends in the "comfortable, modern" room known as El Amigo, and received distinguished guests and members of the diplomatic corps in the great Ambassador's Room.[62] The dearth of free seating in the park, along

Chapultepec Park. Lithograph from C. Castro et al., *México y sus alrededores: Colección de monumentos, trajes y paisajes* (Mexico City: Establecimiento Litográfico de Decaen, 1855–56). (Courtesy of Bancroft Library, University of California, Berkeley)

with prohibitions on use of the grass, represent less overt methods of social control. Although technically a public park open to everyone, Chapultepec was actually a carefully controlled scenario for the benefit of a select segment of the population.

Chapultepec played an important role in the culminating event of the Porfiriato, a centennial celebration in honor of the hundredth anniversary of Mexico's Declaration of Independence and, coincidentally, Díaz's eightieth birthday. The Centenario took place in September 1910, and festivities spanned the whole month. Serious planning for the Centenario began in 1907, when the government established the Comisión Nacional del Centenario. The commission reviewed numerous proposals for centennial projects, from renaming streets to freeing political prisoners. Proposals submitted by members of the elite were, for the most part, accepted. Contributions flowed into the centennial fund from businessmen, financiers, and professional organizations. During the first two weeks of September, in the first phase of the celebrations, the government inaugurated a host of new buildings, including a mental hospital, new schools, and new government buildings, and laid the cornerstone for a new prison. But the real festivities began on 14 September, with a parade from the Alameda to the cathedral, including representatives of "all elements of Mexican society" dressed appropriately to represent their various stations in life. This was followed the next day by an even more elaborate parade representing the stages of Mexican history, as interpreted by the Díaz government. On 16 September, the actual date that the revolution for independence had commenced, the government unveiled and dedicated the impressive *Monument to Independence*, a colossal bronze angel atop a soaring, ornate column, in the final circle before Chapultepec on the Paseo de la Reforma.[63] Celebrations continued throughout the city for the rest of the month, including a memorable event staged in Chapultepec Park on 22 September.

In preparation for the centennial celebration, Chapultepec experienced a flurry of construction activity in the year leading up to the *Centenario. El Imparcial* reported as early as February 1910 that "Sr. Limantour, every third day, in the morning, before going to his office, arrives at the park to discuss work in progress with the director of works, Julio Riouss, the head horticulturalist, Alberto Kersmbum and the engineer Daniel Garza." The projects that Limantour supervised that year included the broad, straight Avenida Central, starting at the glorieta (roundabout) at the entrance to the park, on the Paseo de la Reforma, and ending at the terrain of Los Morales on the northwestern edge of the park. This avenue was planted with large masses of trees, interspersed with openings, to create view corridors. Limantour also supervised the construction of artificial caves and grottoes, made with artificial rocks, and the excavation of the large, cement-lined lake, which had a surface area of 80,000 square meters and a capacity of 120,000 cubic meters of water. A mirador adorned with six Greek columns and a spherical cupola, constructed on the small island in the lake, reached a height of 40 meters above the lake and afforded an impressive view of the "volcanoes, the forest, the lakes and all the beautiful landscape that is forming to be inaugurated during the *Centenario*."[64]

The "garden-party" staged in Chapultepec Park on 22 September 1910 was one of the more colorful events of the Centenario. It started in the afternoon with a grand procession of flower-decorated canoes accompanied by military bands. When night fell, there was a fireworks display simulating an attack on a fort by two battleships. The following description paints a vivid picture:

> The great castle was erected at the edge of the lake, on top of a small hill, and the ships appeared immobile next to it. The combat commenced with a continuous rain of grenades, exploding in the air and falling as colored lights, and projectiles that left luminous trails of gold sparkles. The fort emitted equal fire and the warlike illusion was completed by the acrid odor of gunpowder, the detonations continuing without interruption, and the sound of bugles and drums. That suggestive simulacrum ended with the explosion of the fortress, as though mined, with a blast, enveloped in the flames of a thunderous conflagration. With no dissipation of the smoke of battle, from the center of the lake arose the slender stream of a luminous fountain, brilliantly colored by numerous electric lamps and reflectors, which formed in the airy liquid plume the most beautiful and fantastic combination of lights. Meanwhile, the park was illuminated by infinite electric lights, inserted in the copses, hidden in the shrubbery, and spread around the lawns, which augmented the enchantment of the dazzling picture.[65]

This performance epitomizes the tone of the centennial celebration in general. It was dazzling, extravagant, and illusory, with a focus on appearances that had become characteristic of the Porfiriato. As international visitors began to arrive, beggars were forced off the streets so the city would appear to be prosperous. Some historians have pointed out that the cost of the month-long celebrations "exceeded the entire educational budget for the year 1910. Mexico was at last enjoying its place in the international sun—respect was no longer lacking. But while the champagne was flowing for a few, tens of thousands were suffering from malnutrition. While guests were treated to young female companions, indigenous women in Yucatán were dying in childbirth. While European waiters served at the banquets, urban Mexicans were unemployed. While letters of congratulation arrived on time, 85 percent of the population was illiterate."[66]

Chapultepec Park and Modern Mexican National Identity

Chapultepec Park can be considered a product of the effort to construct a modern Mexican identity in the late nineteenth century, and it embodied the unique political and cultural conflicts that characterized that effort. The progressive bourgeoisie that controlled Mexico during the Porfiriato wanted to restore international esteem for the country. They felt that Mexico's image had been damaged by the fiasco of the French intervention and its tragic ending. To demonstrate that Mexico had entered the modern era, they sought to construct a modern Mexican identity that was both uniquely Mexican and worldly, historically grounded and modern. Chapultepec Park was designed to balance between these poles. Like Mexican national culture in general in the aftermath of Maximilian, the park was shaped in part by a lingering memory of European charges of barbarism following Maximilian's death and a desire to erase an image of Mexico as an uncivilized wilderness.

In his memoirs, Limantour wrote about Chapultepec that "it started from an absolutely wild state, in which the incomparable cypresses died by the hundreds, and was later transformed into one of the most beautiful parks that ever existed."[67] This statement suggests that "wild" was not "beautiful," in Limantour's view. Mauricio Trillo has argued that the Porfiriato built its new modern city, displacing *campesinos*, indigenous communities, and haciendas to the west of the old capital, as an act of frontier expansion in a nineteenth-century sense, imposing civilization on the wilderness. The new city symbolically exorcised the wild and chaotic aspects of Mexican national history, creating a new image of prosperity and stability. It represented "a conquest not only over tradition, chaos and backwardness, but also over nature."[68] In the same vein, transforming Chapultepec Park into a showplace of fashionable European naturalism, interplanting the ancient trees with exotic species, replacing the ancient pools with artificial lakes, even stripping the Spanish moss from the *ahuehuetes*, symbolized the triumph of culture over nature, civilization over wilderness. The frequent comparisons of Chapultepec to the Paris parks of Napoleon III, in the press, guidebooks, and official rhetoric, reveal how important a role Chapultepec played in creating an appearance of modernity, particularly among Mexico's educated, wealthy, worldly

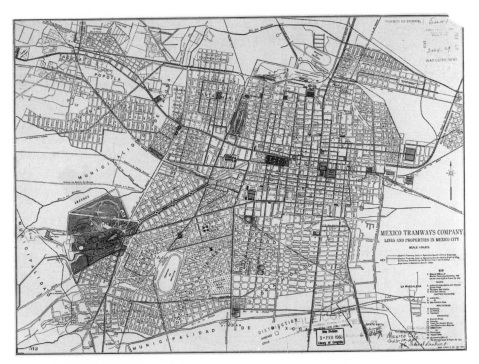

A map of Mexico City by the Mexico Tramways Company, 1910. Published by Rand McNally. (Courtesy of Library of Congress)

elite, including influential foreigners. As a jewel of the new city, insulated from the poverty and backwardness of the urban poor and the increasingly destitute rural sector of the country, the park offered a simulacrum of natural scenery, intended to show the leaders of the modern world that Mexico was no longer a wilderness, but a developed, modern nation.

Chapultepec also proved useful for mythologizing about Mexico's precolonial past. Aztec culture was increasingly accepted, over the course of the nineteenth century, as representing the authentic roots of Mexican culture and considered to be an appropriate foundation on which to build Mexico's modern identity. However, Aztec history was subject to various, and sometimes conflicting, interpretations. Mexico's ancient past had been reinvented many times since the early colonial period and used as a foundation on which to build power structures and justify programs of social control. Increasing interest in archaeology in the nineteenth century contributed tangible evidence of Aztec civilization and culture, but as archaeological evidence mounted, the desire for authenticity sometimes conflicted with the desire for a heroic past. Mexican history painting in the nineteenth century offers ample evidence of the contorted imagery that Mexican artists forced upon both history and the figure of the Indian in an attempt to fit reality to myth. Nineteenth-century intellectuals in Mexico tended to paint the Aztecs as victims of both their own barbaric culture and the barbaric acts of the invading conquistadors. The desperate condition of the contemporary indigenous population in Mexico also undermined efforts to construct national identity based on a heroic Indian past. Under the Porfiriato, the indigenous peoples' worsening condition served as all-too-obvious evidence of the lack of progress in the country, and, to some, also represented the barbarism of the Mexican government in its failure to better the situation of the indigenous population.[69]

Chapultepec offered a solution to this dilemma. Most archaeological evidence of the Aztec presence at Chapultepec had been lost by the second half of the nineteenth century. But the stately *ahuehuetes,* which were actually artifacts of the Aztec period and had been revered throughout history, evoked a suitable sense of dignity and nobility and had stood in silent witness to the events of ancient history. One great *ahuehuete* near Chapultepec had become a nationalistic symbol, as the tree under which, according to legend, Cortés had wept in frustration and humiliation after the Spanish suffered an initial defeat at the hands of the Aztecs on 30 June and 1 July 1520. Although the Spanish regrouped and defeated the Aztecs, the battle of La Noche Triste, as it was called, came to be celebrated as an important Mexican victory, along with the battle of Puebla. *El árbol de la noche triste* (tree of the sad night) became a sacred national monument. It stood for many years on the square of Popotla, in front of the parish church, and in 1872, when the tree was burned by arson, this act of vandalism caused great public outcry and made the headlines of all the major newspapers in Mexico City, which exclaimed: "¡Barbarie!" (barbarity) and "¡Profanación!" (desecration). Today it is the symbol of the metro stop of Popotla, where the remainder of the tree still stands.[70]

In general, the Mexican landscape proved to be a subject amenable to the construction of a modern national identity in the nineteenth century. In 1876, when Díaz became president, landscape painting had begun to replace history painting as the favored school of Mexican painting. Without painting historical events themselves, artists referenced history by painting the locations that had witnessed important historical events and were inextricably associated with them. As Stacie Widdifield has noted, in the paintings exhibited by Mexico in the International Philadelphia Exposition celebrating U.S. independence, "a key role [was] given to landscape painting. Landscapes could provide what history painting could not: the authentic and the national as well as the universal and the international."[71] José María Velasco's painting *El Valle de México,* exhibited in the Philadelphia exposition, won a commendation for merit from the U.S. judges, the only Mexican painting to take a prize at the exposition. Velasco, who had studied at the Academy of San Carlos (later renamed the National School of Fine Arts) from 1858 to 1868, had established his reputation as a landscape painter based in large part on a series of paintings of Chapultepec, and particularly the *ahuehuetes.* The ancient trees fascinated him, and he painted them again and again in the early years of his career. He also painted the castle at Chapultepec numerous times, as well as other images of the forest and pools.

In 1877, Velasco was appointed landscape professor at the Academy of San Carlos, succeeding his mentor and teacher, Eugenio Landesio. Landesio, an Italian schooled in the European tradition of landscape painting, had trained all of his pupils in the European landscape tradition, but found a particularly willing and talented disciple in Velasco. Landesio had been brought from Europe to oversee landscape painting at the Academy of San Carlos in 1855, during a period when foreigners were being sought as a means to add international stature to the Mexican academy. But the political winds changed direction frequently in Mexico, and in the course of his career, Landesio was fired twice from the academy for political reasons. He was first fired when he refused to sign a protest against the French intervention in 1863, and then reinstated when Maximilian arrived in 1864. Ten years later, in 1874, he was fired again when he refused to swear allegiance to the laws of the Reform; apparently he was still viewed as a supporter of Maximilian. Although he always professed neutrality in Mexican politics, Landesio could not avoid being caught up in the culture wars that paralleled political conflicts in Mexico during the nineteenth century. As a foreigner, he was inevitably associated with that segment of Mexican society that sought to introduce more Euro-

The Promenade, Santiago, Chile

The Plaza at Night, Santiago. Harper's New Monthly Magazine, November 1890.

Beautiful girls abound in Santiago, and it is a pleasure to sit and see them pass, and to attribute to them in fancy all the moral and intellectual qualities which they must have in reality. This discreet inspection, however, does not satisfy the youth of Santiago. Following the custom prevalent in Buenos Ayres, the young men simply stand in line along the promenade and stare at the pretty girls as they walk by, in a manner that seems to a stranger to be a little indelicate. Such, it appears, is the creole custom, which it is none of our business to criticize. I cannot, however, help remarking the useless existence led by the very numerous *jeunesse dorée* of the capital, composed of young men who for the most part have spent a year or two in Paris, and now endeavor to continue in Santiago the life of frivolous dissipation which was all they saw of France. These young men have no respect for women.

(From *Harper's New Monthly Magazine*, November 1890)

pean polish to Mexican culture, and his sympathies obviously lay in that direction.[72] Likewise, his favorite pupil, José Velasco, was not immune from cultural politics. Because of his close association with Landesio, Velasco was not promoted to succeed his master as landscape professor in 1874, but after Díaz won the presidency in 1876, Velasco's star rose, and he was eventually appointed director of landscape painting at the academy and became the preeminent Mexican painter under the Porfiriato. Velasco then enjoyed a long period of political favor and received many commissions from the Porfirian elite, including Díaz himself. Velasco's paintings, particularly the great vistas he produced of the Valley of Mexico, portrayed a landscape blessed by nature, with little evidence of poverty or politics. Velasco's great landscape paintings of the Valley of Mexico became emblematic of Mexico as a whole under the Porfiriato. Chapultepec appears in many of these paintings, the castle serenely perched on its hill, high above the sun-baked valley, tranquil and apparently untouched by the problems of the era.

Velasco was a consummate draftsman, and his technical skill won him much praise, but the content of his Mexican landscapes was perceived in some quarters as an endorsement of the policies of the Porfiriato. For example, Ignacio Manuel Altamirano, "well known *puro,* or radical, liberal political figure, who was also lawyer, journalist, poet, playwright, essayist, and art critic," championed the development of a "national" art transcending political rivalries within the country, but he had trouble with the rosy landscapes represented in Velasco's paintings.[73] In one sarcastic review of a Velasco exhibition in 1880, published in the journal *La Libertad,* Altamirano wrote of Velasco's landscapes:

> The valley of Mexico is not the only view our country can offer to the ambition of a painter and the glory of art. . . . There is something newer, more original, so to say, more characteristic of Mexican nature; there are the majestically alpine landscapes of our mountain ranges in cold areas, and there are the soft and paradisiac views of the magnificent and exuberant vegetation of the tropics; one should copy the sterile marshy plains and the yellowish hills of the valley of Mexico, the velvety and brilliant plains of the hot lands, the shadowy ravines, undulating sugar fields, hillocks adorned by flowers, soft rivers running through the woods of banana trees and falling like

foam in between crowded curtains of gigantic lianas; and then we should study, after we finish the Indian's wretched shack made of long shingles or the country house we all know, the cabins made of straw or tiles. . . . If Mr. Velasco persists in reproducing every corner of the valley in his canvases, there will be a day when, even while sleeping, he will be able to paint pepper trees, poplars, *tepozanes* [Empire Blues] and the herbaceous plants adorning the view; his landscapes will bore the public and probably even himself. One day he will furiously throw his brush away while saying: enough of this yellowish land and these *tepozanes*![74]

This review challenging Velasco's repetitive focus on the Valley of Mexico to the exclusion of the rest of the country is a thinly veiled reference to the policies of the Porfiriato. Altamirano mentions the rudeness of indigenous dwellings in oblique reference to the plight of indigenous people under the Porfiriato (Altamirano himself was of indigenous descent). Charges of monotony can be understood as charges of bourgeois monotony, as opposed to the richness and diversity of native Mexican culture. The references to *tepozanes* (*Buddleia*,

The Valley of Mexico from the King's Mill, José María Velasco, 1900. Oil painting. (Reproduction authorized by El Instituto Nacional de Bellas Artes y Literatura, 2009)

MELODRAMATIC LANDSCAPES

spp. "Empire Blue"; commonly called "butterfly bush") seem to hint at Velasco's conservative leanings, perhaps his sympathies for the Emperor Maximilian.

Velasco returned to Chapultepec at various times throughout his career. His paintings added to a collection of images of Chapultepec: it had been painted previously by a number of visiting European and American artists in the first half of the century.[75] But Velasco's representations of Chapultepec carried more weight than those of his predecessors. Velasco was the preeminent Mexican painter of the late nineteenth century, schooled in the European style at the premier Mexican academy, whose work was exhibited to considerable acclaim in international exhibits, including the Paris Exposition of 1889 and the Chicago Exposition of 1893. At the time when landscape was becoming the preferred subject for Mexican painting, his representations of Chapultepec were particularly significant. They helped glorify Chapultepec as an emblem of modern Mexican identity, a site identified with Mexican history, yet burnished with a European polish, the *ahuehuetes* representing ancient Mexico and the castle on the hill representing the progressive ideology of the Porfiriato, with Francophile overtones. Likewise, the park itself embodied these meanings, bridging the difficult gaps between authentic Mexico and European influences, ancient history and modern aspirations.

Chapultepec also served a more mundane purpose, helping to sell real estate in the new western districts of Mexico City. The availability of such a large park with the requisite amenities—naturalistic scenery, riding trails, tennis club, automobile club, etc.—was a selling point for investors in the new districts. And the progressive elite profited directly from the development of this new sector of Mexico City, including Limantour himself, who owned land along Bucareli and saw the value of those lands increase as he awarded contracts for the provision of urban services, including a sophisticated urban park.[76] There was an attempt, at the end of the Porfiriato, to provide a comparable park on the east side of the city, in a poor neighborhood. Miguel Ángel de Quevedo, director of public works for Mexico City, proposed a public park in the barrio of Calzada de la Viga, but when no suitable site could be found there, an alternative site of 96 hectares was selected in Balbuena, a poor barrio east of the city center. The site was designated a workers' park, with the stated hope that it would help make the capital "like the Paris of America."[77] Quevedo estimated the total cost of the Balbuena park at 100,000 pesos. This park never attained anything like the success or stature of Chapultepec, but Limantour may have engaged in land speculation involving this park, for he was subject to a congressional investigation in 1912, for having allegedly profited from its construction.[78]

By the time this investigation took place, the Díaz government had collapsed. Rebellion spread throughout the countryside soon after the Centenario, and Díaz resigned in May 1911, unable to contain the spreading insurgency, which was led by Francisco Madero and supported by the now legendary guerilla leaders Pascual Orozco, Pancho Villa, and Emiliano Zapata, among others. The rebellion was like a spontaneous combustion, as millions of oppressed Mexican peasants and poor workers joined forces and overwhelmed the *rurales* and the national army. The rebels were determined to overthrow the Díaz regime at any cost, convinced that any change would be for the better. Unfortunately, they were not united by a workable plan for governing the country, and Mexico entered another period of political instability, as Díaz sailed away to political exile in Europe.

Chapultepec Park is inextricably tied up in the legacy of the Díaz era. It was a favorite project of the Porfiriato's internationally focused, progressive elite whose tastes, aspirations, and attitudes were those of an international bourgeoisie. This elite "saw their country zooming into modernization; hence they rushed to adopt the styles, attitudes, and amusements of other modernized western nations."[79] But this was Mexico, not Paris or New York. Díaz may have enforced political stability for more than thirty-five years, but his regime exacerbated the culture wars that also characterized nineteenth-century Mexican society. The progressive, Eurocentric elite of the Porfiriato went to war with the traditional, more provincial segments of Mexican society. Chapultepec was one of the fronts in this war. In many ways, it was emblematic of the ideology of the regime of Porfirio Díaz—Eurocentrism, modernism, positivism—yet, it was also representative of the problems of the regime: elitism, conspicuous consumption, a focus on appearances rather than substantive social change. Only later in the twentieth century would Chapultepec become a truly democratic space where all segments of Mexican society would freely mingle.

Central Park &
the Melodramatic
Imagination

ON 27 JUNE 1858, A NOTICE IN THE *New
York Herald* announced the opening of a new pleasure garden in
Manhattan: "the most beautiful, the most attractive, and in all prob-
ability the last great garden that individual enterprise will be enacted
to devote to the health, pleasure and recreation of the citizens of
New York." The advertisement went on to describe the new Palace
Garden:

> Here may be enjoyed the luxury of pure fresh air, laden with the
> perfume of many flowers; here may be seen those brilliantly illumi-
> nated archways with transparent scenic pedestals . . . fountains . . .
> imparting a refreshing coolness to the air, while in the basins beauti-
> ful gold and silver fish may be seen sporting in their native element.
> . . . Upon entering this splendidly decorated garden, the magnificent
> spectacle that bursts upon the beholder's sight appears like a scene
> of enchantment, conjured up, as it were, by the power of another
> Aladdin. (*New York Herald*)

At midcentury, commercial pleasure gardens like the Palace Garden
were still popular among New Yorkers. These privately owned estab-

lishments offered pleasant outdoor settings in which to socialize and stroll along flowery paths, perhaps enjoy light refreshment, view an exhibit, or watch a performance. As the advertisement suggests, however, the Palace Garden represents a late flowering of this genre of urban open space. It opened in the same year that a competition was held to determine the design of the city's new Central Park, which would soon afford a more fashionable setting for outdoor leisure in New York.

New York's Commercial Pleasure Gardens

New York's commercial pleasure gardens had once represented a sophisticated new fashion imported from Europe. They were patterned after various commercial gardens throughout Europe, but the most widely emulated was Vauxhall Gardens in London. This famous pleasure garden was a lively place where Londoners from various walks of life rubbed shoulders at the turn of the nineteenth century. In his popular novel *Vanity Fair*, set early in the nineteenth century, William Thackeray captured Vauxhall Gardens at the height of its

Illustration from the cover of sheet music for "The Palace Garden Polka," 1858. (Music Division, The New York Public Library for the Performing Arts, Astor, Lenox and Tilden Foundations)

A General Prospect of Vaux Hall Gardens, after 1751. Lithograph by John S. Muller, ca. 1715–92, after Samuel Wale, 1721–86. (Yale Center for British Art, Paul Mellon Collection)

popularity. He described its "lamps, which were always lighted; the fiddlers in cocked hats, who played ravishing melodies under the gilded cockle-shell in the midst of the gardens; the singers, both of comic and sentimental ballads, who charmed the ears there; the country dances, formed by bouncing cockneys and cockneyesses, and executed amidst jumping, thumping and laughter; the signal which announced that Madame Saqui was about to mount skyward on the slack-rope ascending to the stars; the hermit that always sat in the illuminated hermitage; the dark walks, so favourable to the interviews of young lovers; the pots of stout handed about by the people in the shabby old liveries; and the twinkling boxes in which the happy feasters made-believe to eat slices of almost invisible ham."[1]

As Thackeray's description makes clear, while a pleasant stroll was a large part of the appeal of Vauxhall Gardens, visitors also expected other forms of entertainment. Not only did these commercial establishments vie for a fashionable clientele by offering increasingly extravagant and louche forms of amusement, but their reputation as a setting for private trysts also constituted a large part of their allure. The

The Flight: Incident on a Party to Vauxhall, Isaac
Cruikshank, 1794. Engraving. (Yale Center for
British Art, Paul Mellon Collection)

earliest pleasure gardens were often attached to country taverns. Some
openly operated as country brothels. Samuel Pepys, a frequent visitor
to London's Vauxhall Gardens (then known as Spring Garden),
emphasized the lure of the ladies. Sir Roger de Coverly, departing the
garden after a visit in 1712, reportedly remarked to "the Mistress of the
House, who sat at the Bar, That he should be a better Customer to her
Garden, if there were more Nightingales, and fewer Strumpets."[2] In
Vanity Fair, the lively foreground barely distracted Thackeray's read-
ers from the erotic background of dark and shady garden paths where
the novel's heroine, Becky Sharp, hoped to snare a vulgar but wealthy
husband, thus improving her social and economic status.

As the nineteenth century progressed, however, London's pleasure gardens became increasingly associated with low life and de-
bauchery, and gradually lost their fashionable clientele. Early in the
century, Vauxhall's reputation had been enhanced by the frequent

attendance of the prince of Wales, whose dissolute life style was legendary. Upon becoming King George IV, he approved the renaming of the garden as the "Royal Gardens, Vauxhall." However, as industrial London grew, the gardens' formerly rural surroundings vanished and their illusions, like worn stage sets, became less and less compelling. Visitors remarked that the grounds appeared tawdry by daylight. Incidents of drunkenness and violence were reported. Proprietors tried to counter public fears by including assurances of safety and gentility in their advertisements; however, such tactics failed to halt the steady decline of pleasure gardens over the course of the nineteenth century. Vauxhall Gardens, London, closed for good in 1858.[3]

Commercial pleasure gardens began to appear in New York early in the eighteenth century. The first examples were small, privately owned gardens, usually an acre or two in size, used for outdoor dining associated with a tavern or inn. Some had originally been private country houses and were turned into commercial venues by enterprising new owners. With shaded walks, lawns, and arbors, they offered a relaxed, informal setting for light meals, private meetings, or special events. They were open for business in the summer only. Admission was usually free; proprietors made their profits from selling drinks and light refreshments or catered meals for larger groups. Sometimes traveling performers stayed at a pleasure garden for a week or two, setting up a tent and charging admission for performances.

In the late eighteenth and early nineteenth century, as their numbers increased, commercial pleasure gardens in New York began to offer an increasing variety of entertainment. Competition for clientele spurred proprietors to greater flights of fancy in a search for novelty and a competitive edge. Transparent paintings were a popular form of illusion in commercial pleasure gardens. Erected at the terminus of walkways, incorporated into the pedestals of statuary or into walls of pavilions or theaters, these trompe l'oeil scenes appeared extremely realistic, at least at first glance, often blending ingeniously into the garden scenery. The technique involved painting on several layers of fabric or glass and shining a light through the layers, which created a three-dimensional effect and an appearance of inner illumination, especially effective at night.[4] Paintings were changed frequently in an effort to keep the garden decor fresh and provide new interest. These paintings transformed pleasure gardens into mysterious and fanciful places. Like the scenery in a theater, they made the garden into an exotic and illusory setting.

During the daylight hours, pleasure gardens hosted concerts, balloon ascensions, and circus acts, from tightrope walking to animal shows. In the evening, artificial illumination transformed the gardens into fantasy settings for balls, concerts, or plays. Fireworks exhibitions drew large crowds to pleasure gardens, especially for annual Fourth of July spectacles when proprietors competed with each other to produce special shows on patriotic themes. Technicians mounted fireworks on scaffolding, telling elaborate stories with sequential images. Moving dioramas were also a popular attraction, such as the one on view at Vauxhall on the Fourth of July 1806. Nearly a thousand feet long, it depicted a procession held in New York in 1788 in honor of the U.S. Constitution.[5] Sometimes painted scenery, dioramas, fireworks, and other illusions were combined to produce multimedia effects. A show mounted in August of the opening season (1805) at Vauxhall Garden, on the Bowery, combined fireworks, panoramas, and mechanical models in a depiction of a naval skirmish in the Bay of Tripoli. The following description from the *New York Daily Advertiser* gives a scene-by-scene account of the elaborate spectacle:

The Intrepid, bomb ketch, accompanied by the Syren Schooner, are seen entering the port of Tripoli—The Syren takes her allotted station near the entrance. The Intrepid advances to the frigate, on which flies the Tripolitan Flag. They board; the Tripolitan flag is struck, and the frigate is discovered on fire. The Batteries commence a brisk fire upon the ketch, who returns the fire, and displaying the American flag, departs successful amidst the fire of the enemy. The Frigate still burning, the masts and rigging give way as she is consumed; the cannon on board are discharged by the heat. Grand Explosion of the Magazine; Spars, rigging, etc. discharging in the air. The hull drifts from her burnt cables and strikes upon a rock at the foot of the Bashaw's Castle. A number of bomb ketches advance in order to attack, and commence the bombardment; the enemy open their fire from the castle and battery. Shells are thrown into the city from the ketches, several of which fall on the houses and set them on fire; the spires and part of the buildings are consumed; the Americans depart with the tide, having accomplished their design, in setting fire to the city; the city still burning, the Timbers, etc. appear in the flames, and fall to pieces as they are consumed.[6]

MELODRAMATIC LANDSCAPES

As the century progressed, garden proprietors focused increasingly on events and performances, building bigger and more elaborate theater buildings and other structures on the premises to house shows and exhibits. Some pleasure gardens evolved into full-fledged performance venues. The word "garden," retained in the names of many New York theaters, such as Madison Square Garden, Atlantic Garden, and Niblos Garden, recalls this era.

Most commercial pleasure gardens stayed open for only a year or two. In cases where they persisted in the same location for several decades, ownership often changed regularly, and this turnover was reflected in frequent name changes. There were at least five Vauxhall Gardens in different locations in New York City. One of these, located on the Bowery, persisted longer than most, weathering major social changes in its neighborhood over a forty-year period. It serves well to illustrate the history of commercial pleasure gardens in New York. Early in the nineteenth century, Vauxhall Garden catered to a fashionable clientele. Located well out of town, it attracted a class of visitors who could afford to come by carriage. A newspaper editorial in 1807 described it as an "elegant place of public amusement . . . [which] may be justly said to rival in point of elegance and beauty any place of the same kind in the European world. . . . In the United States it is without parallel, and in this City there is no place of public resort that offers so great attraction to the gay, the fashionable, and the pleasure-taking world."[7] In 1817, President James Monroe visited on the Fourth of July and the Marquis de Lafayette spent an evening there in 1824.[8] New York guidebooks often recommended Vauxhall Garden as a pleasant destination for an afternoon or evening; one described it as a place "to which the inhabitants resort during the summer evenings, and regale themselves with food, wine, liquors and confectioneries."[9] But as the city expanded, residences gradually surrounded the garden and the character of the neighborhood changed. The Bowery changed as well, and by "ante-bellum days lay with its southern end amid the slums, its northern amid the aristocracy."[10] In 1828, the Vauxhall Garden property was split in two parts by the extension of Lafayette Place. The part lying along the Bowery continued as Vauxhall Garden, but row houses were built on the other parcel, reducing the garden's size by half. Neighbors began to complain of it as a nuisance, particularly objecting to the noise and danger posed by fireworks. By the time it

Miss Mary Taylor and Mr. F. S. Chanfrau. In *A Glance at New York*, by Benjamin Baker, ca. 1848. (Courtesy of Library of Congress)

closed in 1856, the *New York Herald* reported that it had become "the resort of a different class from that which built it up. The fashionables had deserted it and the democracy of society took it altogether to themselves."[11]

In the 1840s and 1850s, guidebook writers and city reporters had begun to draw contrasts between fashionable Broadway and the working-class Bowery, symbolically locating different social classes on the New York map. Fiction writers and dramatists further emphasized this contrast, developing stereotypical characters to represent the two social sets: Broadway dandies versus "Bowery b'hoys." Vauxhall Garden figured prominently in the Bowery imagery, as a favorite working-class pleasure spot. As one guidebook put it, "Here we are at Vauxhall Garden; a sort of ice-creamery, and general rendezvous for the Bowery fashionables, who assemble, mostly at night—not having time during the day like the Broadway dandies."[12] The working-class "Bowery b'hoys" entered popular culture and were immortalized as characters in a popular melodrama by Benjamin Baker, *A Glance at New York*, staged in 1848. In Baker's play, the "b'hoys" and "g'hals" (slang terms derived from the Irish pronunciation of "boy" and "gal") were drawn as stereotypes to represent working-class culture in New York. Significantly, Baker set the final scene of his play in Vauxhall Garden on the Bowery. In the play, the main character, Mose, is the stereotypical Bowery b'hoy, a cocky, boisterous, tough-talking but kindhearted volunteer fireman. In the scene set at Vauxhall Garden, Mose enters the garden with his girlfriend, Lize, looks around at the dining tables set under the trees and arches of colored lamps, and remarks in typical Bowery b'hoy slang: "Say, Lizey, ain't this high?" and Lize responds, "Well, it ain't nothing else."[13] In this bit of dialogue, capturing Mose's reaction to the garden's attempted ostentation, Baker highlights the unpretentiousness of the Bowery b'hoy, whose evident pleasure in the garden's faded decor is meant to appear straightforward and naïve.

In the years leading up to and during the Civil War, writers and newspaper reporters frequently used the Bowery b'hoys and g'hals, as personified by Mose and Lize, to characterize a certain slice of New York society, a native working class whose ranks included "the butcher-boy, the mechanic with his boisterous family—the b'hoy in red flannel shirt-sleeves and cone-shaped trousers—the shop-woman, the sewing and folding and press-room girl, the straw-braider, the type-rubber, the map-colorer, the paper-box and flower maker, the g'hal, in short in all her various aspects and phases."[14] Portrayed in the popular media as honest, independent, direct in speech and manners, simple in taste, this stereotype was contrasted to stereotypes of the unfortunate or degenerate poor at one end of the social spectrum and a pretentious, morally hypocritical upper class at the other end.[15]

In the presidential campaign of 1848, the Whigs held parties at Vauxhall and courted the b'hoys for Zachary Taylor.[16] A novel by Cornelius Mathews, *The Career of Puffer Hopkins*, written in 1842, prefigures that political campaign with the story of a fictional ball at Vauxhall Garden, attended by the would-be working-class politician Puffer Hopkins. The ball is hosted by a political ring called the Round-Rimmers. Mathews's description of Vauxhall Garden satirizes its illusions of grandeur: "Puffer, entering, was overwhelmed with the gorgeousness and splendor of the spectacle that broke upon him. In the first place, the Garden, to which he was a stranger, was filled with trees—which was a novelty in a New York public garden—some short and bushy, others tall and trim, but actual trees; then there were the thousand eyes or better lurking and glaring out in every direction, in the shape of blue and yellow and red and white lamps, fixed among the trees and against the stalls; then there was a fountain, and then, through two rows of poplars, commanding a noble prospective of two white chimney-tops in the rear, there stretched a . . . ballroom floor."[17] By this time, the upper classes had deserted Vauxhall Garden, according to one contemporary observer finding it "vulgar . . . to be seen walking in the same grounds with mechanics, house servants, and laboring people."[18] When Lydia Maria Child visited Vauxhall Garden in 1844, she noted that, "being in the Bowery, it is out of the walk of the fashionables, who probably ignore its existence, as they do most places for the entertainment of the people at large."[19]

Although various entertainments contributed to the allure of commercial pleasure gardens, simply promenading in fresh air along shady walks remained one of the major pleasures that these places offered to visitors. Prior to the opening of Central Park, a popular promenade favored by New Yorkers was a commercial pleasure garden in Hoboken called Elysian Fields, which afforded a much-admired view of the city across the water. Colonel John Stevens owned Elysian Fields and operated a ferry service to Hoboken from the Battery. The sylvan landscape along the Hudson was the main attraction for the hordes of visitors who crowded onto those ferries on pleasant days. But Elysian Fields also had various special attractions. An amusement area on the green, near the '76 House Tavern at the Hoboken ferry terminal, offered a variety of diversions, including a Ferris wheel, merry-go-round, ten-pin alley, wax figures, a camera obscura, a flying machine or "whirligig," and a narrow-gauge track with human-powered cars. There was a steam train on a two-hundred-foot loop.[20] Another popular attraction was Sibyl's Cave, a cavern excavated at a point in the cliff along the promenade, where a spring flowed from the rock. A pavilion near Sibyl's Cave sold refreshments, including liquor for those desiring stronger drink than spring water.

Pleasure garden proprietors usually drew a substantial proportion

A view of Elysian Fields, Hoboken. Engraving by A. Dick. (Emmet Collection, Miriam and Ira D. Wallach Division of Art, Prints and Photographs, The New York Public Library, Astor, Lenox and Tilden Foundations)

of their profit from selling refreshments, especially liquor. Frances Trollope, visiting Elysian Fields during a brief stop in New York in 1830, remarked that, "at Hoboken, as every where else, there are *reposoires*, which, as you pass them, blast the sense for a moment, by reeking forth the fumes of whiskey and tobacco." However, she noted that, at Elysian Fields, "the proprietor of the grounds . . . has contrived with great taste to render these abominations not unpleasing to the eye; there is one in particular, which has quite the air of a Grecian Temple, and did they drink wine instead of whiskey . . . might be inscribed to Bacchus."[21] George Foster, a city reporter for the *New York Tribune* and a major commentator on the New York social scene, also noted that liquor was an important attraction at pleasure gardens. In one sketch, he described the scene at Sibyl's Cave at Elysian Fields: "The little refreshment shop under the trees looks like an ice-cream plaster stuck against the rocks. Nobody wants 'refreshments,' my dear girl, while the pure cool water of the Sibyl's fountain can be had for nothing. What! Yes they do. . . . A little man, with thin bandy legs, whose Bouncing wife and children are a practical illustration of the one-sided effects of matrimony, has bought 'something to take' for the

whole family. Pop goes the weasel! What is it? Sarsaparilla—pooh!"[22]
Like Frances Trollope, Foster emphasized the social aspect of pleasure
gardens over the scenery. The landscape was a setting for social life
and social gatherings, eating, drinking and carousing.

By midcentury, commercial pleasure gardens, in general, were
associated with working-class leisure. Observers tended to emphasize
the "democratic mix" of the crowds, a euphemism for the preponder-
ance of working-class revelers, and to disparage the vulgar tone of the
festivities. Elysian Fields was a favorite destination for working-class
families on a Sunday. Lydia Maria Child, who also visited Hoboken
in 1844, noted that "the boats are crowded all day. The average number that go over every pleasant Sunday, in summer, is over ten thousand. . . . If the influence of groves and streams were all they sought,
it would be well; but unfortunately, drink and cigars abound at Hoboken, and sounds are heard there not at all resembling the worship of
the heart in the stillness of nature." Similarly, George Foster described
the scene at Elysian Fields, Hoboken: "What a motley crowd! Old
and young, men, women and children, those ever-recurring elements
of life and movement. Well-dressed and badly-dressed, and scarcely
dressed at all—Germans, French, Italians, Americans, with here and
there a mincing Londoner, with his cockney gait and trim whiskers.
This walk in Hoboken is one of the most absolutely democratic places
in the world—the boulevards of social equality, where every rank,
state, and condition, existing in our country—except, of course, the
tip-top exclusives—meet, mingle, push and elbow their way along
with sparse courtesy or civility."[23] Large groups sometimes leased
pleasure gardens for social events, picnics, and ethnic festivals. In
May 1851, for example, more than ten thousand Germans gathered at
Elysian Fields to commemorate the holiday of Pentecost. The initially
peaceful picnic turned into a riot. The *Tribune* reported that prior
to the riot, "beer flowed in torrents from the barrels on tap, down
hundreds of thirsty throats." The article gave imprecise and contradictory accounts of the disturbance, but identified the instigators as a
"gang of rowdies" calling themselves the Short Boys, who included
among their members "some German[s], some Irish and some American[s]." As many as twelve persons were reported killed and hundreds wounded, including a justice of the peace, who tried to stop the
violence, and the local sheriff, who called in the local militia in an

New York City—The First Annual Festival of the North German Societies—The Grand Procession Leaving the Germania Assembly, Monday, August 30th, 1875. Illustration by Joseph M. Gleeson. (Picture Collection, The Branch Libraries, The New York Public Library, Astor, Lenox and Tilden Foundations)

attempt to restore order. One tavern in Elysian Fields was completely destroyed during the three-hour battle, and one newspaper reported that "all this time the women and children were screaming with terror and running in all directions from the showers of stones that were flying."[24]

Vivid portrayal in the press of such events fixed pleasure gardens, as a genre, on the social map of the city and in the public imagination. They were identified as working-class venues and linked in public perception not only with boisterous revelry, cheap entertainment, and liquor consumption, but also with unruly and potentially dangerous crowds. When the Palace Garden opened in 1858, its owners tried to counter this perception of commercial pleasure gardens. Advertisements for the new Palace Garden predicted that the new garden would "become the resort of the refined, the fashionable and the intellectual." The proprietors assured New Yorkers that decorum would be maintained: "It will be the aim of the parties who have leased these extensive premises to make them the most desirable resort of any in the city during the summer months, and to effect this objective they have determined to enforce such rules as will assure the strictest order and decorum. Looking to the most respectable portion of the community for encouragement, the proprietors know they must so conduct the management as to give entire satisfaction in every particular, and this they feel confident they are perfectly prepared to do."[25] The proprietors employed a large staff, including guards, to enforce decorum in the Palace Garden. No liquor was sold or consumed on the premises.

The Palace Garden stayed open for only four years. Originally designed to recall the old Vauxhall Garden on the Bowery, it went through several renovations during its brief existence, as its proprietors searched for a more successful formula. A Civil War regiment was billeted there in the summer of 1861. The garden changed ownership and was renamed Nixon's Cremorne Garden in 1962, but it closed for good in December of that year. Noting that the "relentless march of improvements" had eliminated many old pleasure gardens in the city, the proprietors of the new Palace Garden had sought to revive a fading tradition. But they were swimming against the tide. Commercial pleasure gardens would soon vanish from New York.

The Greensward Plan for Central Park

As commercial pleasure gardens like the Palace Garden were disappearing in New York, a new type of pleasure garden appeared. With its acres of meadows and woodlands, Central Park dwarfed older commercial pleasure gardens, both literally and figuratively, ushering in a new era for urban green space in the United States. Like commercial pleasure gardens, Central Park was conceived as an outdoor setting for leisure activities of various kinds and intended for people spanning the social spectrum, but it differed from commercial pleasure gardens in crucial ways that reflected the changing social order in New York.

We now take Central Park so much for granted that it is easy to forget that it was a dramatic gesture, in both conception and realization. The idea of a large park in New York had been debated for years, and it is difficult to pinpoint its exact origin, but the original idea is often credited to William Cullen Bryant, who, as editor of the *New York Post*, wrote an editorial in 1844 calling for a new park in the city. Andrew Jackson Downing also played an important role, writing a series of letters from London in 1849 and 1850 calling for a large park in New York City.[26] Subsequently others joined the debate, and the concept was widely discussed in the public media, and no doubt in many private conversations for many years. Regardless of who first proposed the idea, it is clear that the earliest proponents of the park were well-educated, well-traveled, and familiar with public urban parks in Europe.

By the time the City of New York acquired a site for Central Park, there were many precedents in Europe for this kind of public garden. The royal parks of London had been open to the public for some time. Regent's Park, also in London, had been developed early in the century as part of an exclusive real-estate venture, and was officially designated a public park in 1838. Other new public parks opened in the 1840s in England, in conjunction with real-estate developments. One of these, Birkenhead Park near Liverpool, was very successful in replicating the model of Regent's Park for a middle-class market. Victoria Park opened in London's working-class East End in 1846.[27] As the idea of a new park was debated in New York, the Bois de Boulogne in Paris was receiving considerable international attention (it was remodeled between 1852 and 1856), and public parks were being developed in Germany.

But Central Park was the first large urban park of this kind in the United States, and when the competition for its design was announced in October 1857, it signified the beginning of a new era, not just for New York, but for other cities around the country. Thirty-three proposals were submitted in the competition to design the new park. Most of them included features familiar to New Yorkers from commercial pleasure gardens—formal avenues and promenades, elaborate flower beds, conservatories, parade grounds, statuary, fountains, aviaries, and other embellishments. However, the more embellished proposals were rejected by the park commissioners in favor of a much simpler and more naturalistic design, submitted by Frederick Law Olmsted and Calvert Vaux.[28] Their winning scheme, evocatively called the Greensward Plan, was a simple, cohesive representation of

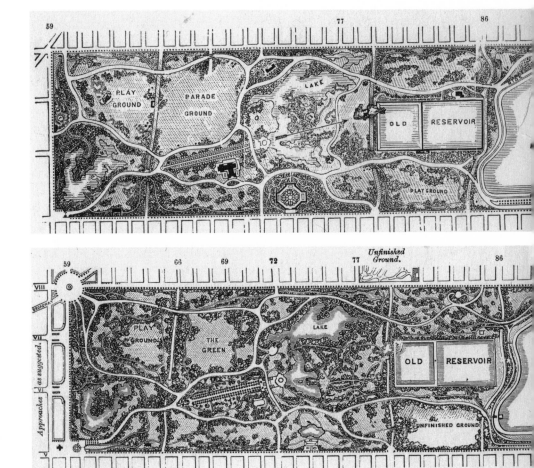

First study and design for Central Park, Calvert Vaux and Frederick Law
Olmsted. Greensward Plan. (Collection of The New-York Historical Society,
negative no. 46063)

rural countryside, presented as a series of prospects, rendered in wa-
tercolorlike landscape paintings: stately trees framing rolling meadows, large bodies of water, wooded islands, a few carefully sited architectural accents.

The competition for the design of Central Park, and the winning
entry itself, sparked considerable debate about landscape aesthetics
among New Yorkers. There were highly vocal proponents of the more
elaborate and embellished style of landscape design. Many were dismayed by the naturalism of the winning design. Some thought the
contrast between the urban fabric of New York and the Greensward

MELODRAMATIC LANDSCAPES

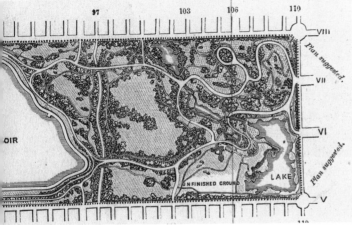

Plan was "grotesque," and argued that Olmsted and Vaux's plan ignored the glory and accomplishment of American culture. Editorials in working-class periodicals such as the *Irish American* and the *Zeitung und Herold* argued that commercial pleasure gardens were an excellent model for Central Park.[29] For these critics, eclecticism and variety were positive attributes. In their view, the pleasure-garden landscape was varied, exciting, and cosmopolitan, offering a medley of statues and busts, architectural monuments, trompe l'oeil panoramas, and changing entertainments. They touted pleasure gardens as popular social settings, places to see and to be seen, and as appropriate venues for cultural events, festivals, and social gatherings. Proponents of pleasure gardens argued that their proven popularity made them an excellent model for Central Park.

Among the park commissioners themselves there was disagreement. Dissenting from the Republican majority, the two Democrats on the park board objected that the Greensward Plan failed to represent the urbane and civilized life of New York and wondered how the rustic style could be modified to create more public access and also to reflect the "highest forms of artificial or civilized life, erected by the wealth and designed by the genius of man." These members were outvoted, although the board made a concession to their protest and directed Olmsted and Vaux to modify the Greensward Plan to create more circulation in the park. As it turned out, these modifications actually made the park even more rustic and picturesque than in the original design.[30] In contrast to the more animated landscape of commercial pleasure gardens, the landscape of Central Park, sparsely populated in the Greensward Plan renderings, was designed to offer an escape from urban crowds and boisterous revelry. Creating a new image for American public space, the designers of Central Park replaced the lively, unpredictable, crowd-filled scenery of commercial pleasure gardens with a monumental, picturesque rendering of Nature.[31] The most rustic part of the park, the Ramble, was the focal point of the design, "the picture that people would come to see."[32]

It is important to recognize, however, that Olmsted and Vaux were not merely designing a picture, or a stage set; they were designing an environment, a place to be experienced with all of the senses. They envisioned the park as a very large expanse of rural countryside where citizens of New York could escape the hustle-bustle and mind-numbing routines of urban life. The landscape of the new park was not intended merely as scenery; it was meant to envelop and surround the visitor and thereby to induce a different state of mind, at least for a few hours. They conceived the Greensward Plan as an antidote to modern urban life. Its landscape was meant to act upon the visitor, and the visitor was expected to engage with it. This was quite a departure from commercial pleasure gardens, where the scenery was little more than an enticement, a decor changed regularly for novelty's sake. The landscape of commercial pleasure gardens was mainly a backdrop for performances, exhibits, and the various social dramas that played out in the foreground, but these dramas were usually quite independent of the scenery in the garden.

By contrast, the Greensward Plan offered New Yorkers a place to interact with nature. Proponents of Central Park in New York had long emphasized nature as the appropriate theme for the park. William Cullen Bryant had envisioned the park as "a piece of conserved nature." Andrew Jackson Downing had called for "space enough to have broad reaches of park and pleasure grounds, with a real feeling of the breadth and beauty of green fields, the perfume and freshness of nature."[33] When the competition was held for the park's design, many New Yorkers expressed their preferences for a more naturalistic landscape, in letters published in the major newspapers, and these letters sometimes conjured images of commercial pleasure gardens as a model to be avoided. One correspondent to the *Tribune* pleaded with New Yorkers not to be "led astray by the claptrap and gewgaw . . . the harrowing spectacle of Nature made mincemeat of—her fair proportions indiscriminately chopped up and served to suit only a vitiated taste." This writer worried that some would-be designers of Central Park "could not resist a Chinese pagoda—an Indian wigwam; they would surfeit us with nymphs and mermaids and dancing fauns—would seek to tickle the fancy at every step by curious grottoes and labyrinths, artificial ponds, innumerable cascades . . . cunning devices studiously disposed to conceal under their meretricious array the chaste beauty of Nature."[34]

The winning Greensward Plan deliberately eschewed the model of commercial pleasure gardens, offering instead a simple design of "bold and sweeping" lines, with vistas showing "great breadth in almost every aspect in which they may be contemplated . . . as this character is the highest ideal that can be aimed at for a park under any circumstances."[35] Well aware of the finer distinctions of landscape aesthetics and versed in the nuances of a discourse on this subject that had been flourishing in Europe, and among cognoscenti in the United States, Olmsted and Vaux created natural scenery with a skilled brush in Central Park. Their winning design appealed to connoisseurs conversant in the fine distinctions between different types of landscape scenery—the beautiful, the sublime, the pastoral, the picturesque. Each of these terms conjured a particular set of meanings and associations to literature and the visual arts, to particular moments

Camels in Central Park

A great centre of attraction yesterday was on the top lawn west of the pavilion, where, at a distance respectfully remote from the music, a docile camel moved around to be admired, and bore upon his back that which at a distance was too undefined in shape to appear other than an exaggeration of the hump, but which on close approach proved to be a man. He drove the animal, or rather directed its course by a coaxing application of a small tree, which he brandished luxuriously in his right hand. He was dressed—about five-sixths of him—in red pantaloons, the other sixth being blue jacket and snowy turban. . . . On inquiry as to what he was, we were told he was an Arab, whereupon having read of travels in Arabia and the manners and customs of the natives, we confronted him, drew our two feet together, bent our body gracefully forward, and stretching our hands out horizontally, with their backs toward the sky, brought them together with superb curves, at the top of the forehead, and with downcast eyes, repeated in purest Arabic the usual salutation, "Salaam malek," expecting of course that he would return it in the customary manner with "Lekma Osalaam," when, to our astonishment, he smote the camel with the heavy wand he bore and said, with one eye on the beast

and the other on us: "Go on out, out o' dhat, will yez?" He was Irish, ignorant Irish; he didn't know a word of Arabic!

(FROM THE NEW YORK TIMES, 28 OCTOBER 1866)

Mowing with the Camel in the New York Central Park. Harper's Weekly, 13 November 1869. (From the author's collection)

in European history or particular precedents on the continent. To those who had seen parks like this in Europe, the Greensward Plan seemed a very sophisticated design.[36]

As the foregoing debate in the editorial pages and letters to the editor suggests, class-based preferences played a role in the reactions to the design of Central Park. They also played a role in the selection of the winning design. The park commissioners, who selected the Greensward Plan, were predisposed by their social status and background to appreciate this design. Appointed by a Republican-dominated state legislature to oversee the development of a large civic park in New York City, the majority were members of a cultural elite that included bankers, wealthy businessmen, and professionals. Olmsted and Vaux also counted themselves a part of this social group, which Olmsted himself referred to as a self-styled "natural aristocracy," including men of "education, good judgment and civic influence," a "natural" class of leaders who believed they had the vision and authority to shape a new era for the city. Some members were descendants of established, wealthy families; others were self-made men. But they distinguished themselves from the "vulgar, presuming and peculiarly snobbish" *nouveaux riches* who lusted after the trappings of European aristocracy and demonstrated social status through conspicuous displays of wealth.[37] The Greensward Plan appealed particularly to these gentlemen because, although it was clearly modeled after parks in Europe and represented the latest style and most sophisticated taste in landscape design, it was not, in their opinion, conspicuous or flashy.

The picturesque qualities of the park, perhaps best exemplified by the Ramble but also apparent in many other aspects, appealed particularly to those with a highly refined and cultivated sensibility at mid-century. An appreciation for picturesque landscape scenery spread among landscape connoisseurs in the United States throughout the nineteenth century, and aficionados particularly valued certain qualities, such as wildness, roughness, and rusticity. Important arbiters of landscape taste in North America, such as William Cullen Bryant and Andrew Jackson Downing, helped cultivate and broaden the picturesque sensibility in the United States, modifying the aesthetic to American needs. It proved an adaptable framework that could encompass the vastness of the wilderness as well as the rough patterns and textures in the bark of a tree trunk. Later in the century, the picturesque sensibility even encompassed the more dramatic signs of human progress, and picturesque landscapes became a marketable commodity consumed in America not only in the form of designed landscapes, but also in books of picturesque views taken around the nation, such as *Picturesque America*, edited by William Cullen Bryant (1872–74). But when the Greensward Plan won the Central Park competition, the picturesque was still a rarefied taste shared by those with the appropriate education and means. Thorstein Veblen observed that only by the end of the century did a taste for picturesque effects trickle down to the middle class, manifest "in such contrivances as rustic fences, bridges, bowers, pavilions, and the like decorative features . . . or by a circuitous drive laid across level ground."[38]

Scholars of the picturesque aesthetic in England have pointed out that it always represented class-based relations to the land, and that, while it initially appealed to an elite sensibility, it was quickly adopted by middle-class consumers. As Elizabeth Helsinger has argued, renderings of the picturesque landscape in England offered a range of possible relations to the landscapes depicted, "from rural laborers through the gradations of a provincial middle class to rural gentry and aristocracy, not to mention the professional travelers and tourists occasionally glimpsed along the way." Yet, commodification of the picturesque enforced a distinction between those who were the viewers (consumers) of the scenery and those who could only be imagined as objects in the landscape. Only the former enjoyed the privilege of "possession and circulation" represented by ownership of an estate or books of picturesque views or by tours of the picturesque countryside.[39]

This analysis, applied to the renderings of the Greensward Plan for the Central Park competition, calls attention to the fact that these drawings represent people as small, insignificant objects in the landscape. Although park promoters employed inclusive rhetoric leading up to the competition for Central Park and stressed the broad appeal of the park and the universal benefits of nature for people across the social spectrum, the Greensward Plan renderings figuratively excluded the masses from the privileges of possession and circulation enjoyed by educated consumers of the picturesque. Although this scenery was ostensibly for "the democracy of society," it could not encompass hordes of visitors without losing some of its aesthetic integrity. Crowds of revelers tended to ruin not only the picture, but also the experience that the designers had in mind. A similar problem arose when the national parks were created. Olmsted played a major role in that movement as well, and by that time foresaw the problem inherent in the very idea of these parks: Although these places were intended for the general public, if they were successful in attracting the public in large numbers, they would likely fail to offer the kind of contemplative experience that they were intended to preserve.[40]

Early proponents of a naturalistic park in the city, such as Downing, had foreseen this problem, to some extent, and worried about the potential disruption of crowds and revelers in such a park, but Downing hoped that the park would "[raise] up the working man to the same level of enjoyment with the man of leisure and accomplishment" and that rules of decorum would keep this problem under control.[41] Olmsted agreed, noting optimistically "that the aesthetic faculties need to be educated—drawn out; that taste and refinement need to be encouraged as well as the useful arts. That there need to be places and times . . . which shall be so attractive to the nature of all but the most depraved men, that the rich and the poor, the cultivated and well bred, and the sturdy and self-made people shall be attracted together and encouraged to assimilate."[42] Olmsted hoped that the park would hold a kind of mystical appeal for visitors, that its design would compel people of various backgrounds and economic levels to come together in harmonious appreciation of beautiful, naturalistic scenery.

Yet many proponents of Central Park, including Olmsted himself, expressed concern about how the park might be received by an untutored public; that is, how working-class visitors might behave in the park when it opened. Could it accommodate boisterous and rowdy crowds like those who frequented commercial pleasure gardens? An editorial in the *New York Times* worried: "As long as we are governed by the Five Points [the Bowery], our best attempts at elegance and grace will bear some resemblance to jewels in the snouts of swine. Better the Park would never be made at all if it is to become the resort of rapscallions . . . if no attempt is to be made to keep it clear of the intemperate, the boisterous and disorderly."[43] The park was conceived rather like a painting in an art museum: Patrons were expected to admire the scenery and somehow pick up good manners from the ambience, to be awed and speak in modulated tones in the presence of such beauty. Proponents hoped that the park would help to elevate those less favored by fortune, by eliciting favorable emotions and drawing out positive sentiment from even the poorest and unluckiest members of society; they hoped that it would be an edifying experience.

As it turned out, crowds of working-class visitors didn't materialize, at least not right away. In the early decades of its existence, Central Park served mainly the segment of New York society that lived by and set the rules of taste and decorum. They came in their carriages to tour the park, appropriating it for their own rituals of social intercourse. Even when the trees were still small, and the park's scenic effects required considerable imagination, they entered into the spirit of the park's illusion. The poor from districts such as the Five Points stayed away for various reasons, including distance, inaccessibility, and the cost of public transportation, but also partly out of preference for commercial pleasure gardens, where they could spend "their limited leisure time and money in ways that were not permitted or encouraged in the park."[44] The scenery in the new park must have looked some-

A Drive in Central Park, Winslow Homer. Lithograph, *Harper's Weekly*, 15 September 1860.

what raw and unappealing at first, especially to those untutored in the aesthetic. But it is also likely that quiet contemplation of nature did not particularly appeal to those used to more lively, boisterous forms of recreation and the more stimulating entertainments offered by commercial pleasure gardens.

The comparison of commercial pleasure gardens with Central Park illustrates, in microcosm, sweeping social and cultural change under way in New York at midcentury, and efforts by a small group of conservative reformers to counteract those changes. The nineteenth century was a period of social and political instability in the United States, and New York reflected the national turmoil. The city grew very rapidly, becoming the major city in the country over the course of the century. It was increasingly a city of immigrants, and it swelled with migrants from the countryside as the United States shifted from a rural to an urban society. During the 1850s and 1860s, increasing political and social upheaval divided the nation, particularly the issue of slavery, and the Civil War threatened to destroy the country altogether. The buildup to the Civil War, and the war itself (1861–65), highlighted the volatility of American society and the fragility of American democracy. In the aftermath of the war, it was unclear how the country would recover and what path it would take.

At the end of the war, in 1865, a small, select group of intellectuals and reformers, Olmsted among them, founded the American Social Science Association (ASSA), based in Boston, for the purpose of studying and shaping American society during that period of such profound political upheaval and social change. The association addressed a range of social issues, sponsoring meetings and collecting and disseminating information on topics ranging from prison discipline and treatment of the insane, to education and sanitary conditions. The ASSA was a vehicle for the kind of social reforms its membership supported, reforms based in scientific and technical knowledge and overseen by a small group of educated and public-spirited leaders. The agenda was broad in conception and high-minded in tone; the ASSA charter emphasized the "responsibilities of the gifted and educated classes toward the weak, the witless, and the ignorant." They were motivated by "a belief that American society urgently needed to fortify itself against the crude and materialistic

Frederick Law Olmsted, John Singer Sargent, 1895.
Oil portrait. (Used with permission from the Bilt-
more Company, Asheville, North Carolina)

impulses of popular culture; and a hope that the tensions of a newly
urban nation might be moderated by structural arrangements, both
political and aesthetic, to foster respect among rival social groups."[45]

Much has been written about Olmsted, his personal background,
his career, and the creation of Central Park.[46] To summarize, Olmsted
was born into an old New England family and followed several career
paths, including scientific farming and journalism, before being appointed as superintendent of Central Park in 1857. Previously he
edited *Putnam's Magazine,* a monthly periodical of commentary on
social, political, scientific, and artistic issues. He authored several
books of social commentary on a variety of topics, including an influential volume on the antebellum South. He ultimately settled on landscape architecture as a means to enact social reform and foster social

order, and Central Park was the project on which he cut his teeth. His experience as superintendent of Central Park was a political education, and he engaged in an ongoing series of battles with the board of park commissioners over how the park should be run. He was particularly aghast at the system of political spoils that increasingly exercised authority over civil service in New York, as the notorious Tweed Ring consolidated its power from 1868 to 1870. The system of political rewards in New York led, in his view, to poor management and poor decisions, and the park suffered as a result.[47] He felt that his expertise was unappreciated and that the purpose of the park—namely, the social reforms he had in mind—was misunderstood or ignored. Finally, in 1878, he was removed from the park department. After a few years in California, he moved his practice to Boston, where he found the political climate more supportive and where his influence and reputation grew as his list of projects expanded to include parks in cities throughout the United States and Canada.

Central Park and subsequent parks developed in other American cities in the nineteenth century by Olmsted and his colleagues are a legacy of what some historians have labeled "conservative reform." This term encompasses the efforts of organizations like the ASSA to manage social change in American society in this period. The genteel reformers of the so-called Gilded Age shared "assumptions about the design of a good society, where hierarchy, deference, and skilled leadership might impose tranquility on a contentious, egalitarian people." They mistrusted "the self-interest of freshly rich merchants and entrenched local politicians." These reformers have been characterized as "an aspiring intellectual elite in a nation which did not want an elite and met its overtures with constant scorn." As one social historian has put it, urban parks are "durable relics" of this movement. The goal of these parks was to affect "the everyday lives of large numbers of people. By providing pleasant and uplifting outlets in the narrow lives of city dwellers, they promised a measure of social tranquility" and "a moderating influence on the behavior of park visitors."[48] Central Park was designed to exert a leveling influence in a city of extremes; it was conceived as a haven of bourgeois decorum and civility in a city perceived as invaded by boisterous, rowdy, potentially riotous workers at one extreme, and vulgar, *nouveaux riches* at the other.

The Melodramatic Imagination

In such a period of accelerated social change, as New York City grew rapidly and its demographics shifted, urban life offered people many opportunities to reinvent themselves, and social roles were relatively fluid. Fortunes rose and fell unpredictably in an economy rocked by several market crashes and the Civil War, and social life demanded skillful role-playing. Social status often depended on keeping up appearances. Historians have often characterized nineteenth-century American culture as highly theatrical, in many ways a culture of performance.[49] Melodramas in the theater gained popularity in this period, and in a parallel development, new public spaces in nineteenth-century cities, such as theaters, shops, restaurants, and parks, all became important stages for public performances of individual social identity as well as performances of collective civic and cultural identity. It is illuminating to compare Central Park to popular melodramas playing in theaters in New York in this period and trace some of the narrative threads that wove together and helped shape performances outside as well as inside theaters. These threads reveal the workings of what Peter Brooks has called the "melodramatic imagination." Somewhat akin to what Fredric Jameson has called the "political unconscious," the melodramatic imagination can be thought of as a network of concealed narrative threads running through various artifacts of nineteenth-century culture, posing imaginary solutions to irresolvable political and social tensions of the historical moment.[50] To understand how the melodramatic imagination manifested itself in the nineteenth century, it is helpful to start by looking at its most overt expression, which was in the theater.

As a theatrical form, melodrama originated in France, probably with Jean-Jacques Rousseau, who devised a new form of theater by setting his libretto of *Pygmalion* to music, looking for a more "natural" alternative to opera in the late eighteenth century. The musical setting was intended to add emotional impact to the spoken word. The real father of melodrama, however, was Guilbert de Pixérécourt, who believed that the theater could be not only a popular form of entertainment, but a means to instruct an emerging middle class in the morals, mores, habits, and manners thought necessary for stability and prosperity in postrevolutionary France. Born into an upper-class family in

Nancy, Pixérécourt developed a healthy respect for the political power of the common people, having witnessed some of the excesses of the revolution. In his popular melodramas, Pixérécourt sought to model good and bad behavior and show "acts of heroism, bravery and fidelity," not only in the context of daily life, but in a clear moral context. As a genre, melodrama looked to nature for a moral context, filling a void left by the collapse of the moral authority of the monarchy and the church.[51]

The early playwrights and critics who promoted melodrama were members of the French bourgeoisie, frightened by political revolution and worried about the aftermath of those events. Growing out of these fears, melodrama was calculated to appeal to the lower classes as a means to foster social stability. Aiming at an uneducated public, playwrights and directors of melodramas in France employed emotion as a means to help audiences relate to characters and situations. They believed that the emotions elicited by the theater could be a force for moral improvement. Tears were viewed as evidence of success, particularly in female spectators. Yet proponents of melodrama recognized that emotions could be fickle and difficult to control. And, while some French critics, by mid-nineteenth century, expressed the view that melodrama produced positive effects in society, even a decline in the crime rate, others charged that melodrama instilled dangerous political ideas in spectators. Actually, by midcentury many in the audience were middle-class (artisans, shopkeepers, salespeople, workers), comfortable enough to buy tickets, with sufficient leisure time and at least some education. Few were really poor, as the cost of theater tickets prevented the poor from attending. The audience for melodrama grew throughout the century to embrace a much broader spectrum of French society, including members of the wealthier classes.[52] As the genre's popularity spread well beyond France, popular productions were translated into various languages, and the same melodramas played in various cities around the world simultaneously.

Melodrama, as a theatrical form, had clearly identifiable characteristics. One characteristic was the use of emotion as a force for moral improvement. Related to this belief in the power of emotion was sensationalism. The goal of sensationalism in the theater was to arouse, astonish, and thrill audiences, to stir emotions and elicit strong emotional reactions. Competition for audiences fed the desire for sensational effects and led to more and more elaborate spectacles. Another characteristic of the genre was its essential optimism; the original creators of melodramas believed in the power of the genre to improve society as well as to entertain. Aiming at broad audiences, producers of melodrama tended to simplify moral choices down to a matter of moral binaries—right versus wrong, good versus evil, virtue versus vice. Dichotomies such as these were not only the stock of melodramatic plots, but also at the root of the characters in melodrama; for example, a standard melodramatic plot pitted a beautiful and virtuous heroine against an ugly and evil villain. Virtue and beauty triumphed in the end.

There are striking parallels between nineteenth-century urban parks and nineteenth-century theatrical melodramas. Like theatrical melodrama, urban parks were intended as a popular, morally edifying form of entertainment for "the people." Like melodrama, parks grew out of bourgeois fears of the power and influence of the people, meaning particularly the lower classes that gained power and influence in the aftermath of the age of revolutions. Both theatrical melodramas and public parks were essentially optimistic in outlook and predicated

In *The Effect of Melodrama*, a painting by Louis-Léopold Boilly, ca. 1830, emotion overcomes a member of the audience. (Musée Lambinet, Versailles)

on a belief in the power of positive influences and role models. Both appealed to the senses and aimed to arouse positive emotions, thus serving as a force for moral improvement. Like melodramas in theaters, parks were conceived, at least rhetorically, to span social boundaries. These parallels suggest a strategy of interpretation that uses the framework of melodrama to look at how parks influenced the dialogue between the classes, negotiated class and gender tensions, and promulgated certain bourgeois notions of morality and character in the larger theater of public space. This framework is particularly helpful for understanding how parks developed into such viable and powerful social institutions in the United States, where they were not imposed by an autocratic government, but grew out of the sociocultural structure of a participatory system of government.

In the United States, melodrama enjoyed increasing popularity as a form of theatrical entertainment as the nineteenth century progressed. The content of popular melodramas reflected changes in the American theatergoing public over the course of the century. According to Bruce McConachie, early in the century paternalistic, fairy-tale melodramas affirmed the authority of upper-class males who made up the majority of theater audiences. Then, in the period prior to the Civil War, heroic and apocalyptic melodramas appealed to a growing working class with themes of liberalism (Jacksonian republicanism, celebration of the independent yeoman-hero) and capitalism (values of independence and masculine honor). By midcentury, coinciding with the development of Central Park, moral reform melodramas were becoming popular.[53]

Moral reform melodramas represented the concerns, values, and morals of the emerging business and professional class in the United States.[54] They dealt with political issues of particular interest to this social class, issues such as temperance, abolition, and the "woman question." They explored problems of social identity and changing class and gender roles. Moral reform melodramas addressed social insecurities fostered by fluctuations in the economy and portrayed the jockeying for social position between those fallen into genteel poverty and those with newfound wealth. Examples include popular plays such as *Fashion* (1845), written by Anna Cora Mowatt, which dealt with questions of authenticity in a society contending with new wealth and social mobility. *Uncle Tom's Cabin* (1852), adapted by George

Intrepid Reporter Finds Story in Central Park

Perils of the Park. National Police Gazette, 19 October 1878. (Courtesy of Library of Congress)

When he saw me sitting alone he endeavored to attract my attention . . . Four times he drove past me, turning within a few yards and repassing. He gave little whistles, coughs and smacking of his lips to make me look, but I still gazed at the top line in my book, which allowed me, without raising my eyes, to see all that was going on before me.

When he passed the fifth time, going towards Seventy-second street, I lifted my head and gazed steadily at him. He nodded his head for me to follow him. An officer

Aiken from Harriet Beecher Stowe's hugely popular novel, was the first real blockbuster of American theater. Widely credited with turning the tide of popular sentiment in favor of abolition, *Uncle Tom's Cabin* truly transformed theatrical melodrama into an agent of moral and political reform. *The Poor of New York* (1857), by Dion Boucicault, explored extremes of wealth and poverty in the modern city and addressed issues of class identity. In analyzing how melodramatic ways of thinking shaped Central Park, it will be useful to refer to speon the path, who could not but see the man's performances, merely looked at me lazily. [He] drove as closely to where I sat as the road would allow and then stopped.

"Good morning," he said. I made no reply, but kept my eyes fastened on my book.

"I would like to take you for a drive," he said, "if you will go down the path while I turn." I got up without replying and looked at the officer. He was watching us.

"Which way?" I asked the man.

"Down towards Seventy-second street," he replied. I walked past the officer, who turned his face, on which rested a broad smile, towards his horse, presenting his back to us. I stopped where the first path crossed the drive and the man came up.

"Aren't you afraid to do this?" I asked as I got into the vehicle with him.

"Why, there's nothin' to be afraid of," he answered, as he arranged the lap robe.

"The officers," I suggested, "aren't you afraid they will arrest you?"

"No, I'm solid with them," he answered, laughing, as if the idea was a good joke.

(From Nellie Bly, "The Infamy of the Park," New York World, 5 August 1888)

cific examples drawn from these three plays. All had extended runs in New York during the second half of the nineteenth century as Central Park was being developed.[55]

As a new cultural institution, Central Park addressed many of the same issues that were being dramatized in these popular moral reform melodramas in the theater: extremes of wealth and poverty in the city, changing class and gender identities, questions of social authenticity, public safety, and so on. The park was conceived as a new genre of public space that could serve as a staging ground for the social roles and social interactions that would define the modern American city. There are a number of parallels between the way social issues, social roles, and social interactions were addressed in the park and in the theater. Both moral reform melodramas in the theater and the new park were forms of cultural production driven by a social agenda of moral reform. Both aimed to influence public perception of pressing social issues. Both framed these issues through the lens of the melodramatic imagination. We can look first at melodramas in the theater, to identify some of the characteristic structures that conveyed moral reform messages in these plays, and then find parallels in the park.

Melodramas in the theater adhered to a highly structured format. Typically they had predictable plots that pitted good against evil and built to vivid, emotional climaxes in which virtue was rewarded and evil punished. Characters were conceived in terms of stereotypes—the suffering heroine or hero, the persecuting villain, the well-meaning comic—and remained true to type in the face of various challenges and hardships. The characters of melodrama were simplified, not psychologically complex or morally conflicted, in comparison to characters in classical tragedies, for example.[56] The staging of theatrical melodramas was spectacular, with striking visual and sound effects employed to heighten the emotional impact of the story. Important scenes, conveying moral messages, were commonly presented as tableaux in which the actors held frozen dramatic poses for several seconds, usually accompanied by uplifting music.

Three aspects of Central Park—its design, its staging, and its cast of characters—offer strong parallels to theatrical melodrama. The design, or concept, of the park is like the plot of a theatrical melodrama: it is the basic scaffolding, the vehicle for conveying important themes and moral messages, the framework within which the action takes place. The staging of the park—the way it was promoted and programmed—is comparable to the staging of a play: The goal is to win the audience, to entertain, to create a memorable experience. The cast of the park is composed of its users, conceived by park proponents as both actors and audience. As actors, park users are expected to enact the performances for which the park is designed. As audience, they are expected to receive its moral messages and to be entertained. Focusing on the three plays mentioned earlier—*Fashion, Uncle Tom's*

Cabin, and *The Poor of New York*—we can see how both the park and melodramas in the theater addressed troubling issues such as extremes of wealth and poverty; changing social class and gender identities; and the shift from a rural to an urban society. We can see the melodramatic imagination at work in both the theater and the park.

The Melodramatic Landscape of Central Park

The nineteenth-century melodramatic imagination produced predictable plots that pitted good against evil, contrasting virtue and vice. Anna Mowatt's popular play *Fashion,* which opened in New York in 1845, offers a typical example. It is about a *nouveau riche* New York matron, Mrs. Tiffany, and her daughter, Seraphina, seeking to establish themselves in fashionable society. Adopting European fashions in dress and manners, Mrs. Tiffany and her daughter intend to secure their social position by snaring a French count as a match for Seraphina. The plot revolves around a series of social deceptions, which are, of course, exposed in the end. The count himself turns out to be an imposter; indeed, nearly everyone in the play turns out to be an imposter of one sort or another. The exception is Adam Trueman, a farmer recently arrived from the country to visit his old friends in the city. Trueman represents social authenticity, as opposed to the falsity of the other characters. He utters the speeches that convey the moral message of the play. His final speech is a defense of American meritocracy as a system that rewards virtue (honesty) in the face of vice (dishonesty and social deception): "We *have* kings, princes, and nobles in abundance—of *Nature's stamp,* if not of *Fashion's*—we have honest men, warm-hearted and brave, and we have women—gentle, fair, and true, to whom no *title* could add *nobility.*"[57] By contrast to the other characters in the play, who are all posing in one way or another, Adam Trueman remains honest and true. He is represented as secure in his social status because, as a yeoman farmer, he is firmly rooted in the soil of rural America. Of course, his honesty and social authenticity are rewarded at the play's end.

The design for Central Park, like the plot of the play *Fashion,* followed a stock format contrasting good and evil by representing the country in moral opposition to the city. Olmsted and Vaux designed the new park as a swath of rural countryside, in striking juxtaposition

A view of "squatters" near Central Park. Harper's Weekly, 26 June 1869.

to the man-made structures of the modern, industrial city. Pushing this contrast to its limit, they emphasized the rural references in the park at every opportunity, staunchly defending it against intrusions that might have lessened this rural-urban dichotomy, such as proposed architectural additions (museums, statuary, monumental gateways) or recreational facilities such as ball fields. Framed like a painting by a grid of urban streets, its transverse roadways hidden below grade so as not to dilute the vividness of its contrast to the city, the park was designed to present "an aspect of spaciousness and tranquility with variety and intricacy of arrangement, thereby affording the most agreeable contrast to the confinement, bustle, and monotonous street-division of the city."[58]

Since the design of Central Park evoked the country to represent rural virtue, it was not designed as a realistic, nuanced, or complex representation of the contemporary rural landscape in the United States. Consider the site on which the park was constructed, a rural site occupied by real rural people.[59] Former residents of the site included a few well-off New Yorkers who had built country homes to escape outbreaks of cholera in the city, but mostly it was home to subsistence farmers and squatters who had constructed dwellings ranging from cottages to shanties. It was the site of Seneca Village, a well-established town, with schools and churches, whose residents included African Americans and Irish immigrants. There were several industries on the site, of an unsightly and foul-smelling sort, such as tanners and bone-boilers. The park removed all reference to these authentic rural conditions, replacing them with a representation of rural scenery designed to represent moral virtue. The goal was to heighten a melodramatic and moral contrast between city and country.

The tendency to reduce complex moral issues to simplistic moral binaries was a hallmark of melodrama. This tendency is also well illustrated by *Uncle Tom's Cabin*, the most popular American melodrama ever produced. Many different stage adaptations of Harriet Beecher Stowe's novel played in theaters throughout the country and around the world, reaching a much wider audience than the book.[60] Aiken's adaptation was the first successful theatrical version of the novel, opening in Troy, New York, and then playing at the National Theater in New York City in 1852. Of all the various theatrical adaptations, it was the most faithful to Stowe's radical abolitionist intentions, but even this staging greatly reduced the moral complexity of Stowe's novel.

Recent scholarship on Stowe's novel has emphasized that her anti-slavery beliefs were part of a much larger social critique "embedded in a nexus of values that challenged the secular, masculine, and capitalist society of the antebellum North."[61] Stowe used slavery as an extreme example of what she saw as the immorality of market-driven capitalism. Although critics have interpreted the novel variously, most agree that Stowe proposed an alternative society, based on Christian values and maternal love, in which economic cooperation triumphs over materialism, exploitation, and individualism. But in reworking Stowe's novel for a theater audience, Aiken avoided any critique of market capitalism. He distilled from Stowe's complicated story a thrilling series of "splendid pictures in a drama packed with lurid action."[62] The play reduced the novel to a series of dramatic scenes, emphasizing contrasts between good and evil. Its effectiveness as a theatrical melodrama lay in its ability to arouse sentiment through sensational staging of the most wrenching, emotional scenes of the novel.

Like Stowe's novel *Uncle Tom's Cabin*, Central Park was intended to be an instrument of social reform and to ameliorate some of the worst social effects of market capitalism. Olmsted was well acquainted with Harriet Beecher Stowe and shared many of her political and moral beliefs. While superintendent of Central Park, and at other times throughout his life, he sometimes railed in private against capitalists and men of commerce because of what he perceived as their self-interest and focus on economics rather than social reform.[63] Compared to Stowe, however, Olmsted was more cautious, or perhaps more conflicted, about criticism of market capitalism. His own anti-slavery sentiments, articulated in three books on the South, written and published prior to the Civil War, were complex and thoughtful; but one of his main arguments against slavery was that it was essentially anticapitalist: It was not good for production because slaves had no financial incentive to work.[64] And although Olmsted argued with capitalists on the park board, he also often noted that the park was a boon to capitalist expansion in New York, boosting real-estate values, making the city more competitive in attracting tourists and capitalist investment, raising it to the standard of European investment capitals.[65]

Central Park was designed to address social problems produced by rapid capitalist expansion, problems such as poor public health, crowded living and working conditions, lack of community, and social alienation among the working classes. Olmsted argued tirelessly that the park could help ameliorate these problems. Yet in his public addresses he often sounded more like George Aiken than Harriet Beecher Stowe, tending to simplify these complex social problems for audiences spanning the political spectrum. Typically, he reduced moral reform messages to simple binary oppositions in a manner characteristic of melodrama. The park represented "good," versus the "evil" of the city: "The more I have seen of them [parks], the more highly have I been led to estimate their value as means of counteracting the evils of town life."[66] And, as already discussed, the design of the park embodied rather simplistic, moralistic messages, reducing complex social problems to a series of dramatic scenes contrasting the country and the city.

The Melodramatic Staging of Central Park

In the theater, melodramas employed striking visual and sound effects to appeal to large audiences and heighten emotional impact. The formula for moral reform melodramas was developed to deliver moral messages in the guise of popular entertainment. Such plays maintained a careful balance between these two potentially conflicting demands. For example, *Fashion* had a moral theme, but it was also a lighthearted comedy about new wealth in New York. It poked fun at the social games that accompanied rising social status, while also showcasing the glamour, ease, and comfort enjoyed by the new American bourgeoisie. Audiences could take vicarious pleasure in the fashionable lifestyle and elaborate parlor games played on stage. Although *Fashion* cautioned audiences about social pretense, the play's happy ending effectively trivialized the dangers of social posturing. The Tiffanys may have had trouble attaining quite the social status they longed for, but their struggles were merely temporary setbacks on the way to social success.

Central Park was staged, like a moral reform melodrama, as a vehicle for moral messages, and also as popular entertainment. Like the play *Fashion*, it delivered its moral messages, while at the same

The Four-In-Hand Club, Albert Berghaus. Lithograph, *Frank Leslie's Newspaper*, 27 November 1875.

time showcasing the new American bourgeoisie. Its rural landscape was intended to signify rural virtue, but it also represented the latest fashion in landscape design imported from Europe. It did for New York what an elegant Parisian headdress did for Seraphina in the opening scene of *Fashion*. It showed that New York was a fashion-conscious, world-class city. The main feature of the park was a series of drives and promenades that served, like drives in the Bois de Boulogne, to show off the fine horses and carriages of wealthy New Yorkers.[67] The park's centerpiece was a mall modeled on the Champs Élysées. Parkside lots quickly became desirable, and the residences that grew up alongside the park became fashionable places to live. Central Park soon became a public drawing room for the new American business class. It offered a stage for the spectacle of American conspicuous consumption, a place to see and a place to be seen, like Rotten Row in London's Hyde Park, the Champs Élysées, and the Bois de Boulogne in Paris.

As Central Park was being discussed and constructed, many upper-class New Yorkers feared that it would be overrun by the lower classes, and proponents of the park feared that the wealthy "might flee the city and bring ruin to the local economy if the park were built."[68] These fears turned out to be unfounded, as the wealthy took to the park gladly, although not always decorously. A report in the *Herald*, some years after the park opened, noted that, "the more brilliant becomes the display of vehicles and toilettes, the more shameful is the display of bad manners on the part of the extremely fine-looking people who ride in carriages and wear the fine dresses."[69] Olmsted himself seems to have struggled to reconcile large congregations of people in the park with his own preference for more solitary pursuits, noting that "purely gregarious recreation seems to be generally looked upon in New England society as childish and savage, because, I suppose, there is so little of what we call intellectual gratification in it. We are inclined to engage in it indirectly, furtively, and with complication."[70] This admission supports Raymond Williams's thesis that a major distinction between working-class and bourgeois culture is that "between alternative ideas of the nature of social relationships," the former "collective and mutual," the latter "individualist."[71] But Olmsted placed great faith in the power of the park and its natural scenery to bring people together, to exert a moderating influence at both ends of the social spectrum, to induce harmony and smooth over social differences and social preferences. This determination, even in the face of obvious inner doubts, seems to indicate the influence of the melodramatic imagination in his thinking.

One of the most spectacular devices of theatrical melodrama was the tableau, or living picture. The theatrical tableau functioned as a sort of melodramatic punctuation at the end of important scenes and at the climax of a play. In moral reform melodrama, the tableau became a powerful vehicle for delivering moral messages. Enhanced by mood-setting music and sometimes prolonged through a series of slow-motion, freeze-frame actions, the tableau of nineteenth-century American melodrama was a precursor of modern cinema.[72] Some of the most famous tableaux in the history of American melodrama— reproduced in countless programs, posters, and souvenirs—were the ones in George Aiken's stage adaptation of *Uncle Tom's Cabin*. In Aiken's play, eight tableaux froze moments of high melodrama in audience memory. Probably the most sensational of these showed Eliza fleeing across the ice-clogged Ohio River with her pursuers close at her heels. But the final tableau of Aiken's production was

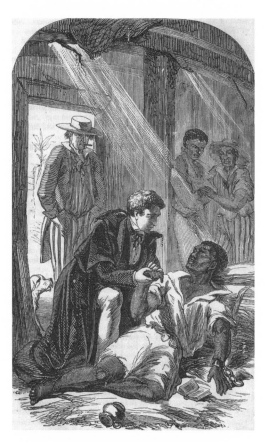

Death of Uncle Tom. Illustration from Harriet Beecher Stowe, *Uncle Tom's Cabin or Negro Life in the Slave States of America* (London: Clarke & Co. Foreign Booksellers, 1852). (Courtesy of Shields Library Special Collections, University of California, Davis)

equally famous, and it carried the moral message of the play. The stage directions for this final tableau specified: "Gorgeous clouds, tinted with sunlight. Eva, robed in white, is discovered on the back of a milk-white dove, with expanded wings, as if just soaring upward. Her hands are extended in benediction over St. Clare and Uncle Tom who are kneeling and gazing up to her. Expressive music. Slow curtain."[73]

This climactic scene condensed the moral impact of Harriet Beecher Stowe's novel into one vivid visual image. In true melodramatic fashion, it played powerfully on audience emotions. Following directly after Uncle Tom's death, it deepened the audience's sense of sorrow by recalling Eva's death earlier in the play. Yet, by suggesting a heavenly reunion, it also provided the uplifting, happy ending that audiences demanded and that Stowe had tried to effect with a drawn-out series of revelations in the final chapters of her novel. This final tableau drives home the play's antislavery message by reference to a higher moral authority.

Like a theatrical melodrama, Central Park was initially presented to the public as a series of memorable visual images, a series of sensational scenes. When Olmsted and Vaux won the competition to design Central Park in 1858, their presentation included a series of watercolor studies showing "effects proposed" for particular sites in the park. While the site plan for the park was in many ways like a script, directing the entire park production, the watercolor studies served as tableaux, highlighting parts of the design, fixing these in public memory and driving home the moral message at the core of the park idea. More effectively than the plan, these studies showed the sensational, visual impact that rural scenery could have in New York, the striking contrast it could offer to its urban context. Each park study was paired with a "before" view. Keyed to particular locations on the Greensward Plan, the "before" scenes were either black-and-white outline drawings or black-and-white photographs. By contrast, the "after" scenes were lushly rendered in watercolor. The effect of this contrast was to show the remarkable transformation of a barren wasteland into a verdant park. The park appears to burst into life. The trees are in leaf; winter has given way to spring. Even the water in proposed lakes seems to come to life, rendered with a highly reflective surface, mirroring lush foliage and capturing nuances of light and shadow. Blank skies, which form a dreary backdrop to the "before" scenes, are transformed by magnificent cloud formations in the watercolor studies, subtly suggesting a celestial presence not unlike the final tableau of *Uncle Tom's Cabin*. As a whole, the effect of these studies is to show a landscape that has moved from shadow into sunshine.

Theatrical melodramas typically unfolded in a series of dramatic, tension-building scenes. The tension was ultimately relieved in a climactic final scene, which delivered the final moral message. In Central Park, the final message had to do with transcending the evils of the

"*Effect Proposed*" for Central Park, Calvert Vaux, 1858. Presentation sketch #4, from the Greensward Plans for Central Park. (© Museum of the City of New York)

city through the humbling and awe-inspiring experience of nature. Each watercolor study for the Greensward Plan built to that message, showing tiny human figures dwarfed by the magnificent, rural scenery of the park. In some of the studies, a lone canoeist suggests human presence. In others, there appear scattered groups of men and women engaged in conversation or strolling beneath stately trees along the edges of great meadows. These studies show the public imagined for the park, the cast of characters for whom the Greensward was designed. The figures exhibit bourgeois respectability in their dress and demeanor. Casually grouped in picturesque poses, they illustrate the anticipated civilizing effect of the park on visitors, the manners and mores that were expected to pertain in this new public space. Like theatrical tableaux, the Central Park studies distill the park's moral and social agenda into a vivid and lasting visual impression. Like the final tableau of *Uncle Tom's Cabin,* they show both the park and its inhabitants blessed by a benevolent Nature.

The design for Central Park appealed to the senses, as a means to

arouse sentiment in its audience. The sensations of the park were designed to contrast markedly with the sensations of the city. The park
was conceived as a place "to which people may easily go after their
day's work is done, and where they may stroll for an hour, seeing,
hearing, and feeling nothing of the bustle and jar of the streets, where
they shall, in effect, find the city put far away from them."[74] The park
offered sensations associated with the country: the sounds of birds,
the sight of trees and pastures, the scent of flowers, the feel of soft
leaves underfoot. These sensations, in contrast to the noises, odors,
and sights of the city, were expected to produce desirable sentiment
in park visitors, to effect calm, diffuse tension, to relieve some of the
stresses of urban life, and, most importantly, to create "a very strong
moral impression through an enlarged sense of the bounteousness of
Nature."[75] And, as the park matured and attendance grew, Olmsted,
like a theater impresario, regarded sentiment in his audience as evidence of the success of his production: for example, "tears of gratitude
in the eyes of poor women, as they watched their children enjoying
themselves."[76]

Like an evening at the theater, Central Park offered diversion and
a temporary escape from the realities of everyday life in nineteenth-
century New York, but fell somewhat short of providing a cure for the
social problems it purported to address. Rosemarie Bank writes about
Uncle Tom's Cabin: "The melodrama's effectiveness, its ability to manifest sensation, is sited with its weakness as a delegitimation of slavery,
rehearsing all the reasons for wide-ranging intervention—broken families, exploited workers, beaten and seduced slaves, corrupted whites,
and racism (vested in degrees of color and in depersonalization)—but
leaving emancipation suspended with Eva, somewhere overhead in
the realm of Providence."[77] A similar analysis can be applied to Central
Park. The park's ameliorative sensations did offer welcome diversion
to New Yorkers of various social classes, but actually did little to alter
social conditions or lessen class divisions in the city. Addressing all
the reasons for social intervention—poverty, inhumane living and
working conditions, depersonalization, poor public health—it left social change somewhere overhead in the realm of Nature.

Like popular melodrama in the theater, Central Park was conceived as a lavish production, staged as a spectacle, and intended for
large audiences. Some contemporary critics of the new park pointed

out that a series of smaller neighborhood parks, spread equitably throughout the city, might have been considerably more effective in actually redressing the social ills that the Central Park targeted.[78] Even Olmsted himself noted that "small grounds so distributed through a large town that some one of them could be easily reached by a short walk from every house, would be more desirable than a single area of great extent, however rich in landscape attractions it might be."[79] But the park was envisioned as a spectacle, not only to evoke the country in contrast to the city and compete with the scale of the new urbanism, but to serve as a grand gesture demonstrating to New Yorkers, and to the world, that this was a socially harmonious, cultured, world-class city.

The Melodramatic Cast of Central Park

One of the defining characteristics of nineteenth-century melodrama was the steadfastness of its character types through various twists and turns of plot. In contrast to the internally conflicted characters of tragedy, "the undivided protagonist of melodrama has only external pressures to fight against: an evil man, a social group, a hostile ideology, a natural force, an accident or chance, an obdurate fate or a malign deity. It is this total dependence upon external adversaries which finally separates melodrama from all other serious dramatic forms."[80] These steadfast character types were appealing because, in a period of rapid social change and widespread social insecurity, they offered continuity and were so predictable.

Questions of social authenticity preoccupied Americans in the nineteenth century. Two market crashes, in 1837 and 1857, produced widespread financial insecurity that, in turn, produced considerable social anxiety. As fortunes fluctuated, sometimes with startling rapidity, appearances became increasingly important as a means to maintain social status through periods of economic instability. The boom-and-bust economy produced new money, and social climbers flourished. But the social anxiety that accompanied social climbing could be acute, as portrayed in the play *Fashion*. Early in the century, middle-class anxiety about authenticity led to condemnation of social role-playing, but by midcentury most middle-class Americans accepted social role-playing as a necessary ritual of social success. Moral reform melodramas often addressed social rituals and their attendant social anxieties, helping to legitimate role-playing in real life, making it more acceptable and diffusing some of its potential to produce anxiety.

Much of the typecasting in nineteenth-century melodrama was class-based. Boucicault's *The Poor of New York* (1857) illustrates some of the popular class-based character types in American melodrama at midcentury. The play was an adaptation of *Les Pauvres de Paris*, the runaway success of the 1856 theater season in Paris. Americanizing the plot, Boucicault set *The Poor of New York* in the boom-and-bust cycles of the American economy in the nineteenth century, specifically the two panics of 1837 and 1857. The characters represent various social classes affected by the cycles of the economy. Mrs. Fairweather, the genteel widow of a sea captain, and her two children, Lucy and Paul, represent the virtuous middle class. They have been deprived of their rightful inheritance by Gideon Bloodgood, who is the prototypical evil banker, a staple of nineteenth-century melodrama. In their desperate poverty, the Fairweathers are forced to take charity from their kindly working-class landlords, Puffy the Baker and his wife. Mark Livingstone, a young man from an old New York family, represents New York's morally upstanding social elite. Tom Badger, played famously by Lester Wallack, is the "brash, opportunistic, wisecracking, full of get-rich-quick schemes, garrulous, and soft-hearted" New York character, a well-known type on the New York stage.[81] He acts with forethought and ingenuity to save the written proof of the Fairweathers' inheritance from a sensational fire set by Bloodgood at the climax of the play.

Following the financial crisis of 1857, American melodrama began to acknowledge the existence of class differences and to introduce the variable of chance as a factor in economic success. Sensation melodramas, like *The Poor of New York*, produced in the second half of the century, portrayed the city as a great theater, a stage on which speculation could produce dramatic reversals of fortune overnight. In *The Poor of New York*, as fortunes rise and fall due to market instability, characters representing different classes are thrown together. Genteel families, suddenly poverty-stricken, find themselves living in proximity to the working class. Unlike earlier moral reform melodramas, such

The Cunning Suitor

Cunning Cupid as Mendicant, how a sly New York heiress, under the eye of a watchful mamma, communicates with her forbidden lover during her airings in the park. National Police Gazette, 8 April 1882.

Love, as everyone knows, is reputed to have laughed at locksmiths ever since locks came into vogue. So modern custodians of young people do not place reliance on bolts and bars. They prefer to keep their eyes peeled and rely on personal shrewdness. Acting on this principle, the mother of a beautiful young society heiress has taken upon herself the duties of duenna in order to keep off a young chap who has been forbidden the house. The young woman favors him, however, and as she takes her morning walk with her mamma every day their path is crossed by a most wretched specimen of the genus tramp. Into his hat, by parental consent, the fair one always drops a few pennies, with sometimes a little perfumed billet, receiving in return a light kiss on her dainty gloved hand. Then the tramp hobbles off, removes his make-up and gloats over the tender phrases of the epistle. The tramp is a good-looking, dashing young fellow who is a talented amateur actor and who is thus making use of his stage experience. An elopement will probably be the next scene in the play.

(From "Cunning Cupid as Mendicant," National Police Gazette, 8 April 1882)

as *Fashion*, which coupled business-class success with old-fashioned virtues like honesty and sincerity, the moral lessons of *The Poor of New York* have more to do with virtue as its own reward.

There are no real poor in *The Poor of New York*. Poverty is represented as a potential hazard of speculation, a temporary economic setback. The Fairweathers are the poor to whom the title refers, but, although they temporarily suffer desperate poverty, they retain their middle-class identity throughout and regain their rightful inheritance at the end of the play. Contrary to its title, the play is really about the vicissitudes of fortune in New York at midcentury. Bad luck befalls rich and poor alike. The working-class characters—Puffy the Baker and his wife—are actually better off financially than the Fairweathers throughout most of the play. But shifts of fortune do not change the basic working-class stereotype that the Puffys represent. As Bruce McConachie points out, they are "business-class wish fulfillments come to life"; they work hard, live comfortably, speak deferentially, and take care of their betters through hard times.[82]

In terms of casting, there are many parallels between *The Poor of New York* and Central Park. The characters that peopled Central Park in the public imagination at midcentury, like the characters in *The Poor of New York*, reflect growing class-consciousness among urban Americans. From its conception, the park was imaginatively peopled in the press with characters from various social classes thrown together in the park as in a melodrama. Working-class characters figured prominently in this melodrama since a major justification given for the park was the need to improve the quality of life for those at the lower end of the economic spectrum. A dominant working-class type that figured in the park's cast of characters was virtuous, hardworking, and deserving, similar to the Puffys in *The Poor of New York*. For example, note this description in a *New York Times* article of 1866: "Of the many charms, health-giving and inspiring as they are, which the park affords, the greatest boon by far is that it is an ever available and quiet resting place for the plodders of the week, men and women, where they enjoy that companionship and interchange of thought denied to them in a great measure during the long hours of toil."[83] However, another working-class type also appeared with regularity, representing business-class anxiety about cross-class interactions in the new public space. A writer in the *New York Herald*, writing around the same time, described this second type:

> When we open a public park Sam will air himself in it. He will take his friends whether from Church Street, or elsewhere. He will knock down any better dressed man who remonstrates with him. He will talk and sing, and fill his share of the bench, and flirt with the nursery maids in his own coarse way. Now we ask what chance have William B. Astor and Edward Everett against this fellow citizen of theirs? Can they and he enjoy the same place? Is it not obvious that he will turn them out, and that the great Central Park will be nothing but a great beer-garden for the lowest denizens of the city, of which we shall yet pray litanies to be delivered?[84]

Both of these characterizations parallel class-based types in contemporary melodrama. They represent, on the one hand, wish fulfillment and, on the other hand, anxiety about the underclass. Like the characters in popular melodrama, they are not fully developed as individuals, but serve the moral narrative by offering contrasts between good and evil, virtue and vice, passivity and aggression.

Such character types also inhabited the imagination of Central Park's designers. In 1870, in a talk before the American Social Science Association in Boston, Olmsted quoted the above description of the fictional Sam's encounter with William B. Astor. He used it as a prelude to declaring that "no one who has closely observed the conduct of the people who visit the Park, can doubt that it exercises a distinctly harmonizing and refining influence upon the most unfortunate and lawless classes of the city,—an influence favorable to courtesy, self-control, and temperance."[85] In Olmsted's reformist (melodramatic?) imagination, virtuous, wish-fulfilling, working-class character types would prevail in Central Park.

Proponents of public parks like Olmsted believed that "decisive intervention by a socially responsible elite was essential if urbanization were to prove beneficent in its social effects."[86] Yet, as Thomas Bender has pointed out, park advocates "combined a sincere feeling for the less fortunate with a somewhat manipulative concern for raising them up to middle-class standards."[87] Fredric Jameson's notion of *ideologemes* helps to explain how this manipulation worked. According to Jameson, *ideologemes* were the structural narratives that served

Music on the Mall, Central Park, New York. *Harper's Weekly*, 9 October 1869.

as the building blocks of nineteenth-century melodrama, working at an unconscious level to "resolve, manage, or repress the evident class anxieties aroused by the existence of an industrial working class and an urban lumpen-proletariat."[88] Middle-class anxiety was a structural narrative underpinning the melodrama of Central Park, expressed through certain recurring melodramatic scenarios, such as the one between the aggressive Sam and William B. Astor. The *ideologeme* embedded in this scenario is "stay in your place." Deference and decorum would be enforced in the park, and rowdiness would not be tolerated.

Jameson writes that "two paradigms, the sentimental and the melodramatic . . . may be said to be the carrot and the stick of nineteenth-century, middle-class moralizing about the lower classes."[89] If the message "stay in your place," delivered via Sam-the-ruffian, operates as a melodramatic "stick," the following text, written by Olmsted in 1870, introduces a "carrot." In this passage, Olmsted explains his intentions for the Dairy—a secluded glen that he and his partner, Calvert Vaux, designed specifically for women and children in Central Park: "On a hot day a mother carrying a sick child, and perhaps leading other children, if she follows the throng, is liable to become more heated and feverish through fatigue, anxiety and various slight embarrassments, than if she remained quietly within a close, dark chamber. If she comes with a party of friends, she will be glad to find some quiet nook in which, while others wander, she can be left with her baby. The class of considerations thus suggested had influenced the treatment of several localities [in Central Park], but had been controlling in a larger way than elsewhere at the point in question."[90] With its heightened sense of drama, exaggerated sentiment, coy references to "slight embarrassments," and stereotypical representation of motherhood, this scenario portrays a sentimental favorite. The Dairy in Central Park was designed for her. She is the "helpless and unfriended" heroine of domestic melodrama: weak and powerless, vulnerable to the worst designs of evil villains, but capable of showing great strength under adversity.[91] She is a repository of virtue, a bastion against immorality, a refuge from the evils of the marketplace.

Olmsted and Vaux proposed the Dairy for Central Park in 1865, and it was completed in 1871. Although intended as a public space, it evoked an idealized private, domestic space. It was designed as a secluded, homelike refuge for women and children within the public landscape of the new park. The building was sited at a distance from the main drive, hidden from view by large masses of rock and dense shrubbery. The designers sought, "by thickening and extending the original sylvan defenses, [to] secure a more decided effect of rural retirement." The building was a wooden structure in the Stick Style. A large veranda provided shelter from the weather. The steeply pitched roof and gables, embellished trusses, and brace supports signified a rural cottage—of the sort that Andrew Jackson Downing had designed as rural retreats for middle-class families who could afford a house in the suburbs surrounding New York. The Dairy's original function was to dispense fresh milk, bread and butter, and other wholesome country fare. The building faced south toward a lawn area enclosed by sheltering plantations on three sides. "Upon the bit of green-sward in front, it had been intended that a cow or two, a ewe with lambs and a few broods of chickens should be kept for the amusement of children, and a small stable had been built for them hard by, which also served to mask a dressing-room and water-closet."[92]

It seems more than coincidental that the design and construction

MELODRAMATIC LANDSCAPES

General View of the Dairy, Central Park, New York, Calvert Vaux, 1869. Drawing. (Milstein Division of United States History, Local History & Genealogy, The New York Public Library, Astor, Lenox and Tilden Foundations)

of the Dairy in Central Park coincided with well-publicized attempts by American women to organize a political movement for the purpose of obtaining political representation. Two years earlier, Susan B. Anthony and Elizabeth Cady Stanton had founded the National Woman's Suffrage Association (NWSA) in New York and had begun publishing their newspaper, the *Revolution* (1868–71). Also in 1868, Jane Croly founded the woman's club Sorosis, in New York, in response to the exclusion of women from Charles Dickens's lecture at the New York Press Club. Other feminist organizations dating to the same period include the American Woman Suffrage Association (AWSA), started in Boston in 1869 by Lucy Stone and Elizabeth Blackwell, and the New England Woman's Club, founded by Caroline Severance in Boston in 1868.[93]

The "woman question" shook the foundations of gender relations and challenged prevailing gender identities in the second half of the nineteenth century in America. These women's organizations strongly challenged the boundaries of the domestic sphere, focusing primarily on suffrage, but also addressing issues of fair employment, equal wages, educational opportunities, and other nondomestic concerns of growing numbers of urban middle-class women. Threats to traditional gender identities in New York in this period came not only from a growing middle-class women's movement challenging traditional gender roles, but from ethnic minorities and rural immigrants as well.[94] In this context, the Dairy in Central Park affirmed a conservative, middle-class view of feminine nature in keeping with the prevailing gender ideology of separate spheres. Although it extended an invitation to women to use the public park, its design was based on the assumption that women and children are a natural unit and that woman's natural place is in the private sphere, at home with children. The message to women, although couched in sentiment, was really: "stay in your place."

As the fashion for large urban parks swept the country in the late nineteenth century, the Dairy was widely emulated throughout the United States, and therefore represents not just an isolated instance, but a new genre of gendered public space.[95] Gendered spaces in parks, like women's lunch rooms in department stores and women's lounges on ferries, were an attempt to choreograph women's social interactions in a rapidly changing urban environment. While such spaces invited women to the city, they also worked symbolically to confine and control women's movements. In fact, nineteenth-century women across all social classes moved much more freely in public than these gendered spaces would suggest.[96] Such spaces represent a complex response to women's self-assertion in the nineteenth century, a kind of wish fulfillment on the part of a male-dominated power structure. As Martha Vicinus has noted, "placed within a realistic contemporary framework, domestic melodrama is a world of wish fulfillment and dreams . . . concerned not with what is possible or actual, but with what is desirable."[97] The Dairy was a little melodrama about domesticity and traditional family values. It was designed around the kind of female character that Olmsted and Vaux hoped would add the right tone to the park. She was the little woman that Ruskin famously described in his essay "Of Queen's Gardens" (1865), "with her child at her breast, and a power, if she would wield it, over it, and over its father, purer than the air of heaven, and stronger than the seas of earth."[98]

Proponents of Central Park rejected the overt theatricality of commercial pleasure gardens, with their dramatic spectacles and elaborate scenic effects, in favor of the more "natural" alternative presented by the Greensward Plan. Yet Central Park was, in many ways, a highly theatrical production. Much like a giant tableau, it fixed in cultural

Descending the Steps, Central Park, Frederick Childe Hassam, 1895. Oil
painting. (Virginia Museum of Fine Arts, Richmond; Gift of the Estate of
Hildegarde Graham van Roijen)

memory some of the important dramatic themes, special effects, and
stereotypical characters that preoccupied the nineteenth-century
melodramatic imagination. Like a successful melodrama in the theater, Central Park spawned many imitations, and a generation of public parks appeared in cities throughout the United States, all employing a similar design formula juxtaposing the country and the city,
reproducing comparable sensations, designed with a similar cast of
characters in mind, representing bourgeois taste and modeling bourgeois decorum. Like popular nineteenth-century moral reform melodramas, such as *Uncle Tom's Cabin*, these parks played to audiences
across the country, from New York to Chicago to San Francisco, and
enjoyed tremendous success in every venue.

Frontispiece of Matthew Hale Smith, *Sunshine and Shadow in New York* (Hartford: J. B. Burr, 1869). (Picture Collection, The Branch Libraries, The New York Public Library, Astor, Lenox and Tilden Foundations)

New York City guidebooks in the nineteenth century often divided the city figuratively into zones of sunshine and shadow, representing virtue and vice. This imaginary map—yet another figment of the melodramatic imagination—worked to contain class-based anxieties about social change and changing morals in the modern city. For example, Matthew Hale Smith, writing in 1869 in *Sunshine and Shadow in New York*, conjured quite different imagery for the Bowery and Central Park. About the Bowery, he noted that "the lowest drinking-places, the vilest concert-saloons, negro minstrelsy of the lowest order, and theatricals the most debasing, distinguish the pastimes of the Bowery. These places, open on Sunday, are jammed to suffocation Sunday nights." On the other hand, writing about Central Park, "the pride of New York," he described, in glowing detail, its transformation from shadow into sunshine, crediting the park commissioners: "On a bare, unsightly, and disgusting spot, they have created an area of beauty, charming as the Garden of the Lord."[99] Such narratives are what Fredric Jameson calls "the political unconscious." They turn a novel, a guidebook, a map, or a park into a vehicle for bourgeois moralizing. In a final glance at Central Park as a nineteenth-century cultural institution, we might recall Jameson's warning: "only a genuine philosophy of history is capable of respecting the specificity and radical difference of the social and cultural past while disclosing the solidarity of its polemics and passions, its forms, structures, experiences, and struggles, with those of the present day."[100]

In recent years, Central Park has been meticulously restored to its nineteenth-century form and is perhaps even more revered today as an American cultural institution than it was at its inception 150 years ago. Comparable parks in other cities have been similarly cherished and preserved for posterity. What do these parks signify in our culture today? Does their sensational juxtaposition of the country and the city still represent a nineteenth-century moralizing narrative? Has the cast of characters changed? If so, is the new cast less stereotypical? In the public imagination, these parks still seem to occupy an elevated plain, inviolate, somewhere in the realm of Providence. Perhaps the melodramatic imagination has not lost its hold on American consciousness?

Conclusion

THESE DAYS, ON A SUNNY SUNDAY AFTER-
noon, the parks in Paris, Mexico City, and New York are even more
filled with people than in the nineteenth century—filled with families
strolling, picnicking, and playing games, with lovers trying to look
inconspicuous, with bird-watchers and amateur horticulturalists focusing on the fauna and flora, with dog walkers and cyclists enjoying
the largesse of the landscape. A few things have changed in these
parks. Some fashions and customs are different, especially for women.
Automobiles have replaced horse-drawn vehicles. The crowds have
become increasingly mixed in terms of income and ethnicity. But, for
the most part, these parks are used much as they were over one hundred years ago. The mixture of families and loners, young and old,
strollers and revelers seems about the same. Children are still especially welcomed. The parks also look much as they did in the nineteenth century: they are soft, absorbent, and green in contrast to the
paved, walled, hard surfaces of the city. They are primarily pedestrian
zones, offering relief from the vehicle-clogged congestion of surround-

Sunday in Chapultepec Park, Mexico City. (Photograph by the author, 2002)

ing city streets. Canopies of trees, curving paths, fountains, and lakes all serve to encourage a different pace, a Sunday pace even on weekdays. Parks are still places dedicated to leisure; they are social spaces and serve as an antidote to the workaday world. Representing "nature" in the heart of the city, the public park still represents the *other* landscape by which the modern city defines itself.

Public parks continue to symbolize certain principles much as they did in the nineteenth century. Important among these is the principle of equity, the most common definition of which is justice according to natural law or right; specifically, freedom from bias or favoritism. This meaning of equity is rooted in the eighteenth-century Age of Enlightenment, with its emphasis on the natural rights possessed by individuals. The public park, as a civic institution, is grounded in the concept of natural law, which guarantees certain basic or universal rights across the social spectrum, rights that transcend political, social, or economic status. Public parks embody the natural right to the pursuit of happiness. People from all walks of life enjoying themselves in a public park on a Sunday afternoon are exercising this right. It is sobering to think about people living in cities without access to this particular method of pursuing happiness: without leisure time and without places like parks where they can spend it.

Yet leisure has always been strongly linked to social status, and what one does in one's leisure time has long been a distinguishing mark of social identity. Writing at the end of the nineteenth century, Thorstein Veblen argued that leisure, more than work, was the distinguishing mark of social class in the United States, noting that, from ancient times, "the rule holds with but slight exception that, whether warriors or priests, the upper classes are exempt from industrial employments, and this exemption is the economic expression of their superior rank."[1] During the nineteenth century, more and more people gained access to leisure. Labor movements fought for laws limiting the length of the workday and the work week. The middle class prospered and developed new ways of using the increased leisure time that accompanied their new prosperity. The public park, conceived in the nineteenth century as an institution dedicated to this new leisure, embodied the nineteenth century's conflicting notions about leisure. On the one hand, the public park was a product of the Enlightenment idea that leisure is essential to happiness and that all individuals, regardless of their social status, should have equitable access to leisure and suitable places to enjoy it. On the other hand, the public park was a public stage for the pursuit of leisure as a mark of social distinction. This conflict, so central to the idea of public parks, remains largely unacknowledged, perhaps because, as Peter Borsay notes in *A History of Leisure*, "leisure is both real and unreal, trivial and serious, and we continue to believe that it is irrelevant at the same time as behaving in a manner which suggests the opposite. . . . It is this ambivalence which makes leisure such a powerful, irreplaceable, and unique aspect of the human makeup."[2]

As parks have become widely established around the world, the origin of the word "park" has been largely forgotten. But in the nineteenth century it was still a word associated with the leisure pursuits of the very privileged, with the aristocracy and owners of large property; a landscape originally designed for riding, hunting, and other time-honored amusements enjoyed by the upper classes. Only as industrial capitalism began to radically change the structure of society in cities around the world in the late eighteenth century did parks

Bicycling in the Park

The Bicycle Path from Prospect Park, Brooklyn, to Coney Island. Illustration by Joseph M. Gleeson, 1896. (Picture Collection, The Branch Libraries, The New York Public Library; Astor, Lenox and Tilden Foundations)

I have taken a slow spin through the Park, enjoying on every side of me the beauties of the earliest dawn of spring. . . . I find there are really very few persons with whom I care to wheel. My theory of the pleasure

became places of leisure for the bourgeoisie, and only in the late nineteenth century did the term "park" come to signify a place available to a broader public that included the emerging middle and working classes. Through all these iterations, parks offered a stage for enacting changing social identities through leisure, albeit with a social script that allowed only so much room for improvisation.

As we have seen, both autocratic and democratic governments created parks ostensibly for public leisure and enjoyment in the nineteenth century, but parks served somewhat different agendas and different publics in the various political and social contexts of Paris, Mexico, and New York. In Paris, the parks lent weight to Napoleon

seems so different from the one which usually obtains. I am a Nature-lover who has always sat at her feet—the wheel is merely a delightful means of getting there. I rode the other day with friends that have an entirely different theory of wheeling (incidentally they have a different theory of life in general). To them the wheel is an end in itself; its charm lies solely in swift riding. To them the Boulevard is the acme of delight because it is asphalted—never mind the ugly stores, never mind the tinkling car bells, never mind the rattling grocers' carts—the road is level and smooth, and that is all one should demand of any road. There is, of course, an elation in swift riding, yet it is always to me completely subjugated by the beauty of the surrounding country. I choose the Riverside Drive, with its superb scenery, every time to the uninteresting Boulevard. I am greedy of every inch of the Drive; I do not turn out to escape a single hill. I crawl down slowly that I may not lose one instant of the sweeping tableau before me. These same friends dislike the Park for its hills. Also, they find the Park bores them because it is always the same. Ye gods! Always the same. I could ride there for a thousand years and each day discover new beauty. To me it is never twice the same.

(FROM ANNIE N. MEYER, MY PARK BOOK)

III's effort to characterize the Second Empire as the "peoples' empire." Spaced equitably over the political and social map of the city, they symbolized *égalité*, that elusive goal of the French Revolution. By the time of the coup of 1851, this goal meant different things to different segments of the political spectrum in France. But for much of the working class, as David Harvey has noted, *égalité* meant at least being "treated as human beings . . . on the same footing as the bourgeoisie." The parks created in Paris during the Second Empire were calculated to demonstrate *égalité* in this sense, providing bourgeois amenities in working-class neighborhoods, and, at the same time, serving the government's need to cultivate its political base.[3] However, while the parks did provide jobs for laborers that flocked to the capital, they also raised the value of surrounding properties and created lucrative ground for bourgeois real-estate speculation. Shady real-estate deals helped to balance a city budget stretched to the limit by the ambitious remodel of Paris undertaken by Napoleon III's government. Defended by Haussmann as symbolic of the emperor's concern for the public good, the parks received their share of criticism during the Second Empire because they were identified with an authoritarian political regime, reflective of bourgeois taste and mores, and surrounded by rumors of corruption and political favoritism.

In Mexico, Chapultepec Park served mainly as a symbol of the Porfiriato's desire to compete in the international marketplace. The transformation of Chapultepec into a modern, urban park symbolized that regime's vision of modernity, which focused primarily on the development of a powerful business and industrial sector that could hold its own internationally among other modern industrial nations. As in Paris, nationalism, politics, and real-estate speculation shaped this park in Mexico City. José Limantour envisioned the park as a means to demonstrate Mexico's sophistication and urbanity to the world and developed it as the centerpiece of a fashionable new residential district designed to entice foreign investors to take up residence in Mexico City. Located on the extreme western limits of the city, Chapultepec Park became a European-style pleasure ground, used primarily by upper-class residents of the city who lived in nearby neighborhoods. The transformation of Chapultepec was emblematic of the ideology of Porfirio Díaz's regime—Eurocentrism, modernism, positivism—yet it was also representative of the problems of the regime: elitism, conspicuous consumption, and a focus on appearances rather than substantive social change. Chapultepec did not do much to address equity issues within Mexico City itself, although the regime's attempt to provide a "workers' park" in the poor barrio of Balbuena indicates that the Porfiriato recognized the social inequities that existed in Mexico City in the nineteenth century.

The social agenda embedded in Central Park reflected the complex social and political context of New York City in the nineteenth century, which differed significantly from Paris and Mexico City. Central Park was overtly intended as a means to redress social inequities. Proponents of this park believed that long hours of work and degrading working and living conditions in New York inhibited the pursuit of happiness for many residents. Olmsted and Vaux designed Central Park as an antidote to the stress and despondency of modern urban life, as "the greatest possible contrast with the restraining and confining conditions of the town, those conditions which compel us to walk circumspectly, watchfully, jealously, which compel us to look closely upon others without sympathy."[4] As the increasing industrialism of the United States in the nineteenth century forced labor from farms to factories, the working classes were increasingly separated from the experience of nature. Olmsted noted that this exacerbated certain inequities that had not been so significant in rural communities. While the upper classes could still escape from the city to enjoy natural scenery, the lower classes did not possess the means to do so; they were, in effect, trapped in the urban environment. Olmsted emphasized that the appreciation of nature should not be restricted to heads of government and the wealthy classes, that it should not be "a monopoly, in a very peculiar manner, of a very few, very rich people."[5]

But Central Park was not purely the product of an altruistic desire to redress social inequity. It was also a covert means of social control in a volatile democracy, an attempt to rein in certain social tendencies and behaviors in the lower classes and immigrants, as well as among the *nouveaux riches*, whose conspicuous consumption and rough manners were anathema to the genteel, intellectual reformers who created Central Park. The new park was a means to manage social changes that were alarming to Olmsted and other members of his social group, a self-identified elite composed of men of means and education who shared a certain vision of civic life and a civil society. In a period during and after the Civil War when social life was far from stable in the United States, when democratic ideals and national sovereignty were being severely tested; and when the franchise was being expanded, Olmsted believed that it was the duty of members of this "new aristocracy" to cultivate a level of "civilization" in the masses, thereby strengthening the whole political system. Olmsted and others in the parks movement believed in the power of parks to elevate the lower classes. Their goal was to "divert men from unwholesome,

Homeless in the Park

Homeless refugees tenting in Golden Gate Park after the earthquake, 1906. Half of stereographic view. (Courtesy of Library of Congress)

Next to viewing the many square miles of ruins that once made San Francisco a city, no better realization of the ruin can be gained than from the refugee camps located in the districts which were untouched by the flames. Golden Gate park was the mecca of the destitute. This immense playground of the municipality was converted into a vast mushroom city that bore striking resemblance to the fleeting towns located on the border of a government reservation about to be opened to public settlement.

The common destitution and suffering wiped out all social, financial and racial distinctions. The man who before the fire had been a prosperous merchant occupied with his family a little plot of ground that

vicious, and destructive methods and habits of seeking recreation."[6] Fear of social disorder was a factor; as Charles Eliot, one of Olmsted's colleagues, put it:

> The tremendous competition for opportunity to work breeds that discontent, and anger, and despair, which lead to anarchy, and feeds the fires of that volcano under the city which the alarmists tell us is soon to break forth. Even if the volcano does not belch forth, civilization is not safe so long as any large part of the population is morally or physically degraded; and if such degradation is increasing in our great towns (and who is to say it is not?), it is plainly the duty and the interest of all who love their country to do what they can to check the drift.[7]

MELODRAMATIC LANDSCAPES

adjoined the open-air home of a laborer. The white man of California forgot his antipathy to the Asiatic race and maintained friendly relations with his new Chinese and Japanese neighbors.

The society belle of the night before the fire, a butterfly of fashion at the grand opera performance, assisted some factory girl in the preparation of humble daily meals. Money had little value. The family who had foresight to lay in the largest stock of foodstuffs on the first day of the disaster was rated highest in the scale of wealth.

A few of the families who could secure willing expressmen possessed cooking stoves, but over 95 per cent of the refugees had to do their cooking on little camp fires made of brick or stone. Kitchen utensils that a week before would have been regarded with contempt were articles of high value.

. . . The grass was their bed and their daily clothing their only protection against the penetrating fog of the ocean or the chilling dew of the morning.

(From Samuel Fallows's introduction to Richard Linthicum, *Complete Story of the San Francisco Horror, by the Survivors and Rescuers*)

The reform agenda embedded in Central Park included a good measure of social conservatism, paternalism, and elitism, and was fueled by an undercurrent of social anxiety. Central Park was an ambitious staging of an ideal of civil society; a production scripted in the language of bourgeois decorum; an attempt to influence society through leisure and entertainment.

Like melodramas in the theater, which were also modified for different audiences, large urban parks were adapted to different political systems and different social contexts and served as vehicles for various social agendas. They often highlighted social problems and economic discrepancies, but mainly they offered diversion and glossed over these issues, much like a good laugh in the theater. As places dedicated to leisure, they could not redress deep social inequities in the workplace, differences in income, substandard housing, the political structure, or structural problems of existing social institutions like schools, hospitals, and prisons. Parks were designed like exquisite theater sets in nineteenth-century cities. Brilliantly and artfully staged representations of the country in the city, they were a spectacle of the melodramatic imagination. Their effectiveness lay in their ability to entertain and make people feel better. They offered nineteenth-century societies a public stage on which to enact the rituals of social identity and social interaction in a rapidly changing urban environment.

We should not forget that the term "equity" has another meaning: it signifies monetary value; specifically, the economic value of a property or of an interest in a property. In the nineteenth century, public parks also represented considerable equity of this kind. The idea of public parks took hold around the world, not only because parks served certain political agendas and represented certain ideals of social justice, but also, in large part, because of real-estate speculators, who began to view parks as urban amenities that could boost property values. As public parks proliferated in cities around the world, they were linked to a wave of real-estate speculation that was international in scope. The public park, as a new public institution, received vital support in the nineteenth century from a powerful and influential bourgeoisie, with increasing international ties, who recognized the potential equity of public parks, not only in terms of political and social capital, but also in economic terms. The members of this class were educated, well-traveled, interconnected, and politically influential. They advocated public parks at least in part because they believed that a park could improve the image of a city, and therefore make it more attractive to new business investors and their families. These citizens supported public parks around the world, under various political systems, with varying degrees of risk and varying amounts of altruism, but often with an eye toward the economic value of property. Many realized direct returns on their investments in the form of rising real-estate equity or other financial gains directly linked to public parks.

Recently, at the end of the twentieth century, the business community has begun to reinvest in these large, old parks, socially, economically, and symbolically. A highly visible example of this renewed interest in parks is the Central Park Conservancy in New York, a non-profit, nongovernmental organization backed by a broad consortium of powerful business interests, which has raised more than $300 million from "individuals, corporations and foundations" since its founding in 1980 and has used those funds to completely renovate the park. The Conservancy now manages the entire park under a contract with the city's Department of Parks and Recreation. The organization's official mission is "to restore, manage, and preserve Central Park, in partnership with the public, for the enjoyment of present and future generations." The Conservancy not only provides "85% of Central Park's annual $25 million annual operating budget," but has responsibility for maintaining the park. Its maintenance crews "aerate and seed lawns; rake leaves; prune and fertilize trees; plant shrubs and flowers; maintain ballfields and playgrounds; remove graffiti; conserve monuments, bridges, and buildings; and care for waterbodies and woodlands, controlling erosion, maintaining the drainage system, and protecting over 150 acres of lakes and streams from pollution, siltation, and algae."[8]

The Central Park Conservancy, as its name suggests, generally takes a reverential view of the park, respecting the nineteenth-century blueprint and perpetuating the nineteenth-century aesthetic that it represents. Like the movement to create the park in the first place, the movement to renovate and conserve Central Park is both public-spirited and calculating. The spruced-up park enhances quality of life for New Yorkers generally. It also boosts real-estate values, the benefits of which are not so equitable. The park offers a powerful symbol of civic pride and makes the city more attractive and more desirable as a place to live, work, and invest. The nonprofit management of the park relieves the overburdened city government, which was obviously unable to maintain the park adequately. Yet the new system changes the nature of public park administration and oversight. A nongovernmental entity now determines how the park is managed, sets priorities, decides which uses are appropriate and whose interests come first. The Central Park Conservancy has made a careful study of Olmsted and Vaux's plans and of Olmsted's eloquent and voluminous writing about how such large urban parks should be designed and managed. Under its direction, Olmsted's exceptional vision has received the kind of recognition and respect in New York that he always felt eluded him in the nineteenth century; his work is now considered sacrosanct and enjoys a protected status above the fray of transient city politics.

It is fair to say that these days Central Park, as managed by the Central Park Conservancy, is a fundamentally conservative, solidly bourgeois institution. It preserves a certain status quo, represents traditional values and customs, resists change, and generally looks backward with nostalgia. Such parks have entered into the pantheon of Western culture and will no doubt be long preserved as cultural icons. As such, these parks do not attract much cultural criticism. Yet, occasionally, something happens to shake up the complacency with which we view them. A recent event in Central Park focused a bright spotlight on this particular park, leaving some witnesses blinking in the unaccustomed glare.

Coda: The Gates

For a two-week period in February 2005, an unusual spectacle provided diversion from the normal winter doldrums in Central Park. The environmental artists Christo and Jeanne-Claude installed a monumental work of art, called *The Gates*, in the park. The artwork consisted of 7,500 brilliant orange gateways, each supporting a curtain of pleated saffron-colored fabric, spaced at about twelve-foot intervals, spanning nearly every path and roadway in the park. The effect was like a giant, networked arbor, snaking along the extensive circulation system that is the structural framework of the park. It was, by most accounts, a beautiful sight. On days when the weather was warm and sunny, it looked as if a swarm of golden-orange butterflies had landed in the park. Against new snow the orange stood out like fire: fire and ice! Each gate framed a slightly different view of the park. From every vantage point, undulating lines of orange were visible in the distance, outlining the topography of hills and valleys and adding depth to what would ordinarily be a flat, gray, leafless vista at that time of year.

It took twenty-six years for the artists to gain approval for *The Gates* in Central Park. They first proposed the project in 1979, and, after lengthy review and discussion of the proposal, the city refused

The Gates, Christo and Jeanne-Claude, Central Park, New York, February 2005. Art installation. (Photograph by the author)

permission in 1981. A 107-page report, issued by the city at that time, gave many reasons for the denial of a permit; these had to do with fears about damage to the park; with the hazard the installation would pose to plants, animals, and people in the park; with crowd control and vandalism. But the overriding reason given was that the gates just were not seen as an appropriate addition to the park, for however brief a time. The project was too large in scope, too invasive, too flashy—just too much. Most worrisome was the precedent it would set; city officials envisioned a rash of proposals for even more invasive projects in the park in the future. The artists persisted, however, and in 2003 they did receive a permit to construct the project. The permit was governed by a forty-three-page contract between the artists and the City of New York, spelling out every detail of concern to the authorities. Having learned much during lengthy discussions with the parks department in the early 1980s, the artists scaled down the project from the fifteen thousand gates originally proposed, and went to extraordinary lengths to make sure that the installation left no lasting marks on the park. The gates were spaced so as not to interfere with any tree limbs. Two cast-iron bases, resting on existing pavement, anchored each gate, eliminating any need to drill holes or dig foundations. The installation was designed to be as light on the land as possible. As with all of the artists' projects, all materials used in the gates were recycled afterward. To avoid ground contamination by chipping paint, the gates were constructed of vinyl, extruded in the orange color. The contract with the city stipulated that the artists would hire staff to pick up any litter and remove all trash, to maintain the usual appearance of the park while the gates were being constructed, for the duration of the installation, and during the dismantling of the project. The contract also stipulated that trucks and other vehicles involved in the installation would stay on hard surfaces at all times and that uniformed monitors would be on hand to discourage any inappropriate behavior by park visitors. The park police provided a security patrol, including twenty officers on horseback and forty-three on scooter patrol, but the artists reimbursed the city for all costs associated with extra security needed for the project and hired thirty-six private security guards to provide around-the-clock surveillance.

The citizens of New York City embraced *The Gates*. Society hostesses planned parties to take advantage of apartments overlooking the park, installing orange decor and selecting menus dominated by saffron. Museums invited knowledgeable art critics and art curators to speak about *The Gates*. Numerous corporate parties, in rented spaces with views of the park, added to the buzz.[9] Stores installed special window displays in tribute to *The Gates*, mostly on the theme of orange. Posters and books about *The Gates* were for sale everywhere. Hermès designed a special Gates scarf and displayed it in their store window on Madison Avenue. DaimlerChrysler donated a $300,000 automobile, a Maybach, to chauffeur the artists around during the installation.

As is their normal practice, Christo and Jeanne-Claude accepted no funding for the artwork from external sources, no sponsorships or donations. They financed the entire project themselves through "sale of preparatory studies, drawings, collages and scale models, earlier works of the fifties and sixties, and original lithographs on other subjects."[10] The artists did authorize, and design, a lot of merchandise, including hats, T-shirts, coffee mugs, postcards, etc. All proceeds from the sale of merchandise went to a charitable foundation established for this purpose, called Nurture New York's Nature and the Arts, and to the Central Park Conservancy. Six hundred workers, organized in teams, installed the gates, erecting approximately one hundred gates per team over the course of a single week. An additional three hundred workers monitored the gates during the two weeks that they were up and then dismantled them and removed all the materials from the park. All workers were paid for their labor and received breakfast and a hot meal at midday at the boathouse in the park.

Reviews of *The Gates* were typically positive, but also somewhat puzzled. Headlines in the *New York Times* reflected the generally noncritical reaction: "In a Saffron Ribbon, a Billowy Gift to the City"; "Dressing the Park in Orange, and Pleats."[11] For the most part, critics were disarmed. Many remarked that the park felt festive, like the scene of a giant party, a parade, or a fireworks display. The *New Yorker* reviewer admitted that, in the face of *The Gates*, "the voluble disaffection of the art critic, me, collapsed, to the relief of my companions." He proclaimed *The Gates* "a populist affront to the authority of art critics." Unable to "think of any other occasion on which he had witnessed so many New Yorkers moving slowly when they didn't have to," he noted that "the crowd's many-voiced sound had an indoor intimacy, like the bright murmur in a theatre, during intermission, when the play is good and everybody knows that everybody knows it."[12] A few critics felt that *The Gates* was too easy to like, and tried to tease out some deeper meaning. For example, Blake Gopnik wrote in the *Washington Post:* "Overall, the event reminded me of a festive parade of flags, such as towns put on to mark important civic holidays. Or of a tall ships' day, or a kite festival, or some newfangled kind of daytime fireworks display. Or, best of all, it reminded me of how nice it feels at Christmastime when lighted garlands stretch out across downtown streets. What it didn't remind me of, much, is the kind of puzzling, complex, probing experience we're supposed to get from significant art." He compared *The Gates* to other works by Christo and Jeanne-Claude, and found the Central Park project wanting because it was not meaningful in any deeper way. Unlike with many of the artists' other projects, such as *Running Fence*, which "seemed to talk about the fencing of the West; about the American Dream's obsession with open space; about competition between man and nature," or *Wrapped Reichstag*, which commented meaningfully on the demise of the Berlin Wall and all it symbolized, Gopnik was not "able to find any similar leverage that the gates might have on the site or times they inhabit." He concluded that "overall, 'The Gates: Central Park' is so clearly about lighthearted civic celebration that . . . it's quite a stretch to give it topicality in our troubled times."[13]

The artists themselves claimed that *The Gates* had no purpose, that they themselves had no ulterior motive, that the project was "only a work of art" and the goal was to create "joy and beauty." They refused to discuss the meaning of the installation or to engage in debates about its social, cultural, or political significance. The press release for the project stated that, "as all true artists do, they created their art for themselves, if other people like it, it is only a bonus."[14] They stuck firmly to this line through numerous interviews and public events surrounding the installation. They did release many impressive statistics about the project: the total cost was $21 million; the gates covered twenty-three miles; all of the gates were sixteen feet tall; widths varied from five feet, six inches to eighteen feet; the fifteen thousand steel bases weighed from 613 to 837 pounds; the extruded vinyl poles would span sixty miles if laid end to end; the project used 1,092,200 square feet of ripstop fabric and 116,389 miles of nylon thread, and so on.

Critics like Blake Gopnik who found *The Gates* unsatisfying as a work of art didn't see much point in adding to the park. As Gopnik put it: "I can't see any lack that the gates fill in Central Park. They just turn up the volume a bit."[15] But what does it mean to "turn up the volume" in Central Park? Could *The Gates* be understood as a parody? A good parody usually involves a slight distortion, a clever twist, a subtle send-up of the target. Viewed as parody, *The Gates* offers some interesting commentary on the park. The artists did celebrate the park as a beautiful object, but they also spoofed it just a little bit.

Christo and Jeanne-Claude clearly studied the history of the park. The official bulletin about *The Gates* posted on the artists' Web page refers to the original proposal by Olmsted and Vaux to install heavy metal gates at all entrances to the park, so that the park could be locked up at night. As it turned out, Olmsted and Vaux did not like Richard Morris Hunt's design for these gates, and eventually the whole idea of locking up the park was abandoned. But many of the names selected for the gates remain in use today: Mariners' Gate, Boys' and Girls' Gate, Artists' Gate, Emigrants' Gate, Explorers' Gate, Inventors' Gate. These names have the effect of selecting certain broadly drawn segments of the population for recognition, while ignoring others. And, in fact, a gate, wherever installed, is a device for selecting or controlling who may enter a place. Installing 7,500 gates in Central Park can be understood, on the one hand, as just turning up the volume on the openness of the park, its lack of selectivity, its accessibility. But, on the other hand, perhaps those many gates represent all of the invisible, symbolic gateways through which each of us enters the park; that is, all of the memories, codes, restrictions, and associations that govern our interactions with the park. Framing the park over and over, the gates represent the many layers of meaning through which we view and experience the park, as a figment of collective imagination and collective memory, and as a landscape to which each of us brings our own set of frames. Although the project was called *The Gates*, the individual structures weren't much like traditional gates, but more like tall, curtained doorways. Many people commented on the orange fabric hanging from each gate, likening it to sails, pleated skirts, or kites. Could it be that the fabric parodied the curtains over our collective eyes, shielding the park from us, obscuring our understanding of the park, causing us to take it at face value, as just a bit of pasture in the city, and leave it at that?

The labor of constructing, maintaining, and dismantling *The Gates* was also a parody of sorts. As discussed earlier, the landscape of nineteenth-century parks has always been depicted as devoid of labor. Parks are first and foremost landscapes of leisure. The original idea, which still holds sway today, was to create places that looked natural, as though no labor were involved in their creation or maintenance. In the case of *The Gates*, the labor employed to erect the park was, in fact, leisure. The work of erecting the gates was a form of recreation for the six hundred people who signed up to help. Most were art lovers and admirers of the artists' work who would have gladly worked without compensation, but the artists insisted on paying these "volunteers." This had something to do with the ability to get insurance for the project, but, on another level, was also symbolic. The gates were imag-

Fairmount Park, Philadelphia

Fairmount Park, Philadelphia. Scribner's Monthly, January 1871.

At the town end the water works are well worthy of a visit. . . . When I first saw it I thought how fortunate the Philadelphians as to their water supply. But I drive through their beautiful Park, and along the bank of their broad River, and what do I see on the high ground above me? Is it

inatively constructed by workers who were not really working; they were taking time off from work. They were actually playing, on vacation, spending their leisure time as they pleased.

As most reviewers noted, the overwhelming impression of *The Gates* was that of a grand spectacle. The scale of the project was spectacular, reaching into every nook and cranny of the park, involving mind-boggling amounts of material, coordination, engineering, etc.

possible, or is it a ghastly dream? I see white marble tombstones in thick array. It is their great Laurel Hill Cemetery, with its adjuncts, covering 130 acres of ground, 110 feet above the river which supplies their town with water, the graves I should judge within little more than 50 yards of the water's edge. And this Cemetery receives a large proportion of the dead of 800,000 people. Rain falls on it: where does it soak to? and where does it afterwards drain to? The thought is too hideous to pursue; but if I were a Philadelphian, I should look askance at my iced water, and my tea would lose its charms. . . .

I am sorry to pick a hole in such pretty combinations as the Park, the Cemetery, and the Water Works, but "honesty obliges." I passed hundreds of light trotting carriages today full of happy Cits, with their wives and children, dashing all unconsciously along the well kept roads. I saw thousands walking and sunning themselves in the trim gardens and by the pretty fountains. What if the destroying angel, in the shape of typhoid and cholera, or other plague, now clearly shown to be transmissible by infected water supplies, struck these happy people through their grave-yard and their river, and the thought had occurred to me, and I had not spoken it out!! Good-bye Philadelphia: no more iced water for me within your borders.

(From H. Hussey Vivian, *Notes on a Tour in America from August 7th to November 17, 1877*)

The orange color was as vivid, striking, and startling as possible. The hype was also appropriately spectacular, involving years of anticipation and a mounting tempo as the date approached. As a dramatic gesture, the fabric, rolled cocoonlike on the crossbar at the top of each gate, was unfurled on the first day in a carefully choreographed manner throughout the park.

Some witnesses were disappointed by the spectacle; to them the whole affair seemed like a giant, pointless, bourgeois extravaganza. Bland. Meaningless. Christo and Jeanne-Claude, chauffeured around the park in an expensive car on loan for the duration of the installation by DaimlerChrysler, seemed to heighten the parody of bourgeois respectability. The endless discussions of the amounts of money involved, from the $21 million supposedly expended on the project by the artists, to the huge revenues that the project brought to the city in tourist dollars, also parodied bourgeois values. Certainly this aspect of the spectacle was not lost on a homeless man pushing his loaded shopping cart through the park during the installation of the gates, who shouted at the workers that the money expended on *The Gates* was "wasted" and would have been better spent on food and shelter for people in need.[16]

In another parody, those who loved *The Gates* spoke of the work in terms that recalled the heightened emotions of nineteenth-century melodrama. Many emphasized the sensuality of the experience and remarked on the way the installation sharpened their appreciation of the beauties of the park. Sentimental expressions of love for the park abounded. Many pointed out how the installation brought people together, softening even hardened New Yorkers and causing everyone to slow down and simply soak up the splendor of the place. *The Gates* were all sunshine, no shadow. The worst sentiment expressed in response to the project was: so what?

The project also highlighted how conservatively the park has been managed for the past twenty-six years, since the Central Park Conservancy took charge. It took Christo and Jeanne-Claude longer to obtain permission to install *The Gates* in Central Park than it took to obtain permission to wrap the Reichstag or install the *Umbrellas* simultaneously in Japan and California, or any of their other projects to date. For them, since the whole process of obtaining permission is part of the artwork, *The Gates* project started in 1979, a year before the Conservancy was officially founded. This extended process adds a layer of meaning to *The Gates*, highlighting the sanctity of the park and, perhaps, through gentle parody, questioning that sanctity.

The Gates project is a fitting coda to this discussion of nineteenth-century urban parks, the point of which is also to probe the sanctity of these parks, although not through parody, but by understanding their origins and revealing some of the meanings embedded in these cherished oases in the midst of modern cities. These meanings have been obscured by nearly two centuries of habit and imitation. It is important, once in a while, to brush off the layers of historic dust that have accumulated on these parks, obscuring the social, political, and ethical issues that once attached to them. Doing so not only reminds us of the historic period that produced them, but also stimulates us to reconsider the values that public parks embody and perpetuate in cities today.

Notes

Introduction

1. Choay, *Modern City;* Olsen, *City as a Work of Art.*
2. Bender, *Towards an Urban Vision;* Schuyler, *New Urban Landscape;* Rosen-zweig and Blackmar, *Park and the People;* Homberger, *Scenes from the Life of a City.*
3. Tate, *Great City Parks.*
4. Barthes, *Mythologies,* 11.
5. Williams, *Country and the City,* 289.
6. Barthes, *Mythologies,* 109–58.
7. See Barrell, *Idea of Landscape;* Hunt, *Garden and Grove;* Hunt and Willis, *Genius of the Place;* and Thacker, *History of Gardens.*
8. Clarke, *Stowe Landscape Gardens,* 4.
9. Bermingham, *Landscape and Ideology,* 14; Copley and Garside, *Politics of the Picturesque.*
10. Lasdun, *English Park,* 104; see also Austen, *Mansfield Park,* 149–50, 173–74.
11. Thurston, *Royal Parks;* Conway, *People's Parks;* Lasdun, *English Park;* Gi-rouard, *Cities & People;* Green, *Spectacle of Nature.*
12. Cranz, *Politics of Park Design.*
13. Clary, *Making of Golden Gate Park,* 2.

14. Calhoun, *Habermas and the Public Sphere*, particularly the essays by Mary Ryan (259–88) and Geoff Eley (289–339).

15. Brooks, *Melodramatic Imagination*, xiii.

16. Blodgett, "Olmsted: Landscape Architecture as Conservative Reform"; Fein, *Olmsted and the American Environmental Tradition;* Foglesong, *Planning the Capitalist City.*

17. Halttunen, *Confidence Men and Painted Women*, 186.

18. Bank, *Theatre Culture in America*, 110, 122.

1   Parks in Paris during the Second Empire

1. Invoking Zola's insights, I share Arnold Hauser's reading: "Zola's literary theories are not entirely free of charlatanism, but his novels have, nevertheless, a certain theoretical value, for, even if they do not contain any new scientific insights, they are, as has rightly been said, the creations of a considerable sociologist" (*Social History of Art*, 4:87).

2. Zola, *La curée* (*The Kill*), 42; *Les Rougon-Macquart: Histoire naturelle et social d'une famille sous le second empire* (Natural and Social History of a Family under the Second Empire). Translations from the French, unless otherwise indicated, are by the author.

3. Achard, "Bois de Boulogne," 1242; de Corval, *Guide dans Paris*, 144–46; Delvau, *Plaisirs de Paris*, 32–33.

4. Texier, *Paris, capitale du monde*, 1.

5. Haussmann, *Mémoires*, 3:172.

6. Jeanne Gaillard refers to Haussmann's *Mémoires* as "misleading but indispensable" in her bibliography: *Paris, la ville*, 660.

7. See the chapter "View From Notre-Dame" in Clarks's *Painting of Modern Life*, 23–78; see also Gaillard, *Paris, la ville*, esp. 559–72.

8. Pinkney, *Rebuilding of Paris*, 25.

9. Ibid., 45–48; Le Dantec and Le Dantec, *Reading the French Garden*, 176–84, 190–92.

10. Pinkney, *Rebuilding of Paris*, 7–19.

11. Haussmann describes his own difficulties in getting around Paris during his student days, in his *Mémoires*, 3:535–36.

12. Texier, *Tableau de Paris*, 65.

13. Zola, *L'Assommoir.*

14. Girard, *Deuxième République*, 145–46.

15. Pinkney, *Rebuilding of Paris*, 93.

16. Des Cars and Pinon, *Paris-Haussmann*, 77.

17. Clark, *Painting of Modern Life*, 45.

18. See Lavedan, *Histoire de l'urbanisme*, 482.

19. Pinkney, *Rebuilding of Paris*, 5.

20. Zola, *L'Assommoir*, 367.

21. For a summary of the opposition to the rebuilding process, see Clark, *Painting of Modern Life*, 23–78; and Herbert, *Impressionism*, 1–7.

22. Some historians have emphasized strategic military considerations as a motivation for the rebuilding of Paris. Haussmann himself mentioned strategic considerations (Clark, *Painting of Modern Life*, 39). Pinkney was skeptical of the importance of such motives in the overall planning process (*Rebuilding of Paris*, 35–38). For further discussion of this issue, see also Gaillard, *Paris, la ville*, 567–72; and Sutcliffe, *Autumn of Central Paris*, 27–33.

23. Pinkney, *Rebuilding of Paris*, 44.

24. Edmond de Goncourt, *Journal: Mémoires de la vie littéraire*, trans. Clark, *Painting of Modern Life*, 35. Clark also includes the original French text.

25. Gautier, "Mosaïque de ruines," 43; Baudelaire, "Le cygne," trans. Keith Waldrop, "The Swan," 115–16.

26. Zola, *La curée*, 90.

27. Malet, *Haussmann et la rénovation de Paris*, 338.

28. Marx, *Eighteenth Brumaire of Louis Bonaparte*, translated and reprinted in *Basic Writings on Politics*, 345–46.

29. Herbert, *Impressionism*, 141.

30. For a summary of the shifting opposition, see Elwitt's introduction to *Making of the Third Republic*, 1–18.

31. Girard, *Deuxième République*, 175.

32. Alphand, *Promenades de Paris*, lix. Page citations are to the 1984 reprint edition.

33. Rosen, *History of Public Health*, 189–90.

34. Ibid., 263–66.

35. Sutcliffe, *Autumn of Central Paris*, 27–30.

36. Green, *Spectacle of Nature*, 66; emphasis in original.

37. Ibid., 74.

38. Haussmann, *Mémoires*, 3:210.

39. See map of barricades thrown up during that uprising, showing heavy concentration of activity in the eastern districts of Paris, in Girard, *Deuxième République*, 36–37.

40. Elwitt, *Making of the Third Republic*, 8.

41. Pinkney, *Rebuilding of Paris*, 94–95.

42. Conway, *People's Parks*, 41–42.

43. Haussmann, *Mémoires*, 3:211.

44. Galignani, *New Paris Guide*, 586.

45. Delvau, *Plaisirs de Paris*, 35.

46. Ibid., 36.

47. Girard, *Deuxième République*, 235.

48. In reporting the cost of the Bois de Boulogne, Alphand deducted 8,779,365 francs (an amount realized from sale of property) from the total cost of

14,352,004 francs incurred in renovating and enlarging the park (*Promenades de Paris*, 6). In the case of the Bois de Vincennes, Alphand reported a cost of 23,742,740 francs, from which he deducted an expected 12 million francs to be realized from resale of property (172).

49. Ibid., 6, 171–72.

50. Haussmann, *Mémoires*, 3:212.

51. Alphand, *Promenades de Paris*, 194.

52. Haussmann, *Mémoires*, 3:233.

53. The story of this arrangement is recounted by Malet, in *Baron Haussmann et la rénovation*, 191–93.

54. The Péreire brothers, who became enormously rich in real estate and then went bankrupt in 1867, were a model for Zola's main character, the *nouveau riche* speculator Aristide Saccard, in *La curée* (374 n. 27).

55. Walter, "Parc de Monsieur Zola," 18.

56. Delvau, *Plaisirs de Paris*, 45.

57. As a young man in 1868, Zola himself lived not far from Park Monceau, in Batignolles. When Zola wrote *La curée*, in 1870, the zone along the park was not completely built up. Number 63 rue de la Monceau, the Hotel Violet, was built in 1864 and may have been a model for Saccard's hotel in the novel. It was demolished in 1910 (Walter, "Parc de Monsieur Zola").

58. Haussmann, *Mémoires*, 3:233.

59. Ibid., 234; Alphand, *Promenades de Paris*, 203.

60. Girard, *Deuxième République*, 140–48.

61. Lazare, *Quartiers de l'est de Paris*, trans. Clark, *Painting of Modern Life*, 29. Clark also includes the original French text.

62. W. Robinson, *Parks, Promenades and Gardens*, 60.

63. Clark, *Painting of Modern Life*, 29; Gaillard, *Paris, la ville*, 57–58.

64. Haussmann, *Mémoires*, 3:237.

65. This series of events is recounted by Pinkney, *Rebuilding of Paris*, 102–4.

66. Duveau, *Vie ouvrière*, 466–67.

67. Alphand includes drawings and costs for grills, ha-has, gatehouses, and superintendent cottages in *Promenades de Paris*; see, for example, 7, 65, 77, 198, and 204.

68. Herbert, *Impressionism*, 150.

69. Alphand, *Promenades de Paris*, i, xxvii, xxxiii.

70. Ibid., liii.

71. Herbert, *Impressionism*, 149.

72. Green, *Spectacle of Nature*, 95.

73. Ibid., 105, 111.

74. Pinkney, *Rebuilding of Paris*, 94; Choay, "Haussmann et le système des espaces verts," 84.

75. Herbert, *Impressionism*, 154.

76. Ann Bermingham argued that Uvedale Price's 1842 satire of the "Brownian garden" was based in anti-Jacobin fear; Price thought English landscape gardens of the *nouveaux riches* were too conspicuous at a time when social inequity was engendering popular uprising in France (*Landscape and Ideology*, 67).

77. Duveau, *Vie ouvrière*, 10.

78. Herbert, *Impressionism*, 154.

79. Alphand, *Promenades de Paris*, 203.

80. Marceca, "Reservoir, Circulation," 59; Grumbach, "Promenades of Paris," 66.

81. Robinson, *Parks, Promenades and Gardens*, 61.

82. Haussmann, *Mémoires*, 3:236.

83. Alphand, *Promenades de Paris*, 32, 33.

84. See Weibenson, "Parc Monceau et ses 'Fabriqués.'"

85. Fournel, *Paris nouveau et Paris futur*, 111.

86. Haussmann, *Mémoires*, 3:232.

87. Fournel, *Paris nouveau et Paris futur*, 123–24.

88. Delvau, *Plaisirs de Paris*, 31.

89. Gaillard, *Paris, la ville*, 572.

90. Tuckerman, *Maga Papers*, 157.

91. Herbert, *Impressionism*, 144.

92. Clark, *Painting of Modern Life*, 24.

2 Chapultepec Park and the Staging of Modern Mexico

1. Ezcurra, *De las chinampas*, 32–33. Translations from the Spanish, unless otherwise indicated, are by the author.

2. Torre, *Chapultepec*, 15.

3. M. Meyer, Sherman, and Deeds, *Course of Mexican History*, 54–56.

4. Durán, *Historia de las Indias*, 245–46; Solís Olguín, "Chapultepec," 41; Torre, *Chapultepec*, 15–29.

5. M. Meyer, Sherman, and Deeds, *Course of Mexican History*, 83–84.

6. Ibid., 83.

7. Teja Zabre, *Chapultepec: Guía*, 59.

8. Torre, *Chapultepec*, 39–40, 57–61.

9. Ibid., 64–69.

10. Ibid., 90–91; M. Meyer, Sherman, and Deeds, *Course of Mexican History*, 338.

11. M. Meyer, Sherman, and Deeds, *Course of Mexican History*, 339.

12. Sierra, *Political Evolution*, 322.

13. M. Meyer, Sherman, and Deeds, *Course of Mexican History*, 379–81.

14. Corti, *Maximilian and Charlotte*, 830.

15. Widdifield, *Embodiment of the National*, 8–9.

16. Maximilian to the Archduke Karl Ludwig, 10 July 1864, in Corti, *Maximilian and Charlotte*, 431.

17. Kollonitz, *Court of Mexico*, 187; Hyde, *Mexican Empire*, 148.

18. Kollonitz, *Court of Mexico*, 193.

19. Blasio, *Maximilian, Emperor*, 30; Torre, *Chapultepec*, 99.

20. Teja Zabre, *Chapultepec: Guía*, 125; cited in Torre, *Chapultepec*, 102.

21. Elton, *With the French in Mexico*, 37.

22. Kollonitz, *Court of Mexico*, 186–94.

23. Corti, *Maximilian and Charlotte*, 431.

24. Blasio, *Maximilian, Emperor*, 31–34.

25. Maximilian to Karl Ludwig, letter, 24 February 1865, in Corti, *Maximilian and Charlotte*, 465; Hyde, *Mexican Empire*, 172.

26. Leduc and Lara y Pardo, *Galván Almanac*, 242; quoted in Torre, *Chapultepec*, 85–86.

27. Anderson, *An American in Maximilian's Mexico*, 31.

28. Duplessis, *Aventuras Mejicanas*, quoted in Torre, *Chapultepec*, 95.

29. Elton, *With the French*, 38.

30. Torre, *Chapultepec*, 117.

31. Beezley, *Judas at the Jockey Club*, 107.

32. *El Constitucional*, 12 November 1867; *La Revista Universal*, 14 August 1868; in Díaz y de Ovando, "Visión de Chapultepec," 2–3.

33. *El Diario Oficial*, 16 August 1868; *La Opinión Nacional*, 19 August 1868; in Díaz y de Ovando, "Visión de Chapultepec," 3–4.

34. Beezley, *Judas at the Jockey Club*, 26–31, 41–52.

35. M. Meyer, Sherman, and Deeds, *Course of Mexican History*, 451.

36. Johns, *City of Mexico*, 18, 23–24.

37. See M. Meyer, Sherman, and Deeds, *Course of Mexican History*, 426, 439–49, for political analysis of the policies of the Porfiriato.

38. Beezley, *Judas at the Jockey Club*, 27.

39. Gooch, *Face to Face*, 68, 158; Johns, *City of Mexico*, 17–20, 29; M. Meyer, Sherman, and Deeds, *Course of Mexican History*, 454–59.

40. Johns, *City of Mexico*, 30.

41. Torre, *Chapultepec*, 117, 118, 131–35.

42. *El Siglo Diez y Nueve*, 7 June 1876, in Díaz y de Ovando, "Visión de Chapultepec," 4.

43. Torre, *Chapultepec*, 141; *El Lunes*, 16 May 1881, in Díaz y de Ovando, "Visión de Chapultepec," 4.

44. Rivera Cambas, *México pintoresco*, 319–20.

45. *El Nacional*, 25 March 1887, in Díaz y de Ovando, "Visión de Chapultepec," 5.

46. Riedel, *Practical Guide*, 356.

47. Díaz y de Ovando, "Visión de Chapultepec," 6.

48. Riedel, *Practical Guide*, 354–55.

49. *El Nacional*, 10 June 1897, discussed in Díaz y de Ovando, "Visión de Chapultepec," 5; Limantour correspondence in archive at Centro de Estudios de Historia de México, Condumex, Chimalistac.

50. Johns, *City of Mexico*, 27–28.

51. *El Mundo Ilustrado*, 14 October 1899, in Díaz y de Ovando, "Visión de Chapultepec," 6.

52. Torre, *Chapultepec*, 139–51; Díaz y de Ovando, "Visión de Chapultepec," 6–7; Prantl and Groso, *Ciudad de México*, 717; *Gobernación: Obras Públicas*.

53. Terry, *Terry's Mexico*, 381, 384–85.

54. Ibid., 384, 386.

55. Ibid., 390.

56. Riedel, *Practical Guide*, 354; *El Imparcial*, 2 April 1901, in Díaz y de Ovando, "Visión de Chapultepec," 6.

57. Terry, *Terry's Mexico*, 381; Vázquez, *México y sus alrededores*, 73.

58. Prantl and Groso, *Ciudad de México*, 717.

59. Gooch, *Face to Face*, 192; Terry, *Terry's Mexico*, 236; Lear, "Workers, *Vecinos* and Citizens," 104–5; Romero, "Labor and Wages in Mexico," 515–16.

60. Terry, *Terry's Mexico*, 380.

61. Lear, "Workers, *Vecinos* and Citizens," 130.

62. Prantl and Groso, *Ciudad de México*, 716.

63. Trillo, "1910 Mexico City," 76–78.

64. *El Imparcial*, 17 February 1910, in Díaz y de Ovando, "Visión de Chapultepec," 7–8.

65. *Crónica oficial de las fiestas . . . de México*, 283–84, cited in Díaz y de Ovando, "Visión de Chapultepec," 9.

66. M. Meyer, Sherman, and Deeds, *Course of Mexican History*, 479.

67. Limantour, *Apuntes*, 90.

68. Trillo, "1910 Mexico City," 86.

69. Widdifield, *Embodiment of the National*, 78–121.

70. Ibid., 59–60.

71. Ibid., 68.

72. Piolle, *José María Velasco*, 30, 114.

73. Widdifield, *Embodiment of the National*, 40.

74. Review by Ignacio Manuel Altamirano, *La Libertad*, translated and quoted in Piolle, *José María Velasco*, 275.

75. Piolle, *José María Velasco*, 61; Torre, *Chapultepec*, 83–93.

76. Johns, *City of Mexico*, 30; Lear, "Workers, *Vecinos* and Citizens," 100.

77. Trillo, "1910 Mexico City," 87; Beezley, *Judas at the Jockey Club*, 64–65.

78. Lear, "Workers, *Vecinos* and Citizens," 145; Trillo, "1910 Mexico City," 87.

79. Beezley, *Judas at the Jockey Club*, 14.

3   Central Park and the Melodramatic Imagination

1. Thackeray, *Vanity Fair*, 67.
2. Sir Roger de Coverly, quoted in Edelstein, *Vauxhall Gardens*, 11–12.
3. For the complete history of Vauxhall Gardens, London, see Southworth, *Vauxhall Gardens;* and Wroth, *London Pleasure Gardens.*
4. Orme, *Essay on Transparent Prints.*
5. Garrett, *History of Pleasure Gardens*, 298.
6. *New York Daily Advertiser*, 5 August 1805, in Garrett, *History of Pleasure Gardens*, 289–90.
7. *New York People's Friend*, 6 June 1807, in Garrett, *History of Pleasure Gardens*, 299.
8. Garrett, "History of Pleasure Gardens," 309, 335.
9. *Blunt's Stranger's Guide to . . . New York*, 136.
10. Harlow, *Old Bowery Days*, 319.
11. *New York Herald*, 24 March 1856.
12. Bobo, *Glimpses of New-York*, 166.
13. Baker, *A Glance at New York*, 30.
14. Foster, *New York by Gas-light*, 155.
15. For an analysis of the "new urban semiotic" created by urban reporters such as George Foster and Matthew Hale Smith in New York in the mid-nineteenth century, see Blumin, "Explaining the New Metropolis," 9–38.
16. *New York Herald*, 24 March 1856.
17. Mathews, *Career of Puffer Hopkins*, 35.
18. Greene, *A Glance at New York*, 216–17; quoted in Garrett, *History of Pleasure Gardens*, 390.
19. Child, *Letters from New York*, 171.
20. Winfield, *Hopoghan Hackingh*, 68; Mann, "John Stevens, Pioneer," 61–78.
21. F. Trollope, *Domestic Manners of the Americans*, 2:202.
22. Foster, *New York by Gas-light*, 54.
23. Child, *Letters from New York*, 173; Foster, *New York by Gas-light*, 53–54.
24. *New York Tribune*, 27 May 1851; *New York Herald*, 27 May 1851.
25. *New York Herald*, 25 October 1858; 27 June 1858.
26. Rosenzweig and Blackmar, *Park and the People*, 15.
27. Lasdun, *English Park*, 160–63.
28. Actual plans still exist for only three of the competition entries, but verbal descriptions of the other thirty entries are available in the New York Public Library. For a good description and analysis of the various competition entries, see Rosenzweig and Blackmar, *Park and the People*, 111–17.
29. Rosenzweig and Blackmar, *Park and the People*, 144; editorials quoted ibid., 100, 111.
30. Ibid., 144, 145.

31. Olmsted, "The Greensward Plan: 1858," in his *Creating Central Park*, 140–49.

32. Calvert Vaux to Clarence Cook, 6 June 1865, in Rosenzweig and Blackmar, *Park and the People*, 133.

33. Rosenzweig and Blackmar, *Park and the People*, 99; Downing, *Rural Essays*, 150.

34. *New York Tribune*, 27 February 1856.

35. Olmsted, *Creating Central Park*, 119.

36. Ibid.; Copley and Garside, *Politics of the Picturesque*; Bermingham, *Landscape and Ideology*; Green, *Spectacle of Nature*.

37. Quotations are from Olmsted, "Letter to Oliver Wolcott Gibbs," in his *Defending the Union*, 467.

38. Veblen, *Theory of the Leisure Class*, 84.

39. Helsinger, "Turner and the Representation of England," 105.

40. See Sax, *Mountains without Handrails*; and Runte, *Yosemite, the Embattled Wilderness*.

41. Downing, *Rural Essays*, 152.

42. Olmsted, *Slavery and the South*, 244.

43. "Central Park Misgivings," *New York Times*, 21 April 1857, 4; quoted in Homberger, *Scenes from the Life of a City*, 259.

44. Rosenzweig and Blackmar, *Park and the People*, 233.

45. Blodgett, "Olmsted: Landscape Architecture as Conservative Reform," 875, 870.

46. See, for example, Olmsted, *Olmsted, Landscape Architect, 1822–1903*, ed. Olmsted Jr. and Kimball; Rybczynski, *Clearing in the Distance*; Fein, *Olmsted and the American Environmental Tradition*; and Olmsted, *Creating Central Park*.

47. See Olmsted, "Spoils of the Park," in his *Slavery and the South*, 117–55.

48. Blodgett, "Olmsted: Landscape Architecture as Conservative Reform," 871–72, 877; Foglesong, *Planning the Capitalist City*, 106.

49. Halttunen, *Confidence Men and Painted Women*, 186; Bank, *Theatre Culture in America*, 110.

50. Brooks, *Melodramatic Imagination*; Jameson, *Political Unconscious*.

51. Marcoux, "Guilbert de Pixérécourt," 52–57; Hyslop, "Pixérécourt and the French melodrama debate," 62–70.

52. Hyslop, "Pixérécourt and the French Melodrama Debate," 73–80.

53. See McConachie, *Melodramatic Formations*.

54. For a description of the postbellum middle class, see Blumin, *Emergence of the Middle Class*, 258–97.

55. Page references to *Uncle Tom's Cabin* and *The Poor of New York* are to versions reprinted in Gerould, *American Melodrama*. Page references to *Fashion* are to the version reprinted in Mowatt, *Plays*.

56. See J. L. Smith, *Melodrama*.

57. Mowatt, *Plays*, 61; emphasis in original.

58. Olmsted, *Second Annual Report*, in his *Creating Central Park*, 212–13.

59. See Rosenzweig and Blackmar, *Park and the People*, 59–91.

60. See Birdoff, *World's Greatest Hit*; Gossett, *"Uncle Tom's Cabin" and American Culture*.

61. McConachie, "Out of the Kitchen," 5.

62. Birdoff, *World's Greatest Hit*, 50.

63. See, for example, Olmsted, *California Frontier*, 604–5.

64. See Rybczynski, *Clearing in the Distance*, 117.

65. See Olmsted, "Public Parks and the Enlargement of Towns," in his *Civilizing American Cities*, 94.

66. Ibid., 75.

67. For a discussion of the "bourgeois" design of parks in Paris, see Schenker, "Parks and Politics."

68. Foglesong, *Planning the Capitalist City*, 106.

69. *New York Herald* [before 1870], quoted in Olmsted, *Civilizing American Cities*, 94–95.

70. Olmsted, *Civilizing American Cities*, 185.

71. Williams, *Culture and Society*, 325–26; discussed in Borsay, *History of Leisure*, 87.

72. See McCullough, *Living Pictures*.

73. Gerould, *American Melodrama*, 133.

74. Olmsted, *Civilizing American Cities*, 102.

75. Olmsted to Mary Perkins Olmsted, 25 September 1863, in his *Creating Central Park*, 186.

76. Olmsted, *Civilizing American Cities*, 79.

77. Bank, *Theatre Culture in America*, 151.

78. See Rosenzweig and Blackmar, *Park and the People*, 55.

79. Olmsted, *Civilizing American Cities*, 74.

80. J. L. Smith, *Melodrama*, 8.

81. Gerould, *American Melodrama*, 13.

82. McConachie, *Melodramatic Formations*, 216.

83. "Central Park," *New York Times*, 22 April 1866.

84. *New York Herald* [1858], quoted in Olmsted, *Civilizing American Cities*, 88.

85. Olmsted, *Civilizing American Cities*, 96.

86. Boyer, *Urban Masses and Moral Order*, 238.

87. Bender, *Towards an Urban Vision*, 179.

88. Jameson, *Political Unconscious*, 186.

89. Ibid., 186.

90. Olmsted, "Review of Recent Changes, and Changes Which Have Been Projected, in the Plans of Central Park," in his *Olmsted, Landscape Architect, 1822–1903*, ed. Olmsted Jr. and Kimball, 243.

91. See Vicinus, "Helpless and Unfriended."

92. Olmsted, "Review of Recent Changes," in his *Olmsted, Landscape Architect, 1822–1903*, ed. Olmsted Jr. and Kimball, 243, 244.

93. See Buechler, *Women's Movements in the United States;* and Croly, *History of the Woman's Club Movement.*

94. See Stansell, *City of Women*, 219–20.

95. See Schenker, "Women's and Children's Quarters."

96. See Ryan, *Women in Public.*

97. Vicinus, "Helpless and Unfriended," 131–32.

98. Ruskin, *Sesame and Lilies*, 174.

99. M. H. Smith, *Sunshine and Shadow*, 215, 361.

100. Jameson, *Political Unconscious*, 18.

Conclusion

1. Veblen, *Theory of the Leisure Class*, 1.

2. Borsay, *History of Leisure*, xiii.

3. Harvey, *Paris, Capital of Modernity*, 73, 86.

4. Olmsted, *Writings on Public Parks*, 189.

5. Olmsted, *California Frontier*, 504.

6. Horace Cleveland, quoted in Foglesong, *Planning the Capitalist City*, 115.

7. Charles Eliot, quoted in Foglesong, *Planning the Capitalist City*, 116.

8. See "About CPC" at the Conservancy's Web site: www.centralparknyc.org/site/PageNavigator/aboutcon_cpc.

9. *New York Times*, 11 February 2005.

10. Artists' Press Release, www.christojeanneclaude.net.

11. *New York Times*, 13 February 2005.

12. Schjeldahl, "Gated," 30.

13. Gopnik, "Christo's Gates."

14. Christo and Jeanne-Claude, "The Gates Views."

15. Gopnik, "Christo's Gates."

16. Incident witnessed by the author while working on the installation.

Bibliography

Achard, Amedée. "Le Bois de Boulogne, les Champs-Élysées, le bois et le cha-
teau de Vincennes." In *Paris Guide*, 1228–65. 1867.

Alphand, Adolphe. *Les promenades de Paris*. Paris: J. Rothschild, 1867–73.
Reprint, Princeton: Princeton Architectural Press, Princeton University, and
Columbia University, 1984.

Anderson, William Marshall. *An American in Maximilian's Mexico, 1865–1866:
The Diaries of William Marshall Anderson*. Edited by Ramón Eduardo Ruiz.
San Marino, Calif.: Huntington Library, 1959.

Appelbaum, Stanley, ed. *Scenes from the 19th-Century Stage in Advertising
Woodcuts*. New York: Dover, 1977.

Arellano Zavaleta, Manuel. *Chapultepec: Época prehispánica*. Mexico City:
Libros de Mexico, 1972.

Arias, Santa, and Mariselle Meléndez, eds. *Mapping Colonial Spanish America:
Places and Commonplaces of Identity, Culture, and Experience*. Lewisburg,
Pa.: Bucknell University Press, 2002.

Austen, Jane. *Mansfield Park*. 1814. Ware, Hertfordshire: Wordsworth Classics,
1992.

Baker, Benjamin A. *A Glance at New York*. New York: S. French, 1848.

Bank, Rosemarie K. *Theatre Culture in America, 1825–1860*. Cambridge: Cambridge University Press, 1997.

Barnes, Eric W. *Anna Cora: The Life and Theatre of Anna Cora Mowatt*. London: Secker and Warburg, 1954.

Barrell, John. *The Idea of Landscape and the Sense of Place, 1730–1840: An Approach to the Poetry of John Clare*. Cambridge: Cambridge University Press, 1972.

Barthes, Roland. *Mythologies*. New York: Hill and Wang, 1994.

Barton, Mary. *Impressions of Mexico, with Brush and Pen*. London: Methuen, 1911.

Baudelaire, Charles. *Les Fleurs du mal*. 1861. Translated by Keith Waldrop as *The Flowers of Evil*. Middletown, Ct.: Wesleyan University Press, 2006.

Beauvoir, Simone de. *The Second Sex*. Translated and edited by H. M. Parshley. New York: Knopf, 1953.

Beezley, William. *Judas at the Jockey Club and Other Episodes of Porfirian Mexico*. Lincoln: University of Nebraska Press, 2004.

Bender, Thomas. *Towards an Urban Vision: Ideas and Institutions in Nineteenth-Century America*. Lexington: University Press of Kentucky, 1975.

Berg, Barbara J. *The Remembered Gate: Origins of American Feminism, The Woman and the City, 1800–1860*. New York: Oxford University Press, 1978.

Bermingham, Ann. *Landscape and Ideology: The English Rustic Tradition, 1740–1850*. Berkeley and Los Angeles: University of California Press, 1986.

Birdoff, Harry. *The World's Greatest Hit: Uncle Tom's Cabin*. New York: S. F. Vanni, 1947.

Blasio, José Luis. *Maximilian, Emperor of Mexico*. Translated and edited by Robert H. Murray. New Haven: Yale University Press, 1934.

Blodgett, Geoffrey. "Frederick Law Olmsted: Landscape Architecture as Conservative Reform." *Journal of American History* 62, no. 4 (1976): 869–89.

Blumin, Stuart M. *The Emergence of the Middle Class: Social Experience in the American City, 1760–1900*. Cambridge: Cambridge University Press, 1989.

———. "Explaining the New Metropolis: Perception, Depiction, and Analysis in Mid-Nineteenth-Century New York City." *Journal of Urban History* 11 (1984): 9–38.

Blunt, Edmund M. *Blunt's Stranger's Guide to the City of New York*. New York: Edmund M. Blunt, 1817.

Bly, Nellie. "The Mystery of Central Park." Serialized in *New York Evening World*, 18–30 July 1889.

Bobo, William M. *Glimpses of New-York City*. New York: J. J. McCarter, 1852.

Borsay, Peter. *A History of Leisure*. Basingstoke, England, and New York: Palgrave MacMillan, 2006.

Boyer, Paul S. *Urban Masses and Moral Order in America, 1820–1920.* Cambridge: Harvard University Press, 1978.

Brooks, Peter. *The Melodramatic Imagination: Balzac, Henry James, Melodrama and the Mode of Excess.* New Haven: Yale University Press, 1976.

Buechler, Steven M. *Women's Movements in the United States.* New Brunswick, N.J.: Rutgers University Press, 1990.

Butler, Judith. *Gender Trouble: Feminism and the Subversion of Identity.* New York: Routledge, 1990.

Calhoun, Craig, ed. *Habermas and the Public Sphere.* Cambridge: MIT Press, 1994.

Campos, Ruben M. *Chapultepec: Its Legend and Its History.* Translated by Luis Bozzo Jr. Mexico City: Talleres Graficos del Gobierno Nacional, 1922.

Castro, C., J. Campillo, L. Auda, and G. Rodríguez. *México y sus alrededores: Colección de monumentos, trajes y paisajes.* Mexico City: Establecimiento Litográfico de Decaen, 1855–56.

Certeau, Michel de. *The Practice of Everyday Life.* Translated by Steven Rendall. Berkeley and Los Angeles: University of California Press, 1984.

Child, Lydia Maria. *Letters from New York.* New York: C. S. Francis and Co., 1844.

Choay, Francoise. "Haussmann et le système des espaces verts parisiens." *Revue de l'art* 29 (1975): 83–99.

———. *The Modern City: Planning in the 19th Century.* New York: Braziller, 1970.

Christo and Jeanne-Claude. *The Gates Views: A Companion to the Gates Map.* United Arts Group, 2004.

Clark, Timothy J. *The Painting of Modern Life: Paris in the Art of Manet and His Followers.* Princeton: Princeton University Press, 1984.

Clarke, George, Jonathan Marsden, Richard Wheeler, Michael Bevington, and Tim Knox. *Stowe Landscape Gardens.* London: National Trust, 1997.

Clary, Raymond H. *The Making of Golden Gate Park: The Early Years, 1865–1906.* San Francisco: Don't Call It Frisco Press, 1984.

Codex Telleriano-Remensis. Facsimile ed. Translated and with an introduction by Ernest A. Hamy. Paris: Burdin, 1899.

Códice Azcatítlan. [Paris]: Societé des Americanistes, 1949.

Colegio de México. *Atlas de la Ciudad de Mexico.* Mexico City: Colegio de Mexico, [1987].

Conway, Hazel. *People's Parks: The Design and Development of Victorian Parks in Britain.* Cambridge: Cambridge University Press, 1991.

Copley, Stephen, and Peter Garside, eds. *The Politics of the Picturesque.* Cambridge: Cambridge University Press, 1994.

Corti, Egon Caesar. *Maximilian and Charlotte of Mexico.* 2 vols. New York and London: Knopf, 1928.

Cranz, Galen. *The Politics of Park Design: A History of Urban Parks in America.* Cambridge: MIT Press, 1982.

———. "Women in Urban Parks." *Signs* 5, no. 3 (1980): 579–95.

Croly, Jane Cunningham. *The History of the Woman's Club Movement in America.* New York: Henry G. Allen, 1898.

Cueva, Hermilo de la. *Chapultepec: Biografía de un bosque.* Mexico City: Talleres de Editorial B. Costa-Amic, 1962.

Daniels, Howard. "European Parks." *Horticulturist and Journal of Rural Art and Rural Taste* 15, no. 11 (1860): 529–32.

Davidoff, Leonore, and Catherine Hall. *Family Fortunes: Men and Women of the English Middle Class, 1780–1850.* Chicago: University of Chicago Press, 1987.

de Corval, René. *Guide dans Paris aux Monuments et Curiosités.* Paris: E. Maillet, 1867.

Delvau, A. *Les Plaisirs de Paris: Guide practique et illustré.* Paris: Achille Faure, 1867.

Des Cars, Jean, and Pierre Pinon. *Paris-Haussmann.* Paris: Picard, 1991.

Díaz del Castillo, Bernal. *The True History of the Conquest of New Spain.* London: Printed for the Hakluyt Society, 1908–16.

Díaz y de Ovando, Clementina. "Visión de Chapultepec." In *Chapultepec en la historia y en el arte,* 1–10. Mexico City: Instituto Mexicano Norteamericano de Relaciones Culturales, 1979.

Downing, Andrew J. *Landscape Gardening and Rural Architecture.* New York: Dover, 1991.

———. *Rural Essays.* New York: G. P. Putnam, 1853.

Duplessis, Paul. *Aventuras Mejicanas.* Translated by D. F. Tubino and D. M. Pizarro. Seville: Est. tip. de La Andalucía, 1862.

Durán, Diego. *Historia de las Indias de la Nueva España e islas de tierra firme.* 2 vols. Edited by Angel María Garibay Kintana. Mexico City: Porrúa, 1967.

Duveau, Georges. *La vie ouvrière en France sous le Second Empire.* Paris: Gallimard, 1946.

Eagleton, Terry. *The Ideology of the Aesthetic.* Oxford: Basil Blackwell, 1990.

Eco, Umberto. *Travels in Hyperreality.* Translated by William Weaver. San Diego: Harcourt Brace Jovanovich, 1986.

Edelstein, T. J. *Vauxhall Gardens.* New Haven: Yale Center for British Art, 1983.

Elton, J. F. *With the French in Mexico.* London: Chapman and Hall, 1867.

Elwitt, Sanford. *The Making of the Third Republic: Class and Politics in France, 1868–1884.* Baton Rouge: Louisiana State University Press, 1975.

Ernst, Robert. *Immigrant Life in New York City, 1825–1863.* Syracuse, N.Y.: Syracuse University Press, 1994.

Evans, Susan Toby. "Aztec Royal Pleasure Parks: Conspicuous Consumption and Elite Status Rivalry." *Studies in the History of Gardens and Designed Landscapes* 20, no. 3 (2000): 206–28.

Ezcurra, Exequiel. *De las chinampas a la megalópolis: el medio ambiente en la Cuenca de México.* Mexico City: Fondo de Cultura Económica, 2000.

Fein, Albert. *Frederick Law Olmsted and the American Environmental Tradition.* New York: George Braziller, 1972.

Fernández, Miguel Angel. *Documentos para la historia de Chapultepec.* Mexico City: INAH, 2000.

Fernández, Miguel Ángel, and José de Santiago. *Historia de un Bosque.* Mexico City: Instituto Nacional de Antropología e Historia, 1979.

Foglesong, Richard E. *Planning the Capitalist City: The Colonial Era to the 1920s.* Princeton: Princeton University Press, 1986.

Foster, George. *New York by Gas-light: With Here and There a Streak of Sunshine.* New York: Dewitt and Davenport, 1850.

Fournel, Victor. *Paris nouveau et Paris futur.* Paris: Jacques Lecoffre, 1865.

Fredeen, Charles. *Nellie Bly: Daredevil Reporter.* Minneapolis: Lerner, 2000.

Gaillard, Jeanne. *Paris, la ville, 1852–1870: L'Urbanisme Parisien à l'heure d'Haussmann.* Paris: H. Champion, 1977.

Galignani & Co., A. & W. *New Paris Guide.* Paris: Galignani, 1866.

Garrett, Thomas M. "A History of Pleasure Gardens in New York City, 1700–1865." Ph.D. diss., New York University, 1978.

Gautier, Théophile. "Mosaïque de ruines." In *Paris et les Parisiens au XIXe siècle: Moeurs, Arts et Monuments,* by Alexandre Dumas, Gautier, Arsène Musset, Paul de Enauit, and Louis du Fayl, 38–43. Paris: Morizot, 1856.

Gerould, Daniel C., ed. *American Melodrama.* New York: Performing Arts Journal Publications, 1983.

Girard, Louis. *La Deuxième République et le Second Empire, 1848–1870.* Paris: Hachette, 1981.

Girouard, Mark. *Cities & People: A Social and Architectural History.* New Haven: Yale University Press, 1985.

Gobernación: Obras Públicas, Junta Superior del Bosque del Chapultepec. Archivo Histórico de la Ciudad de Mexico, Casa de Heras y Soto, 1903–14.

Goldsmith, Barbara. *Other Powers: The Age of Suffrage, Spiritualism, and the Scandalous Victoria Woodhull.* New York: Knopf, 1998.

Goncourt, Edmond de, and Jules de Goncourt. *Journal des Goncourts: Mémoires de la vie littéraire.* 9 vols. Paris, 1912.

Gooch, Fanny. *Face to Face with the Mexicans.* New York: Fords, Howard and Hubert, 1887.

Gopnik, Blake. "Christo's Gates: A Little Creaky." *Washington Post*, 13 February 2005.

Gossett, Thomas F. *Uncle Tom's Cabin and American Culture*. Dallas: Southern Methodist University Press, 1985.

Green, Nicholas. *The Spectacle of Nature: Landscape and Bourgeois Culture in Nineteenth-century France*. Manchester and New York: Manchester University Press, 1990.

Greene, Asa. *A Glance at New York*. New York: A. Greene, 1837.

Grizzard, Mary F. M. *Spanish Colonial Art and Architecture of Mexico and the U.S. Southwest*. Lanham, Md.: University Press of America, 1986.

Grumbach, Antoine. "The Promenades of Paris." *Oppositions* (Spring 1977): 50–67.

Habermas, Jürgen. *The Structural Transformation of the Public Sphere: An Inquiry into a Category of Bourgeois Society*. Cambridge: MIT Press, 1989.

Hadley, Elaine. *Melodramatic Tactics: Theatricalized Dissent in the English Marketplace, 1800–1885*. Stanford: Stanford University Press, 1995.

Halttunen, Karen. *Confidence Men and Painted Women: A Study of Middle-class Culture in America, 1830–1870*. New Haven: Yale University Press. 1982.

Hankins, Marie Louise. *Women of New York*. New York: Marie Louise Hankins and Co., 1861.

Hanna, Alfred J., and Kathryn A. *Napoleon III and Mexico*. Chapel Hill: University of North Carolina Press, 1971.

Harlow, Alvin F. *Old Bowery Days: The Chronicles of a Famous Street*. New York and London: D. Appleton, [1931].

Harvey, David. *Paris, Capital of Modernity*. New York: Routledge, 2003.

Hauptman, Ira. "Defending Melodrama." In Redmond, *Melodrama*, 281–89.

Hauser, Arnold. *The Social History of Art*. Vol. 4, *Naturalism, Impressionism, the Film Age*. New York: Vintage, 1958.

Haussmann, Georges Eugène, Baron. *Mémoires du Baron Haussmann*. 3 vols. Paris: Victor-Havard, 1890–93.

Helsinger, Elizabeth. "Turner and the Representation of England." In *Landscape and Power*, edited by W.J.T. Mitchell, 103–25. Chicago: University of Chicago Press, 1994.

Herbert, Robert L. *Impressionism: Art, Leisure and Parisian Society*. New Haven: Yale University Press, 1988.

Homberger, Eric. *Scenes from the Life of a City: Corruption and Conscience in Old New York*. New Haven: Yale University Press, 1994.

Hunt, John Dixon. *Garden and Grove: The Italian Renaissance Garden in the English Imagination, 1600–1750*. Philadelphia: University of Pennsylvania Press, 1996.

———. *Gardens and the Picturesque*. Cambridge: MIT Press, 1992.

Hunt, John Dixon, and Peter Willis, eds. *The Genius of the Place: The English Landscape Garden, 1620–1820.* Cambridge: MIT Press, 1988.

Hyde, H. Montgomery. *Mexican Empire.* London: Macmillan, 1946.

Hyslop, Gabrielle. "Pixérécourt and the French Melodrama Debate: Instructing Boulevard Theatre Audiences." In Redmond, *Melodrama,* 61–85.

International Bureau of the American Republics. *Argentine Republic: A Geographical Sketch, with Special Reference to Economic Conditions, Actual Development, and Prospects of Future Growth.* Washington: U.S. Government Printing Office, 1903.

Jameson, Fredric. *The Political Unconscious: Narrative as a Socially Symbolic Act.* Ithaca: Cornell University Press, 1981.

Johns, Michael. *The City of Mexico in the Age of Díaz.* Austin: University of Texas Press, 1997.

Kaplan, E. Ann. *Motherhood and Representation: The Mother in Popular Culture and Melodrama.* London: Routledge, 1992.

Kasson, John F. *Amusing the Million: Coney Island at the Turn of the Century.* New York: Hill and Wang, 1978.

———. *Rudeness and Civility: Manners in Nineteenth-Century Urban America.* New York: Hill and Wang, 1990.

Kollonitz, Paula, Countess. *The Court of Mexico.* London: Saunders, Otley and Co., 1867.

Kroeger, Brooke. *Nellie Bly: Daredevil, Reporter, Feminist.* New York: Times Books, 1994.

Landes, Joan B. *Women and the Public Sphere in the Age of the French Revolution.* Ithaca: Cornell University Press, 1988.

Lasdun, Susan. *The English Park: Royal, Private & Public.* London: Deutsch, 1991.

Lavedan, Pierre. *Histoire de l'urbanisme à Paris.* Paris: Hachette, 1975.

Lazare, Louis. *Les Quartiers de l'est de Paris et les communes suburbaines.* Paris, 1870.

Lear, Jon Robert. "Workers, *Vecinos* and Citizens: The Revolution in Mexico City, 1909–1917." Ph.D. diss., University of California, Berkeley, 1993.

Le Dantec, Denise, and Jean-Pierre Le Dantec. *Reading the French Garden: Story and History.* Translated by Jessica Levine. Cambridge: MIT Press, 1990. Originally published as *Le roman des jardins de France* (Paris: Plon, 1987).

Leduc, Alberto, and Luis Lara y Pardo. *Galván Almanac for 1838.* In *Dictionario de geografía, historia y biografía mexicanas.* Paris: Librería de la Vda. de C. Bouret, 1910.

Limantour, José Yves. *Apuntes sobre mi vida pública.* Mexico City: Porrúa, 1965.

Linthicum, Richard. *Complete Story of the San Francisco Horror, by the Survivors and Rescuers.* Introduction by Samuel Fallows. Chicago: Hubert D. Russell, 1906.

Lombardo de Ruiz, Sonia. *Atlas Histórico de la Ciudad de México.* In collaboration with Yolanda Terán Trillo. Edited by Mario de la Torre. 2 vols. Mexico City: Smurfit Cartón y Papel de México, 1996.

Loudon, J. *Gardening for Ladies and Companion to the Flower Garden.* New York: John Wiley, 1843.

Malet, Henri. *Le Baron Haussmann et la rénovation de Paris.* Paris: Les Éditions Municipales, 1973.

Mann, William. "John Stevens, Pioneer in Steam-Powered Navigation, and His Pleasure Park, Elysian Fields, in Hoboken, New Jersey." *CELA Conference Proceedings 1995* 7 (1995): 61–78.

Marceca, Maria Luisa. "Reservoir, Circulation, Residue: JCA Alphand, Technological Beauty and the Green City." *Lotus* 30, no. 1 (1981): 57–63.

Marcoux, J. Paul. "Guilbert de Pixérécourt: The People's Conscience." In Redmond, *Melodrama*, 47–59.

Martin, Theodora P. *The Sound of Our Own Voices: Women's Study Clubs, 1860–1910.* Boston: Beacon Press, 1987.

Martineau, Harriet. *Harriet Martineau on Women.* Edited by Gayle Graham Yates. Douglass Series on Women's Lives and the Meaning of Gender. New Brunswick, N.J.: Rutgers University Press, 1985.

Marx, Karl. *Basic Writings on Politics and Philosophy.* Edited by Lewis S. Feuer. Garden City, N.Y.: Doubleday, 1959. Originally published in 1852 as *The Eighteenth Brumaire of Louis Bonaparte.*

Mathews, Cornelius. *The Career of Puffer Hopkins.* New York: Wilson, 1842.

McConachie, Bruce A. *Melodramatic Formations, American Theatre and Society, 1820–1870.* Iowa City: University of Iowa Press, 1992.

———. "Out of the Kitchen and into the Marketplace: Normalizing *Uncle Tom's Cabin* for the Antebellum Stage." *Journal of American Drama and Theatre* 3 (1991): 5–28.

———. "Pixérécourt's Early Melodramas and the Political Inducements of Neoplatonism." In Redmond, *Melodrama*, 87–103.

McCullough, Jack W. *Living Pictures on the New York Stage.* Ann Arbor, Mich.: UMI Research Press, 1983.

McWilliam, Rohan. "Melodrama and the Historians." *Radical History Review* 78 (2000): 57–84.

Meyer, Annie N. *My Park Book.* New York: Edwin W. Dayton, 1898.

———. *Woman's Work in America.* New York: H. Holt, 1891.

Meyer, Michael C., William L. Sherman, and Susan M. Deeds. *The Course of*

Mexican History. New York and Oxford: Oxford University Press, 1999.

Meyerowitz, J. J. *Women Adrift: Independent Wage Earners in Chicago, 1880–1930.* Chicago: University of Chicago Press, 1988.

Mill, John Stuart. *The Subjection of Women.* 1869. New Brunswick, N.J.: Transaction, 2001.

Millett, Kate. *Sexual Politics.* New York: Simon and Schuster, 1969.

Mitchell, Catherine C., ed. *Margaret Fuller's New York Journalism.* Knoxville: University of Tennessee Press, 1995.

Mowatt, Anna C. *Plays by Anna Cora Mowatt.* Boston: Ticknor and Fields, 1854.

Myerson, Joel, ed. *Critical Essays on Margaret Fuller.* Boston: G. K. Hall, 1980.

Noble, Iris. *Nellie Bly: First Woman Reporter.* Detroit: Messner, 1956.

Odell, George Clinton D. *Annals of the New York Stage.* New York: Columbia University Press, 1927–49.

Olmsted, Frederick Law. *The California Frontier, 1863–1865.* Vol. 5 of *The Papers of Frederick Law Olmsted.* Baltimore: John Hopkins University Press, 1990.

———. *Civilizing American Cities: Writings on City Landscapes.* Edited by S. B. Sutton. New York: Da Capo Press, 1997.

———. *Creating Central Park, 1857–1861.* Vol. 3 of *The Papers of Frederick Law Olmsted.* Baltimore: Johns Hopkins University Press, 1983.

———. *Defending the Union, The Civil War and the U.S. Sanitary Commission, 1861–1863.* Vol. 4 of *The Papers of Frederick Law Olmsted.* Baltimore: Johns Hopkins University Press, 1986.

———. *Frederick Law Olmsted, Landscape Architect, 1822–1903.* Edited by Frederick Law Olmsted Jr. and Theodora Kimball. New York: Benjamin Blom, 1970.

———. *Slavery and the South, 1852–1857.* Vol. 2 of *The Papers of Frederick Law Olmsted.* Baltimore: Johns Hopkins University Press, 1981.

———. *Writings on Public Parks, Parkways, and Park Systems.* Supplementary Series 1, *The Papers of Frederick Law Olmsted.* Baltimore: Johns Hopkins University Press, 1997.

Olsen, Donald J. *The City as a Work of Art: London, Paris, Vienna.* New Haven: Yale University Press, 1986.

Orme, Edward. *An Essay on Transparent Prints.* London: privately printed, 1807.

Peiss, Kathy Lee. *Cheap Amusements: Working Women and Leisure in Turn-of-the Century New York.* Philadelphia: Temple University Press, 1986.

Pinkney, David H. *Napoleon III and the Rebuilding of Paris.* Princeton: Princeton University Press, 1958.

Piolle, María Elena Altamirano. *José María Velasco: Landscapes of Light, Horizons of the Modern Era*. Mexico City: Museo Nacional de Arte, 1993.

Prantl, Adolfo, and José L. Groso. *La Ciudad de México: Novísima guía universal de la capital de la República Mexicana*. Mexico City: Librería Madrileña, 1901.

Rabinovitz, Lauren. *For the Love of Pleasure: Women, Movies and Culture in Turn-of-the-Century Chicago*. New Brunswick, N.J.: Rutgers University Press, 1998.

Rahill, Frank. *The World of Melodrama*. University Park: Pennsylvania State University Press, 1967.

Redmond, James, ed. *Melodrama*. Themes in Drama 14. Cambridge and New York: Cambridge University Press, 1992.

Riedel, Emil. *Practical Guide of the City and Valley of Mexico*. Mexico City: I. Epstein, 1892.

Rivera Cambas, Manuel. *México pintoresco, artístico y monumental*. Mexico City: Imprenta de la Reforma, 1880.

Robinson, David J., ed. *Migration in Colonial Spanish America*. Cambridge Studies in Historical Geography 16. Cambridge and New York: Cambridge University Press, 1990.

Robinson, William. *The Parks, Promenades and Gardens of Paris*. London: John Murray, 1869.

Romero, Matias. "Labor and Wages in Mexico." In *Mexico and the United States*, by Romero, 1:495–558. New York and London: G. P. Putnam's Sons, 1898.

Romero Flores, Jesús. *Chapultepec en la historia de México*. Mexico City: Secretaria de Educación Publica, 1947.

———. *México: Historia de una gran ciudad*. Mexico City: Ediciones Morelos, 1953.

Rosen, George. *A History of Public Health*. Baltimore: Johns Hopkins University Press, 1993.

Rosenberg, Rosalind. *Beyond Separate Spheres: Intellectual Roots of Modern Feminism*. New Haven: Yale University Press, 1982.

Rosenzweig, Roy, and Elizabeth Blackmar. *The Park and the People: A History of Central Park*. Ithaca: Cornell University Press, 1992.

Runte, Alfred. *Yosemite, the Embattled Wilderness*. Lincoln: University of Nebraska Press, 1990.

Ruskin, John. *Sesame and Lilies*. New York: C. E. Merrill, 1891.

Russell, Charles Edward. *Why I Am a Socialist*. New York: George H. Doran, 1910.

Ryan, Mary P. *Women in Public: Between Banners and Ballots*. Baltimore: Johns Hopkins University Press, 1990.

Rybczynski, Witold. *A Clearing in the Distance: Frederick Law Olmsted and America in the Nineteenth Century.* New York: Scribner, 1999.

Sahagún, Bernardino de. *Florentine Codex: General History of the Things of New Spain.* Translated by Arthur J. O. Anderson and Charles E. Dibble, 13 parts. Salt Lake City and Santa Fe: University of Utah Press and School of American Research, 1950–82.

Salm-Salm, Princess Felix. *Ten Years of My Life.* London, 1876.

Sanders, William T., Jeffrey R. Parsons, and Robert S. Santley. *The Basin of Mexico: Ecological Processes in the Evolution of a Civilization.* New York: Academic Press, 1979.

Sax, Joseph L. *Mountains without Handrails: Reflections on the National Parks.* Ann Arbor: University of Michigan Press, 1980.

Schafer, Amanda R. "From, For and of the Megacity." *Praxis: Mexico City* 1, no. 2 (2001): 5–13.

Schenker, Heath. "Feminist Interventions in the Histories of Landscape Architecture." *Landscape Journal* 13, no. 2 (1994): 107–12.

———. "Parks and Politics in Paris under the Second Empire." *Landscape Journal* 14, no. 2 (1994): 201–19.

———. "Women's and Children's Quarters in Golden Gate Park, San Francisco." *Gender, Place and Culture* 3, no. 3 (1996): 293–308.

Schjeldahl, Peter. "Gated." *New Yorker,* 28 February 2005.

Schneirov, Richard. *Labor and Urban Politics: Class Conflict and the Origins of Modern Liberalism in Chicago, 1864–97.* Urbana: University of Illinois Press, 1998.

Schuyler, David. *Apostle of Taste: Andrew Jackson Downing, 1815–1852.* Baltimore: Johns Hopkins University Press, 1996.

———. *The New Urban Landscape: The Redefinition of City Form in Nineteenth-century America.* Baltimore: Johns Hopkins University Press, 1986.

Sharp, William. "Structure of Melodrama." In Redmond, *Melodrama,* 269–80.

Sierra, Justo. *The Political Evolution of the Mexican People.* Austin: University of Texas, 1969.

Smith, James L. *Melodrama.* Critical Idiom series no. 28. London: Methuen, 1973.

Smith, Matthew Hale. *Sunshine and Shadow in New York.* Hartford: J. B. Burr, 1869.

Smith, William Henry. *The Drunkard, or, The Fallen Saved!: A Moral Domestic Drama.* Boston: Jones, 1847.

Solís Olguín, Felipe. "Chapultepec: Espacio ritual y secular de los *Tlatoani* Aztecas." *Arqueología Mexicana* 10, no. 57 (2002): 36–40.

Sorkin, Michael, ed. *Variations on a Theme Park: The New American City and the End of Public Space.* New York: Hill and Wang, 1992.

Southworth, James G. *Vauxhall Gardens: A Chapter in the Social History of England.* New York: Columbia University Press, 1941.

Srebnick, Amy G. *The Mysterious Death of Mary Rogers: Sex and Culture in Nineteenth-Century New York.* New York: Oxford University Press, 1995.

Stansell, Christine. *City of Women: Sex and Class in New York, 1789–1860.* Urbana: University of Illinois Press, 1987.

Stokes, I. N. Phelps. *The Iconography of Manhattan Island, 1498–1909.* 6 vols. New York: Arno Press, 1967.

Susman, Warren I. "'Personality' and the Making of Twentieth-Century Culture." In *New Directions in American Intellectual History,* edited by John Higham and Paul K. Conkin, 212–26. Baltimore: Johns Hopkins University Press, 1979.

Sutcliffe, Anthony. *The Autumn of Central Paris: The Defeat of Town Planning, 1850–1970.* London: Edward Arnold, 1970.

Tate, Alan. *Great City Parks.* London and New York: Spon Press, 2001.

Teja Zabre, Alfonso. *Chapultepec: Guía histórica y descriptiva con un plano pictórico del bosque.* Mexico City: Talleres de Impression de Estampillas, 1938.

Terry, T. Phillip. *Terry's Mexico: Handbook for Travelers.* Boston: Houghton Mifflin, 1909.

Texier, Edmond. *Paris: Capitale du monde.* Paris: J. Hetzel, 1867.

———. *Tableau de Paris.* 1853. Reprint, Paris: Inter-Livres, [1988].

Thacker, Christopher. *The History of Gardens.* Berkeley and Los Angeles: University of California Press, 1985.

Thackeray, William M. *Vanity Fair.* 1847. New York: Signet Classics, 1981.

Thurston, Hazel. *Royal Parks for the People: London's Ten.* Newton Abbot, England, and North Pomfret, Vt.: David and Charles, 1974.

Tira de la peregrinacion mexica. Mexico City: Librería Anticuaria de G. M. Echaniz, 1944.

Torre, Mario de la, ed. *Bosquejos de Mexico: Colección de grabados y litografías del siglo XIX del Banco de México.* Mexico City: Banco de México, 1987.

———. *Chapultepec: Historia y presencia.* Mexico City: Smurfit Cartón y Papel de México, 1988.

———. *Testimonios de Viaje: 1823–1873.* Mexico City: Smurfit Cartón y Papel de México, 1989.

Trabulse, E. *Cartografía mexicana: Tesoros de la nación, siglos XVI a XIX.* Mexico City: Archivo General de la Nación, 1983.

Trillo, Mauricio Tenorio. "1910 Mexico City: Space and Nation in the City of the *Centenario.*" *Journal of Latin American Studies* 28 (1996): 75–104.

Trollope, Anthony. *Australia and New Zealand.* 2 vols. London: Chapman and Hall, 1876.

Trollope, Frances. *Domestic Manners of the Americans*. London: Whittaker, Treacher, 1832.

Tuckerman, Henry T. *Maga Papers about Paris*. New York: G. P. Putnam, 1867.

Vázquez, S. G. *México y sus alrededores: Guía descriptiva ilustrada*. Mexico City: Imprenta Lacaud, 1910.

Veblen, Thorstein. *The Theory of the Leisure Class*. New York: Dover, 1899.

Vicinus, Martha. "Helpless and Unfriended: Nineteenth-Century Domestic Melodrama." *New Literary History* 12 (1981): 127–43.

Vivian, H. Hussey. *Notes on a Tour in America from August 7th to November 17th, 1877*. London: Edward Stanford, 1878.

Von Joest, Thomas. "Haussmann's Paris: A Green Metropolis?" In *The Architecture of Western Gardens*, edited by Monique Mosser and Georges Teyssot, 387–98. Cambridge: MIT Press, 1991.

Walter, Rodolphe. "Le Parc de Monsieur Zola." *L'Oeil* 272 (March 1978): 18–25.

Ward, David. *Poverty, Ethnicity, and the American City, 1840–1925*. Cambridge: Cambridge University Press, 1989.

Weibenson, Dora. "Le Parc Monceau et ses 'Fabriqués.'" *Les Monuments Historiques de la France* 5 (1976): 16–19.

Widdifield, Stacie G. *The Embodiment of the National in Late Nineteenth-century Mexican Painting*. Tucson: University of Arizona Press, 1996.

Wilentz, Sean. *Chants Democratic: New York City & the Rise of the American Working Class, 1788–1850*. New York: Oxford University Press, 1984.

Williams, Raymond. *The Country and the City*. New York: Oxford University Press, 1973.

———. *Culture and Society*. New York: Columbia University Press, 1983.

———. *The Long Revolution*. London: Chatto and Windus, 1961.

Winfield, Charles H. *Hopoghan Hackingh: Hoboken, a Pleasure Resort for Old New York*. New York: Caxton Press, 1895.

Wolfe, Eric R., ed. *The Valley of Mexico: Studies in Pre-Hispanic Ecology and Society*. School of American Research Advanced Seminar Series. Albuquerque: University of New Mexico Press, 1976.

Wolter, Jürgen C., ed. *The Dawning of American Drama: American Dramatic Criticism, 1746–1915*. Westport, Ct.: Greenwood Press, 1994.

Wroth, Warwick W. *The London Pleasure Gardens of the Eighteenth Century*. London and New York: Macmillan, 1896.

Zola, Émile. *La curée*. Paris: Gallimard, 1981.

———. *L'Assommoir*. London: Penguin, 1970.

Index

Bryant, William Cullen, 131, 135, 137, 138
Bucareli Promenade (Mexico City), 84
Bucareli y Ursúa, Antonio María, 73
buildings: athletic facilities, 100; baths, 80; Dairy, 167–69, 169, 170; observatories, 69, 97; pavilion, 167; refreshment areas, 43, 127. See also Castillo de Chapultepec, El

California. See San Francisco (Calif.)
camels, **136**, 136
capitalism: class shifts in, 36; in France, 57, 60; leisure in context of, 177–78; Stowe's view of, 154; urban park as product of, 7. See also social classes
Carlota (Charlotte, empress of Mexico): Chapultepec and, 80–87, 101; rise and fall of, 78, 79
Carmontelle, Louis (Carrogis), 61–62
Castillo de Chapultepec, El: construction of, 73–74; as Maximilian's residence, 80–82; during Mexican-American War, 74–76, 75; as military academy, 75, 76, 92; during Porfiriato, 96, 104–5; vista of, 76
Castro, Casimiro, et al., *México y sus alrededores*, illustrations from, 72, 76, 84, 85, 88, 91, 96, 102, 105
caves and grottos, 49, 62, 106, 126, 127
Central Park (New York): activities depicted in, 23, 148, **148–49**, 152, 167, 187; aerial view of, 2; artists' depictions of, 140, 156, 171; bonfire incident in, 1, 3; camels in, **136**, 136; conception for, 130–31, 139–40, 180–81; Dairy of, 167–69, 169, 170; design competition for, 118, 131, 138, 204n28; discourse on, 132–34, 135, 137; gates of, 190–91; lawn care in, **136**, 136; melodrama compared to,

22–24, 144, 150–51; melodramatic character types of, 164, **164**, 165–70; melodramatic landscape of, 151, 153–55; melodramatic staging of, 155–57, 159–62, 170–71; paradox of people in, 138–40; pathways and roads in, 4, 137, 140, 153, 156; people displaced by, 153; picturesque qualities of, 134, 137–39; as public space and cultural institution, 148–49; restoration of, 173, 185–86; scholarship on, 21; social and political context of, 19–20, 141, 143, 144, 149–50, 162, 180–81; social control in, 181–83; superintendency of, 142–43; working-class access to, 140–41. See also *Gates, The* (Christo and Jeanne-Claude); Greensward Plan (Central Park)
Central Park Conservancy, 185–86, 189, 194
Chadwick, Edwin, 37
Champs-Élysées (Paris), 26, 39, 85, 86, 156
Chanfrau, F. S., 124
Chapultepec Park (Mexico City): activities in, 102, **102–3**, 176; aqueducts of, 69, 70–73, 72, 74, 84, 98; artists' depictions of, 83, 102, 105, 111, 113–15, 114; baths of, 80, 82, 87, 97–98; Centenario projects in, 106–7; cypresses and forests of, 71–72, 82–84, 83, 86–87, 97, 101, **102–3**, 110; Maximilian's romanticism and, 80–87; *Los Niños Héroes* monument at, 75–76, 100; observatory of, 97; perspective on, 105; plan of, 99; precolonial past of, 68–70, 109–10; as prototypical nineteenth-century park, 67–68; public access to, 87–88, 88, 102–4; as public property, 71–72, 74; renovations in Porfiriato, 22, 88, 96–101;

Golden Gate Park (San Francisco), *182*, **182–83**
Goncourt, Edmond de, 34
Gopnik, Blake, 189–90
Great Britain: industrialization in, 56–57, 60; Mexico's crisis and, 77; political power changes in, 15, 17; public health survey of, 37. *See also* English landscape design; Liverpool, Birkenhead Park of; London; Sydenham, Crystal Palace Park of
Great Exhibition (Britain, 1851), 60
Green, Nicholas, 38–39, 54–56
Greensward Plan (Central Park): character types imagined in, 166, 167–68; debate on, 132–34, 137; "effects proposed" for, 159–60, *160;* figures diminished in, 138–39, 160; gates in, 190–91; layout of, *132–33;* style of, 131–33, 170; vision for, 134–35, 137, 181–82, 185–86. *See also* Central Park (New York); Olmsted, Frederick Law; Vaux, Calvert
Groso, José L., 67
grottos and caves, 49, 62, 106, 126, 127
Grumbach, Antoine, 60
guidebooks. *See* travel books and guides
Gutiérrez Nájera, Manuel, 93–94

Habermas, Jürgen, 18
hacienda system, 90–91
Halttunen, Karen, 20
Harper's New Monthly Magazine, text/illustrations from, **44–45,** *45,* *112,* **112**
Harper's Weekly, text/illustrations from, *79, 94,* **94–95,** *136, 152, 167*
Harvey, David, 179
Hassam, Frederick Childe, *Descending the Steps, Central Park, 171*
Hauser, Arnold, 198n1

Haussmann, Georges Eugène (Baron): on balancing boulevards, 39, 42; on Bois de Vincennes, 43; criticism of rebuilding under, 34–35, 49–51; Exposition of 1867 and, 60; legacy of, 22, 66; memoir of, 27, 29, 198n11; on military considerations, 199n22; on Parc des Buttes Chaumont, 61; on Parc Montsouris, 50; on public good, 180; on public health, 37; on real estate around parks, 47–48, 49; rebuilding of Paris under, 27, 29–30, 32–33; resignation of, 29, 35
Haussmannization, use of term, 29, 64–65
Hearne, Thomas, *Gothic House Landscaped in a Picturesque Manner, 14*
Helsinger, Elizabeth, 138
Herbert, Robert L., 52, 65
Hermès International, 188
Hoboken (N.J.), Elysian Fields of, 126–29, *127*
Hofmann, Julius, 81
homelessness, *182,* **182–83**
Homer, 12
Homer, Winslow, *A Drive in Central Park, 140*
Hotel Violet (Paris), 200n57
Hunt, Richard Morris, 190
Hyde Park (London): 1838 view of, *15;* as model for Napoleon III, 42, 57; other parks compared with, 45, 156; as theatrical stage, **44–45**

ice skating, *23, 94,* **94–95**
ideologemes (concept), 166–67
Illustrated London News, illustration from, *54*
Imparcial, El, 106
indigenous peoples, during Porfiriato, 88, 90–91, 92–93, 107, 108, 110, 114

Mill, John Stuart, 92

Milton, John, 12

Moctezuma I, 70, 71

modernity: appearance of, 32; Chapultepec Park as symbol of, 75, 88, 100–104, 108–11, 113–16, 180; Paris parks as symbol of, 45–46; urban amenities as signifiers of, 4–5. *See also* social and moral reform

Monroe, James, 123

Monroe Doctrine, 77

monuments and statuary, 75–76, 99, 100, 106, 110

Mowatt, Anna C., 151. See also *Fashion* (Mowatt)

Muller, John S., *A General Prospect of Vaux Hall Gardens*, 119

music, 90, 93–94, *118*, 144, *167*

Napoleon III: Exposition of 1867 and, 60; ideological limits of, 65; London parks admired by, 42, 56, 57; Maximilian backed by, 68, 77–79; political interests of, 21, 26–27, 29, 35–36, 39, 42–46, 63–64, 178–80; property taken by, 47–48; rebuilding of Paris under, 22, 27, 29, 33–35, 50–51; Zola's chronicle of life under, 25–26

National Police Gazette, text/illustrations from, *148*, *164*, **164**

National Theater (New York), 153–54

National Woman's Suffrage Association (NWSA), 169

naturalistic landscape: of Central Park, 132–35, 137; of Chapultepec renovations, 100; characteristics of, 3–5, 9, 14–15, 137–38; city evils transcended in, 159–60; of current public parks, 175–77; English foundations of, 10–15, 17; fabrication of, 6, 8–9; political meaning of, 11–14; sentiments aroused by, 160–62; wildness erased in, 108–9. *See also* rural landscape

naturalness: commodification of, 54–56; French interpretation of, 65; industrialization as counterpoint to, 57, 60; mythology of, 6, 7–8

New England Woman's Club, 169

New Jersey. *See* Elysian Fields (Hoboken, N.J.)

New York City: aerial view of, *2*; bicycle path in, *178*, **178–79**; call for park in, 131; commercial gardens of, 22–23, 117–18, *118*, 121–30; economic crises in, 162, 165; gender identities in, 169–70; German festival in, 128–29, *129*; landscape design discourse in, 132–34, *135*, *137*; naming parks of, 123; origins of parks in, 23; social and political context of, 19–20, 141, 143, 144, 149–50, 162, 180–81; sunshine and shadow zones of, *172*, 172–73. *See also* Bowery, the (New York); Central Park (New York)

New York Daily Advertiser, 122

New York Department of Parks and Recreation, 185

New Yorker, 189

New York Herald, 117, 124, 157, 166

New York Post, 131

New York Press Club, 169

New York Times, 1, 139, 165, 189; text from, **136**

New York Tribune, 127–29, 135

New York World, text from, **148–49**

Niblos Garden (New York), 23, 123

Niños Héroes, Los (monument), 75–76, 100

Nixon's Cremorne Garden (New York), 130

Noriega, Tomás, 97

Nurture New York's Nature and the Arts, 189